T0305110

The Political Economy of Professional Sport

NEW HORIZONS IN THE ECONOMICS OF SPORT

Series Editors: Wladimir Andreff, *Department of Economics, University of Paris 1 Panthéon Sorbonne, France* and Marc Lavoie, *Department of Economics, University of Ottawa, Canada*

For decades, the economics of sport was regarded as a hobby for a handful of professional economists who were primarily involved in other areas of research. In recent years, however, the significance of the sports economy as a percentage of GDP has expanded dramatically. This has coincided with an equivalent rise in the volume of economic literature devoted to the study of sport.

This series provides a vehicle for deeper analyses of the demand for sport, cost–benefit analysis of sport, sporting governance, the economics of professional sports and leagues, individual sports, trade in the sporting goods industry, media coverage, sponsoring and numerous related issues. It contributes to the further development of sports economics by welcoming new approaches and highlighting original research in both established and newly emerging sporting activities. The series publishes the best theoretical and empirical work from well-established researchers and academics, as well as from talented newcomers in the field.

Titles in the series include:

The Political Economy of Professional Sport

Jean-François Bourg

Researcher, Centre for the Law and Economics of Sport (CDES – University of Limoges) and member of the International Association of Sports Economists, France

Jean-Jacques Gouguet

Professor, University of Limoges, Researcher, Centre for the Law and Economics of Sport (CDES – University of Limoges) and General Secretary of the International Association of Sports Economists, France

Translated by Gerry Goodman

NEW HORIZONS IN THE ECONOMICS OF SPORT

Edward Elgar
Cheltenham, UK • Northampton, MA, USA

First published in French titled *Économie politique du sport professionnel*
© Vuibert, Paris 2007

Published by
Edward Elgar Publishing Limited
The Lypiatts
15 Lansdown Road
Cheltenham
Glos GL50 2JA
UK

Edward Elgar Publishing, Inc.
William Pratt House
9 Dewey Court
Northampton
Massachusetts 01060
USA

A catalogue record for this book
is available from the British Library

Library of Congress Control Number: 2009937899

Mixed Sources
Product group from well-managed
forests and other controlled sources
www.fsc.org Cert no. SA-COC-1565
© 1996 Forest Stewardship Council

ISBN 978 1 84720 956 6

Printed and bound by MPG Books Group, UK

Contents

Acknowledgements

The authors would like to thank the Conseil Régional du Limousin and the Faculty of Law and Economics of Limoges, without whose assistance this translation would not have been possible.

Introduction

There is now a great wealth of economic literature about professional sport, and the economic community cannot remain indifferent to with the rise of this true twentieth-century phenomenon in society. Since the mid-1950s, we have witnessed a transposition of the instruments of economic analysis to the field of sport. The basic problem is to know whether such a transposition has been effective in understanding recent developments concerning the place of sport in modern society.

The argument put forward in this book is that professional sport is an extremely complex phenomenon with many facets, because of its internationalization, funding and organization, and so on. Faced with such complexity, it seemed to us that an overall, applied approach would be preferable to a partial and theoretical approach to the economic models that are at the heart of Anglo-Saxon sports literature.

Nevertheless, beyond this need to widen the analysis, the problem of a certain number of values and aims assigned to economic activity has to be taken into account; these define what some have since called humanistic economics (Généreux, 2001); or, even more radically, "downscaling" (*décroissance*) (Latouche, 2004). Would not sport be a very good field of study, not only to understand all the abuses of expanding the market economy, but also to think about an alternative? This comes back to the circular causality of the relationship between sport and society:

- On the one hand, sport, as we know, is the product of a market society. The aim here is not so much to promote the constituent values of sporting culture (fair play and respect for the opposition, and so on), as to produce a profitable spectacle, even if it means ignoring certain unfortunate consequences such as doping, cheating, money-laundering and corruption, and the like.
- On the other hand, it is surprising to note how much vocabulary relating to sporting competition has now entered that of economic competition: consider the current usage of such expressions as, "a level playing-field", "may the best man win", "competitive balance" and "faster, higher, stronger", amongst others. This means that sport embodies the ideal approach to the market economy

(pure and perfect competition, equal opportunity, efficiency and competitiveness, and so on).

In order to denounce this liberal and productivist ideology, which suggests that the market has the ability to regulate the economy provided that the market is not itself subjected to regulations, we have chosen a certain number of specific features of professional sport to show that this mass phenomenon is truly in tune with the society that produces it. It is therefore to be feared that, beyond equally ideological views about sporting values, we cannot really think of another place for sport in society, unless the rules of the game of the productivist market economy are modified.

To test such a hypothesis, we have chosen those points that appear to us the most fundamental in defining a sporting culture:

- the aim of sporting activity;
- the demand for social justice;
- the struggle against a dual society.

In terms of aims, we will try to answer the question: sport in the service of what? We begin from the statement that professional sport is wholly a business. Besides, there is a real instrumentalization of sporting values as a means for profit maximization. The problem is, therefore, to know how to move towards a more human sport by organizing it in a new way:

- Either from an internal point of view: sports bodies suffer from a total lack of democracy. What governance for sport has to be put in place to create more transparency?
- Or from an external point of view: over the last few years, new actors have really taken control of sports bodies – mainly the media, but also other major actors in the funding of sport (sponsors and multinational marketing agencies, and so on). What impact do they have on the working of the sporting system and how can more autonomy be regained?

In terms of social justice, a lot of discrimination exists in the field of sport and the requirement for equity is not, at the present time, respected. We discuss ways of combating the most serious cases; this can be done by analysing two problems: Third World exploitation through sport and lack of true sporting ethics.

With respect to a dual society, we criticize the attacks on the demand for balanced competition. Indeed, it is easy to see that the search for profit maximization benefits the richest. If we take the example of football, giving back a place to those who have been left out of the equation involves prior study of several types of proposal: regulating the labour market, controlling transfers, regulating the job of intermediaries (agents), redistributing income, supervising accounts and so on. The deregulation of the markets over the last few years has been favourable to the richest, significantly accentuating disparities with the poorest and destroying competitive balance.

In order to deal with these questions, this work has been organized into three major parts: development, organization and ethics. In the first part (Chapters 1–3), we deal with the general relationship between sport and economic development, in order to explain the place of sport in modern society. Indeed, the sporting spectacle has today acquired such a scale in the daily life of individuals that this phenomenon cannot be treated as simple entertainment intended for crowds who are more or less at a loose end. Professional sport is now subject to numerous pressures from powerful actors operating within a complex worldwide economy and there cannot be a simple vision of it, without falling into false reductionism. Three stages are required to deal with this relationship between sport, economics and development.

The first chapter is a historical approach to professional sport, in order to discover its origins and explain its development. One realizes that, as well as an essentially political instrumentalization, sport as a spectacle is in step essentially with an economic and financial logic. Therefore it is necessary to explain the nature of the relationship between sport and economics, taking into account whether one admits that sport is an economic activity like any other, or not. Two questions arise:

- Has professional sport a certain autonomy with regard to the development of the economic system, which would justify the idea of a sporting exception? Professional sport is not entirely an economic activity like any other and would demand special regulation, the main components of which we try to identify, along with its development.
- Is professional sport completely determined by this development of the economic system and its main characteristics concerning state intervention, globalization and competition and the like, thereby leading to the treatment of professional sport as a true industry?

The second chapter presents an analysis of the economic impact of professional sport in order to assess its potential in creating jobs or in value-added: this by itself is being hotly debated by the authors of such studies. It is particularly interesting to note that whereas the scientific community

of economists concludes that there are only very minor economic consequences for such events, private survey firms find major ones. This reflects
the fact that this type of calculation is used to justify public decisions to
support sporting spectacles – which is not legitimate.

The third chapter is an analysis of underdevelopment in sport, carried
out by studying the spatial distribution of its competitors, performances
and the organization of major competitions. It is far from certain that
developing countries have a real interest in entering the medals race or
organizing sporting mega-events. Imbalances in world sport, both in terms
of competitors and in terms of sporting events, need to be studied through
an analysis of the relationships between economic development and sporting development. It is also a question of illustrating the diversity of Third
World countries in their role on the international sporting scene.

In the second part (Chapters 4–6), we analyse the main difficulties posed
by the organization of professional sports. It is a question of showing that
the choice of model between regulation and the market is not a neutral
one and can have consequences for achieving competitive balance. The
main difficulty lies in how best to reconcile economic competition and balanced sporting competition. Yet, after reading the first part of the book, it
would appear that the economic and social stakes involved in professional
sport are such that many actors clash in trying to promote a model of the
organization of sport that is favourable to them. In order to analyse such a
complex system, we break its working logic down into three basic steps:

1. Where does the funding for professional sport come from?
2. How do those involved negotiate sharing out the income thereby
    made available?
3. What are the consequences of such a distribution on competitive
    balance?

The fourth chapter tries to show that the way of funding professional
sports has significantly evolved over the last 20 years and has seen the rise
in the power of television, which has become the principal source of funds
for professional sport. This control of sport by television must therefore
be questioned, by analysing the working of the sports broadcasting market
and that of broadcasting rights.

The simultaneous conversion of television and professional sport to the
market economy during the 1980s caused a breakdown in the competitive
balance between clubs. This was linked to the logic of audience maximization by channels, which bought and broadcast preferably, if not uniquely,
matches by major clubs. This polarization increased financial and sporting
inequality, and reduced the uncertainty of the result and interest of the

spectacle. That is why, more than ever, regulation is necessary – as much to reduce the consequences for television viewers of the abuse of the dominant position and restrictive practices of channels, as to organize sporting competition in an optimal way for sporting authorities.

The fifth chapter is interested in the terms of collective bargaining for the revenue created by the sporting spectacle. Thus, actors with divergent interests confront one another in the sports labour market: players, intermediaries and club owners, and so on. It would therefore be interesting to understand how, according to the balance of power between these different groups, player transfers, salaries and the part played by intermediaries and so on, are negotiated amongst themselves; and what consequences this can have on the general development of the system. In particular, it is the risk of accentuating the separation between clubs or between players and so forth, which in the end calls into question the achievement of competitive balance.

The sixth chapter tackles the question of the illusion of competitive balance in professional sport. This idea is really at the heart of sporting ideology; it is the "glorious uncertainty of sport". Therefore, a balanced competition between two protagonists would guarantee not just the quality of the spectacle – but, above all, the profit. Questions have to be asked not only about the reality of such a balance, but also the effectiveness of the means implemented to achieve it; which poses the whole problem of the choice of organization model and regulatory instruments.

In the third part (Chapters 7 and 8), we wonder whether an alternative to the present governance of sport is possible, so that the deadlocks into which traditional models have led us can be avoided. To do that, it seems to us that a return to ethics is essential.

Sporting ethics are based on a double foundation. One is objective: sporting rules, which act as a regulatory standard and that are essential for ensuring that competitions remain ordered and honest. The other is subjective: the sporting spirit, which represents the system of values that are generally associated with it. Sport and ethics – these two concepts seem, therefore, to go hand in hand, as is emphasized in the Charter of the Olympic Games:

> The Olympic Spirit is a philosophy of life, inspiring and combining in a balanced whole the qualities of the body, the will and the spirit. Combining sport with culture and education, the Olympic Spirit is meant to be the creator of a lifestyle based on the joy of effort, the educative value of good example and respect for universal, fundamental ethical principles.

Chapter 7 returns to the problem of defining sport and its status as either a public good or a private good. Sport has progressively become a total social phenomenon, which has really invaded the daily life of all people in the world. The basic problem is therefore to know what part economic and financial stakes play in such a generalization of sport as a spectacle; and what place is there for another conception of sport as a global public good.

Chapter 8 deals with one of the most controversial attacks on sporting ethics: resorting to doping. With the many scandals that have affected international sport in recent years (the Tour de France, Italian football, rugby in the Southern Hemisphere and athletics and the like), doping appears to be a massive and organized practice, and not an isolated act. That is why it is the main negative externality of the sporting spectacle.

A series of questions are raised by such consequences. For example, is there an incompatibility between doping behaviour and sporting ethics? What is the extent of the phenomenon? Are the new forms of doping that result from the progress of science (for example, gene therapy and cellular therapy) created by the sudden appearance of new attacks on medical ethics and sporting fairness? How and why did one arrive at such practices? How does the doping industry work? Does the champion who takes drugs have a rational behaviour? What is the social cost of doping? Can high-level sport without doping be imagined?

To summarize, the aim of this book is to show that professional sport is a very complex phenomenon with many specificities according to its place in modern societies, its organization with the research of competitive balance and its governance, which needs an alternative. Professional sport is now under the pressures of many economical powerful actors inside a very complex economy. The choice of a model of organization between market and regulation is not neutral and has heavy consequences on the realization of competitive balance. Finally, it appears that professional sport, in contradiction with what is announced in the official sporting doctrine, has denied its main ethical foundations of its origins and has to be reformed.

1. The economic history of professional sport

In the twentieth century, professional sport progressively became a societal phenomenon, characterizing the best of contemporary lifestyles or even the true values of modernity – to such a point that some authors are only too ready to talk of professional sport in the twentieth century as being not only a new ideology, but also an illusion of civilization. For Robert Redeker, therefore:

> The 20th century has been the century of sport. This century was sporting in the same way that the Middle Ages were religious; but while religion produced major works (in architecture, arts, poetry, theology and philosophy) which defined a civilization, sport produced nothing of the sort. (Redeker, 2002, p. 61)

Above all, professional sport can be defined as a spectacle (Yonnet, 1998). The extent of such a spectacle in social life, via the major media (the written press, radio, TV and Internet) is an expression of the increasingly tight links between the sphere of sport and those of politics and economics. This penetration of sport, by forms of logic that are alien to it, deserves a historical analysis that focuses on two questions:

- What are the origins of professional sport and can it be considered a universal phenomenon?
- To that end has professional sport, which has increasingly become an issue in society, been instrumentalized?

1 THE ORIGINS OF PROFESSIONAL SPORT

Professional sport is seemingly as old as the world itself. Nevertheless, can it be said, for example, that the Olympic Games played the same role in Ancient Greece as they do today, as these two periods are both treated as "decadent" (Veyne, 1976)? From an analytical point of view, this poses the problem of the idea of history. For some, history presents a certain continuity and sport has always been a part of human activity. For others, history is not continuous and, as far as sport is concerned, the origin of contemporary sporting spectacle is to be found in the break that was the Industrial Revolution in the second half of the eighteenth century.

The Continuity of History

From the ancient game to modern sport

From a perspective of the linear progression of history, games can be considered to be part of human nature. People have always played games and designed spectacles: the Olympic Games for the Greeks, the circus games for the Romans and tournaments in the Middle Ages, and so on. It is possible, therefore, to consider that sport is only a modernized form of ancient traditional games: rugby and soule, tennis and court tennis, rowing and boating, football and calcio, are examples.

Sociologist Roger Caillois[1] is amongst those who have best expressed this idea of continuity. His stimulating analysis shows that not only have games always existed in all human communities, but, above all, that the type of game adopted by such and such a society conveys a choice of values and culture that could have influenced its development. In Caillois, there is a double idea: on the one hand, the continuity between ancient games and modern sport; on the other, the ability of sport, as a cultural element, to produce social change.

To go further and establish his argument, Roger Caillois distinguishes between four different types of game (see also Table 1.1):

- *Agôn*, which is a competition between opponents for which competitive balance is guaranteed, thanks to precise rules. "The player relies only on himself; he strives and perseveres."[2]
- *Alea*, to describe games of chance. It is fate or chance that enables one of the participants to win. "The player relies on everything, except himself, and he gives himself up to powers over which he has no control."[3]
- *Mimicry*, designating pretence or role-playing games. "The player imagines he is someone else and he invents an imaginary universe."[4]
- *Ilinx*, giddiness or disruption of perception, to describe games intended to create strong emotions in someone who plays them. "The player is pleased to feel the stability and balance of his body temporarily shattered, to escape the tyranny of his perception and to cause his awareness to be diverted."[5]

For Roger Caillois, the choice of one of these four game models by a society is not neutral, compared with its development strategy. Thus, it is that modern civilization has succeeded in establishing itself, thanks

Table 1.1 Four types of games

	Cultural Forms Remaining on the Fringes of the Social Mechanism	Institutional Forms Included in Social Life	Corruption
Agôn (Competition)	Sport	Commercial competition Exams and open competitions	Violence, desire for power, cunning
Alea (Luck)	Lotteries, casinos Racecourses Betting	Speculation on stock exchange	Superstition, astrology, and so on
Mimicry (Pretence)	Carnival Theatre Cinema Cult of the star	Uniform Ceremonial labels, performance professions	Alienation, split personality
Ilinx (Giddiness)	Mountaineering Ski – acrobatics Exhilaration of speed	Professions, where dominating giddiness is implied	Alcoholism and drugs

Source: Caillois (1967b), p. 122.

to adopting the agôn (moderated by the alea), that is, free competition between equal individuals, which confirms meritocracy. Neoclassical economic theory expressed this later, by asserting that each factor of production must be remunerated according to its marginal productivity in a free market. On the other hand, traditional societies founded on the mimicry/ ilinx pair have been overwhelmed by the former pair (Augustin, 1995).

Roger Caillois expresses it very clearly:

> Games in stadia create and offer an example of limited, regulated and specialised rivalry. Stripped of all feelings of hate and personal rancour, this new space of competitiveness inaugurated a school of loyalty and generosity. At the same time, it spreads the custom and respect for arbitration. Its civilising role has been highlighted many times. Indeed, formal games appeared in nearly all major civilisations.[6]

Ancient Greece was, therefore, the cradle both of civilization and of modern sport and it can, therefore, be admitted that there is a certain continuity between the ancient Olympics and those of the present day. In order to justify such continuity, Isabelle Queval (2004) puts forward three arguments:

- Competition, glory and challenge are invariants of human nature, which have always, since prehistoric times, expressed themselves in the same forms of game: "A permanent feature of human beings is that men have played and play."[7]
- Since Greek civilization, looking for balance has focused on ideas such as health, beauty and form. This is an ideal to be attained and can be expressed in the adage, "a healthy mind in a healthy body".
- We have inherited from Greek thinking, a fundamental distinction between, on the one hand, educating the body and, on the other, physical achievement. In the modern era, what remains is the distinction between physical activity that is more or less recreational, and professional sport based on the pursuit of good performance.

The topicality of discussion

It is interesting to notice that sporting metaphors, which are references to competition, efficiency and performance, have nowadays seeped into all areas of social life (work, school, university and political life, and so on). For Isabelle Queval, this signifies that "the striking feature of this universe is the permanence and exacerbation of the idea of surpassing oneself. This is what appears in modern sport. The ideas of effort, progress and limits to be exceeded are all there in current language".[8]

The same author also notes that an ad hoc vocabulary is responsible for describing the champion's way of surpassing him or herself: "pushing your limits, giving your all, tearing each other apart, going beyond yourself and sublimating yourself, etc. You have to be the best".[9] Now, this same vocabulary is used in the world of work. Jean-Marie Brohm (1976) has already developed a theory based on this kind of overflowing of sporting vocabulary to characterize social activities: in 1976, he wrote that "elections are also likened to matches, with their scores and possible knock-outs; businesses establish 'records'; and finance ministers clash with each other during the 'rounds'".[10]

It would seem, therefore, that since the Greeks, the values represented in sport correspond to an invariant in human nature, which is always looking to surpass itself in competition with someone else or with itself. The aim of such "doing better" can vary over time and, for symbolic, religious or political reasons, one moves progressively to economic objectives. This makes it possible to understand that this idea of doing better in sport naturally serves the economic logic, which little by little has come to govern all modern societies.

At the present time, this symbiosis between sport and society has perhaps never been so complete. In some ways, sporting spectacles are an ideal of the functioning of the market economy, as is asserted by neoclassical theory in its model of pure and perfect competition:

- Anyone can win; the perfect market has achieved equality of opportunity.
- In these conditions, it is the best who wins and all participants are paid according to their merit.
- In order to win, it is necessary to submit to the worship of the performance.

All things considered, it appears that the constituent values of sport have been put forward as a lever for social change since antiquity, whatever the very different explanations that can be given for such a change. There is a kind of continuity in the legacy of ancestral values: competition, surpassing yourself, performance and so on.

This theory of continuity has, of course, been denounced by many schools of thought that, on the contrary, defend the theory of a break. Modern sport, as we know it, was born during the Industrial Revolution in Britain. Jean-Marie Brohm (1976) declares as follows:

> Even if it is true that human beings have always done physical exercise within a recreational, competitive, practical or war-like framework (team games, hunting and ritualistic physical exercises), it is false to claim that sport is "as old as the world itself" or that it is "part of humanity". . . . Sport, as an institution, is the product of an historic break. Sport appeared in England, the "traditional place" of the capitalist production process in the modern industrial era.[11]

In an approach that is less critical than reasoned, most historians themselves underline this critical moment at the start of the industrial era, which favoured the start of the era of "modern sport". In fact, social, economic and political changes, particularly in the second half of the nineteenth century, deeply influenced the development of physical and sporting practice, sometimes reinterpreting them. This approach does not prevent a longer history, including old and modern jousting in the same field. It does, however, underline that a key hurdle was overcome, a little more than a century ago.[12]

The Break of the Industrial Revolution

The birth of "modern sport"

The context: from factory system to Fordism   According to historians, the factory system refers to the type of industrialization that was in place in

Britain from the mid-eighteenth century and that reached its full potential in the mid-nineteenth century. Forms of rural industry persisted for a long time, but the Industrial Revolution of the eighteenth century, which was characterized by the rapid mechanization of cotton and the introduction of steam, progressively changed production systems.

The logic of mechanization favours concentration, and the factory system ended by being dominant. This new method of production could be defined as a combination of the following elements: the concentration and control of workers, the size and volume of greater production, the division of labour, mechanization and new forms of energy (in the beginning, steam).

The factory could be distinguished from the manufactory or mill, which used manual labour and traditional forms of energy. Larger-scale production made it possible to make economies, standardize products, lower costs and to exploit the full potential of new machines.

The workforce expanded and the relationship between owners and workers, in conflict about sharing the surplus between salaries and profits, was one of the key aspects of industrial capitalism. Instead of paying for piece-work, as in home working (which comes back again to controlling production, without being on the spot), the owner now paid by the hour or the day, since they could control the time actually worked by the worker.

Lastly, the unit of production became the factory alone, which was different from the unit of consumption, the household; this was contrary to the system of working at home where these two units were mixed up, and it implied a radical change in lifestyle that heralded modern society.

It was precisely from that time that Fordism, which was a new stage in the process of the division of labour, could be described as industrial concentration, mass consumption and, overall, a new way of regulation. This new stage in the organization of labour completed Taylorism, the scientific organization of work, through body assembly plants and assembly line work – the work of Henry Ford. First introduced into the automobile industry in 1913, it mainly became more widespread from 1920 onwards and became both the symbol of modern industry and of modifications to working conditions; two characteristics captured by Charlie Chaplin in *Modern Times* (1936).

From the point of view of production, Fordism depends on a considerable development of machines and on a detailed division of labour. True machine systems, linked to each other by a conveyor, mean that it is no longer the worker who moves, but the product in the process of being made, circulating before a series of workers, tied to their work stations. They were enslaved by the rhythm of work imposed by the machine, which could be used all the time without stopping (for example, shift work).

From the distribution point of view, Fordism popularized the expression, "five dollars a day", by Henry Ford, which was an expression of a radical transformation of the method of the functioning of capitalism. In the manufacturing system, gains in capitalism are obtained by minimizing wage costs and by looking for new markets beyond the world of the workers. The Fordian choice of paying high wages is linked to a management imperative: stabilize wages and lower the turnover rate.

Finally, Fordism appeared to be a way of regulation that succeeded in harmonizing the conditions of accumulation (in order to produce gains in productivity and the conditions of distribution in order to sell all the products created).

One can see, behind these two basic transformations of capitalism, a debate that still exercises economists: was it evolution or revolution? Can other equally important ruptures be identified in history? Was there one industrial revolution or several?

It now seems that the idea of a succession of industrial revolutions in history can be accepted:

- The first, linked to the steam engine, is associated with the manufacturing system. From the 1770s to the mid-nineteenth century, Britain established this new form of capitalist production. It enabled it to strengthen its domination of the world economy and to establish it on a totally new basis. The spread of British sports is one of the indicators of this domination.
- The second industrial revolution, linked to electricity and the automobile, is associated with Fordism. In the United States, during the 1920s, an economic system based on mass standardized production was established, which corresponded to mass standardized consumption; which, in its turn, required the growth of spending power of employees. The United States became the real melting-pot of modern capitalism and dominated the world economy. But US sports did not follow the British example.
- It is interesting to wonder whether we are, at the present time, living at the start of a third industrial revolution, based on new information technologies (computing, genetics and nanotechnology, and so on). This cluster of innovations will, perhaps, lead to a flexible mode of accumulation, based on organizing continuous-flow production over thousands of kilometres. This search for maximal flexibility involves, above all, a generalized mobility of people, goods and capital. Nevertheless, faced with the rising tide of environmental problems, debate is emerging about the end of globalization and the need to relocate the world economy.

In conclusion, the important thing is to understand that this development of modes of production is the determining factor in explaining the development of professional sport. Changes in lifestyles, accommodation, transport and the increase in leisure time, and so on, have led to a demand for sporting spectacle.

The emergence of the professional sports system   Even if, from a technical point of view, one defends the theory of the "break" in terms of the social representation of sport, new codifications partly have their roots in traditional games, but their development was drastically modified. The example used most often in literature is, of course, football.

Before the football era, there was "soule", a violent and scarcely codified game in which the men of a village or district opposed those of another community; and it possibly enabled a certain number of contentious issues to be settled (Wahl, 1991; Vigarello, 2002). This preindustrial form of football and rugby was banned several times in Britain and France and contrasted with the form that emerged in public schools (that is, independent, as opposed to a state school, in the British sense) in the early nineteenth century.

In a general way, the well-known analyses of Norbert Elias and Eric Dunning (Elias and Dunning, 1994) distinguish between the main characteristics of traditional games and sports, which are summarized in Table 1.2 by Jean-Pierre Augustin (1995).

In order to put in place this new concept of modern sport, institutions appeared as early as the mid-eighteenth century (see Table 1.3). However, it was from the second industrial revolution in the mid-nineteenth century onwards that the organization of sport, in the pyramidal shape that we know today, became established by the public schools.

Public schools laid the first foundations of modern sport and its organization. Indeed, it was in these institutions that the qualified labour needed by an industrial society was trained. Engineers, doctors, lawyers and civil servants and the like were needed and this required a cultural modification in the ways of apprenticeship in these disciplines that involved resorting to sporting practices. In fact, a new teaching method was gradually being worked out in British schools to channel pupils' enthusiasm, strengthen their moral qualities, give them a sense of responsibility and initiative and introduce them to social life.

Bernard Rosier and Pierre Dockes (1983) have expressed it well:

[Then] began the time of "disciplines", of manipulated bodies, placed in a chequering of space and time, dislocated – relocated, serialised and specialised by coding activities, which were at last combined to be rationally used as elements

Table 1.2   Structural differences between traditional games and modern sports

Traditional Games	Modern Sports
Informal organization implicit in local social structure	High specificity. Formal organization Institutions differentiated on the local, regional, national and international levels
Simple, unwritten rules, legitimized by tradition	Written rules legitimized by rationality and bureaucratic means
No precise limitation on pitch, length of time or participants	Pitch, playing time, number of participants clearly defined
Very strong influence of social and natural differences on game	Rules minimize social and natural differences
Weak differentiation of roles	Specificity of roles
Little distinction between players and spectators	Strict distinction between players and spectators
Informal control by players themselves	Formal control by officials certified by the institution
Level of tolerated physical violence very high. Spontaneous emotion	Level of tolerated physical violence low Highly controlled emotion
Emphasis on physical strength rather than skill	Emphasis on skill rather than physical strength
Individual identity subordinate to group identity	Great importance of individual identity

Source: Augustin (1995), p. 14.

of collective strength. . . . One can scarcely imagine nowadays the enormous effort of training, the importance of the coercion that had to be imposed on these men, women and children to make paid workers out of them, having internalied the disciplinary rules and accepting as something natural the present form of wage-earner exploitation.[13]

Sport took part in this business of transforming the working class, through using its free time: sport enabled the conditions of the worker to be raised by reducing alcoholism and other illnesses; and sport disciplined the body and the spirit.

It was in such a context that sport, which was first of all reserved for the elite, became more democratic and professional (Augustin, 1995). In 1863, the Football Association was founded (de La Porte, 2006). From 1871 onwards, it organized the national cup, which was won until 1882 by amateur teams from the South, generally made up of former school pupils. But, in 1882, there was the victory of a semi-professional team from the

Table 1.3   Organization of British sport

Disciplines	First organizations	Date
Equestrianism	Jockey Club	1750
Golf	Royal and Ancient Golf Club	1754
Cricket	Marylebone Cricket Club	1788
Mountaineering	Alpine Club	1857
Football	Football Association	1863
Athletics	Amateur Athletic Club	1866
	Amateur Athletic Association	1880
Swimming	Amateur Metropolitan Swimming Association	1869
Rugby	Rugby Football Union	1871
Sailing	Yacht Racing Association	1875
Cycling	Bicyclists' Union	1878
Skating	National Skating Association	1879
Rowing	Metropolitan Rowing Association	1879
Boxing	Amateur Boxing Association	1884
Hockey	Hockey Association	1886
Tennis	Lawn Tennis Association	1888
Badminton	Badminton Association	1895
Fencing	Amateur Fencing Association	1898

Source: Thomas (1997), p. 61.

North. Moreover, for the reasons mentioned earlier, football became a way to socialize. Finally, professionalism progressed and in 1888, professional football set up it own organizations, with the creation of the English Football League. The British national sports associations codified their rules and the sports were exported throughout the British Empire, Europe and to other continents. Sport was an activity that was defined by institutionalized physical competitions, democratically organized with unified rules and scheduled matches. This system became established late in France, but by the end of the century, its pyramidal organization was already in place with its clubs, leagues and central executive committees. Sport triumphed over old games with its own temporality and spaces, independent of traditional festivals and social constraints in general.

All those involved in sport were equal again in competition, independent of their social status. Georges Vigarello recalls that between 1850 and 1914, sport acquired its own temporality in reference to non-working time, with the development of sporting calendars that regulated competitions in a specific way. The example of football can be taken to illustrate this spread of the British model of the organization of sport (Augustin, 1995; Wahl and Lanfranchi, 1995).

It was first of all in those towns and cities in France where the British were well established that clubs were set up: Le Havre (1872), Paris and Bordeaux (1877). Afterwards, the popularization of football was increased by the patronage of the Catholic Church, which was feeling threatened by secular, non-religious schools. It created places to attract young people, thanks to football clubs and particularly as part of the Fédération gymnastique et sportive des patronages de France (FGSPF). It is estimated that in 1914, 600 football teams were regularly playing in the 5000 existing Catholic youth clubs.

The French Trophy, the forerunner of the French Cup, was created as early as 1907. The French Football Federation itself was created in 1919. It was therefore a little later, compared with in Great Britain, that French football saw significant development with the democratization of the game, the change in the social make-up of the players (the arrival of workers) and the generalization of "false" amateurism. Moreover, with the growing success of the sporting spectacle and the growth of ticket sales, the rules of market economics started to make themselves felt in football, with expenses being refunded, match bonuses and the start of blackmail by players who had the right to change clubs without limit, in the name of individual freedom.[14]

Moving from false amateurism, professionalism was born in 1932 in France, at the initiative of the directors of the most powerful clubs, who wanted to impose their power on the players. But the forced mobility of the players, who were in no position to refuse their transfer, gave rise to the beginnings of a players' organization – in the form of a membership organization in 1934 and then a union in 1936.

Besides this example of success, the spread of the British model nevertheless came up against a traditionalist culture in France, which rejected sporting modernity with its individualism and spirit of competition. Conversely, its gymnastic culture was heavily influenced by military values and extolled the virtues of discipline, group cohesion and nationalism. So it was that in France, after its defeat in 1870, gymnastics was instrumental in worshipping revenge and love of country.[15] This made it possible to understand why the supporters of traditional education viewed with disquiet the arrival of the British model, which was synonymous with individualism, freedom and initiative.

According to Jean-Pierre Augustin (1995), other obstacles had to be overcome: the supporters of medical gymnastics and the defenders of traditional, national games. It was in this context that, in the 1930s, there appeared a new dispute between supporters of amateurism and supporters of professionalism. For a long time, professionalism appeared in France to be incompatible with a sporting moral code. Money only served to corrupt the professional, as opposed to the disinterested and virtuous amateur. Despite this opposition, the major sports spectacles such as we know today appeared. Indeed, very quickly, public feeling towards them became fervent, particularly with the search for a champion (Yonnet, 2004). Georges Vigarello (2002) gives the example of the "false" Olympics of 1900 in Paris, which showed the Games in their infancy resulting from the antagonism between the spectacular conception of the organizers of the World Fair and the much more traditionalist and narrow-minded, even elitist, idea of the followers of Baron de Coubertin. These Games were dominated by gymnastics, mass spectacle and military. The purely sporting and individualist confrontation had to wait a little while longer.

As well as this first example, the importance of the rise in free time for the consumption of new sports spectacles can be seen in the two other illustrations provided by Vigarello: the Tour de France (from 1903) and the Football World Cup. In the latter case, it was with the 1934 World Cup in Rome that the principle of national supporters' trips seemed to become generalized. New tourist facilities were even created (access to the stadium, trips, lodging and tourist visits).[16] Sport, as spectacle and as mass culture in the contemporary sense, was not far away.

It is equally important to point out another significant example of an obstacle to the spread of a model of sports organization, by comparing Europe and the United States. A certain number of sports, originating in Britain, did not succeed in becoming established. The most striking case was the US refusal to accept the most popular sport: football, renamed soccer. Conversely, the rise of the most typically US sporting spectacle (especially, baseball) was an expression of both the rejection of British and of cricket. If basketball (1891) and volleyball (1893) are excluded, the two other major professional sports originating in the United States, baseball and American football, did not really succeed in becoming established in Europe.

As Jean-Pierre Augustin (1995, p. 140) has emphasized, this means that "in the case of team sports, the symbolic process of community identification based on the club, the stadium and the local community appears to be fundamental". Among many examples, Olivier Chovaux (2006) recently described this in the case of football culture in the north of France. However, we will show that in the present day, the growing influence of television has weakened this territorial identification.

Suggested explanations
We have just shown, in a general way, that sport is a reflection of the society into which it fits. Faced with the emergence of the industrial society

and capitalism, there are four approaches that enable us to understand the place of sport in the economy that are worth remembering. These approaches are traditionally set out by sociologists (Defrance, 1995) and could constitute the basis of a broadened political economy of sport, more appropriate to giving the sense of sport in contemporary society than most narrow analyses, based on neoclassical orthodoxy. The four approaches are: rationalized sport (Max Weber), sport as a product (Karl Marx), civilized sport (Norbert Elias) and institutionalized sport (Joseph Schumpeter).

Rationalized sport   In order to link sport and capitalism in many ways, one could do no better than return to the brilliant work of Max Weber. First of all, there is recourse to the Weberian concept of the ideal type, which, applied to capitalism, can be characterized by three distinct features: rationalizing work, new accountancy techniques and an ideology that transforms the attitude of people towards work and profit. Sport has not escaped such rationalization, either on the level of internal organization – if one thinks of scientific preparation or measuring performances, in particular – or on the level of its overall social significance or the image of sport on the individual level – if one envisages victory and success as signs of predestination.

In a general way, the organization of modern sport conforms completely with Weberian analysis. Even more, the twentieth century pushed the principle of rationalization to the extreme, tying up with the Courbertinian adage: "higher, faster, stronger". We are witnessing an excess of rationalization, which is now called "scientific preparation" rather than doping. Once again, we are witnessing the risk of unfortunate consequences, resulting from this search for performance at all costs.

It seems to us that it would be preferable to replace rational management of performance by reasonable management (Latouche, 2001). This means establishing limits, respecting ethical barriers and avoiding the excessive accumulation of wealth. In the field of professional sport, many examples could be given of such excesses that are justified by market rationality. We will return to these points in the third part of the book.

Sport as a product   This is a classic of general Marxist analysis. In this type of approach, sport cannot be tackled in an autonomous way on technical bases, as the sporting field only reflects another reality – that of the functioning of capitalism. In order for a Marxist to understand the development of sport, one has to understand the development of different modes of production.

Let us just recall that in the Marxist dialectic, changes in society come from the development of contradictions between productive forces and productive relations (the two elements that characterize a mode of production).

The essential argument of Marx is to assert that, in such a development, it is the productive forces that play the role of the motor of history: if the labour mill produced slavery, the steam engine produced capitalism and the proletariat. It is for this reason that a Marxist affirms that sport is a product, the result of the logic of the working of the capitalist production process and it follows all the steps through the different stages: competitive, monopoly, state monopoly, transnational and world capitalism. As for its function, sport plays a part in reproducing the whole system by offering externalities to capitalists (for example, health and education), as well as being a good instrument of social standardization. From a Marxist point of view, sport thus becomes an element of the extended reproduction of the labour force.

This idea of sport was mainly developed in France by a critical school of thought called Freudo-Marxist, started by Jean-Marie Brohm (see Brohm, 1976). The analysis, even there, was essentially concerned with top-level sport, as the driving force of mass sport, with the result that, overall, sport was likened to an ideological apparatus of state.

Civilized sport   The essential contribution of Norbert Elias (Elias and Dunning, 1994) was to show how the development of sport cannot be understood without reference to the regulation of violence in society as a whole. Elias established a parallel between the development of rules codifying modern sport and the development of mores. He established that, as the tolerated thresholds of violence progressively reduced in contemporary civilization, sport has also become more civilized.

This process started in Britain during the Industrial Revolution. Many examples of it could be given. Thus, bare-knuckle boxing, which is very close to street-fighting, became civilized through very restrictive regulations; the rugby played in public schools distanced itself completely from the village confrontations that expressed themselves in a violent way in the game of "soule".

From an economic point of view, such a sociological analysis could perfectly be included in the French approach to regulation. It must be remembered that the aim of regulation theory is to understand how every age can produce procedures and institutional forms that make it possible to regulate the violence born of the clash of social groups, for the appropriation of the economic surplus. Can the violence generated by the search for vested interest, involving everyone fighting against everyone else, be regulated?

Institutionalized sport One can draw on the work of the French school of regulation (Boyer and Saillard, 2002) to analyse the development of professional sports since the end of the nineteenth century. The theory of regulation begins with the criticism of neoclassical analysis and with the claim of the market to be self-regulating in order to reach some balance: the market economy is not a place of expression of the natural laws of harmony; the invisible hand regulating rational optimizing agents, pursuing their own interest, comes under ideology.

In its place, it is proposed to take into account structures, inside which the behaviour of economic actors can be analysed. Therefore, we return to the idea of François Perroux (1970) about implicitly prescriptive conceptualization in economics: the balance of exchanges between rational agents in a perfectly competitive market is an illusion. Indeed, economic relations in modern industrial societies, developing in unequal and imperfect social structures, appear as power struggles and as unstable and temporary compromises. At best, the optimal is reduced to the tolerable.

What is at stake in the concept of regulation is, therefore, to know whether in such a context, the conditions for economic balance in fundamentally confrontational societies can be achieved. How can a diversity of mixed social groups, organized into a hierarchy, which are in permanent conflict, be integrated into a whole (system) capable of maintaining its cohesion over time, whilst proving resistant to exogenous shocks (technology, population and competition, and the like)?

The theory of regulation gives a response by going back to the historical analyses of the school of Annales. Fernand Braudel (1967–79), in particular, convincingly showed that history is the result of the tangle of several systems obeying different logics and temporalities (short term, long term, very long term or historical periods). In particular, the great institutions of society evolve over the long term. Their role is to produce regulatory procedures for economic agents, while conforming to very long-term structures. However, for reasons of inertia, it may be that these institutions contradict these very long-term structures and therefore no longer manage to regulate the economic system in the short term. Economists of regulation speak about "a great crisis" to characterize such a historical period. It is then a question of setting up new institutions that conform to the very long-term historical development, so that regulation of the economic system would again be possible – until the next great crisis.

The great crisis of the inter-war period was confined to the welfare state and Fordism in the broadest sense; it was this latter system itself that suffered a crisis in the middle of the 1970s and the emergence of a new model was spoken of: flexible accumulation. It should be remembered that the crisis of efficiency that Fordism underwent was different in nature from the market crisis of the inter-war period. That was why the virtuous circle of growth was transformed into a vicious circle. During the "the thirty glorious years" (1947–74), sufficient gains in productivity made it possible to maintain a harmonious relationship between variables of accumulation (profits) and distribution (wages). The whole was mutually reinforced and we spoke of a "golden age" of capitalism and growth. On the other hand, from the mid-1970s onwards, we saw a collapse of productivity gains in industrialized economies, which resulted in a zero-sum game for the distribution of the national value-added between wages and profits. Moreover, it occurred within the framework of a systematic internationalization of production.

We are, therefore, in a dead-end, from which society is struggling to escape. This relates primarily to the regulation of our economies conceived within a national framework – whereas, at the present time, we are living in a world economy. According to regulation theorists, it is necessary to invent a new compromise since the Fordian compromise no longer works. Two large sets of problems have to be resolved: on the one hand, the crisis internal to every economy, with its national specificities (labour organization, welfare state and model of consumption, and so on); on the other hand, the international crisis, with the need to form international regulatory institutions in order to regulate the major problems of the moment (mainly, underdevelopment in the Southern Hemisphere and the problem of the planetary environment).

Can such a working framework be applied to understanding the historical development of professional sport? In order to answer such a question, we repeat the questions already asked by one of the founders of regulation theory, Michel Aglietta (1976), and adapt them:

- What are the forces that transform the system and guarantee its cohesion over a long period?
- Are the conditions and the procedures of this cohesion likely to evolve?
- Under what conditions and according to what processes of qualitative change do they occur in the mode of production?
- Can one identify stages in the development of capitalism and is this method relevant in interpreting the place and development of professional sport in this capitalist mode of production method?

It therefore seems to us that the working framework of the school of regulation is relevant to the analysis of the development of professional sport in the economy, over the long term. In order to do this, we have used four institutional forms: wage relationship, forms of competition, the nature of state intervention and the way of integrating national economies in the world economy.

Wage relationship   According to Robert Boyer (1986), the wage relationship is made up of all the legal and institutional conditions that govern the use of salaried work, as well as the reproduction of the conditions of existence of workers. In analytical terms, five elements characterize the historical configurations of the wage relationship: the type of means of production, the form of the social and technical division of labour, the methods of mobilization and attachment of employees to the company, the determining factors of earned income (direct and indirect) and the salaried way of life. In a general way, the main long-term transformations of the wage relationship, which have an influence on professional sport, concern:

- The development of the standard of household consumption, compared with the increase in free time, the monthly payment of salaries, the rate of equipment of households in consumer durables and so on. All these factors created a demand for sporting spectacle.
- The development of the conflicts in the share of the value-added between wages and profits. It is still a fundamental element that makes it possible to understand the economic context of a certain period.
- The development of the organization of labour, characterized by regular advances in recognizing workers' rights.

It is in this changing context that it is necessary to put the development of professional football in perspective. From 1880 to the present day, the determining factors of wage relationship have been: the setting up of the players' union, the frequency of the spectacle and its growing crowds and the growing importance of the indirect spectacle (television).

Forms of competition   Over the long-term period that interests us, continuous debate has concerned the forms of the market between competition and monopoly. The best-known point relates to the antitrust laws in the United States (Sherman Act 1890, Clayton Act 1914 and Federal Trade Commission Act 1914).

The debate has reached us in Europe and concerns the competition policy of the European Commission. The same issues involving sport can again be found: broadcasting rights, TV programmes, the labour market in sport and transfers.

For the Commission, the professional sports sector is subject to the Treaty's competition rules for the economic activities that it creates. The application of these rules is made on the basis of general principles, while taking into account the specificities of the sector (see above).

State intervention   In the late nineteenth century, state intervention was minimal. Fordism succeeded in the post-war period, in which the state moved from its role as simple arbiter to participating in economic and social activity. Over the last few years, the crisis in Fordism has caused new forms of state intervention to be considered – which some authors call its modernization.

The state intervened very little in the sporting field with regard to professional sport during the first period of our history; this field being considered as belonging to the private sector. The state had difficulties, post-war and in the 1960s, with the sporting movement that claimed to be autonomous. However, some reforms concerning transfers came about following disputes with players. The 1990s saw some new vague attempts by the state to intervene in sport. Nevertheless, it can be said that, overall, professional sport remains little affected by such interventions.

International integration   The major upheaval in our time is the movement from nation states regulating their own economies to a financial globalization dominated by multinationals. It can clearly be seen that the professionalization of sport has been largely influenced by this internationalization and financialization – this phenomenon has been well analysed (Bourg and Gouguet, 2005). It has been the most commented on consequence of the Bosman Case[17] (1995): increase in salaries, transfer fees and the separation of players and clubs between rich and poor, and so on. It is with regard to this context that the need to invent new regulatory tools to regulate the labour market needs to be discussed; or even to imagine another system for organizing professional sport.

The interaction of these four institutional forms, which are supposed to produce regulatory procedures, enables us to understand the emergence of provisional compromises that allow disputes arising from the opposing interests of different actors involved in the sporting spectacle to be managed.

2   THE INSTRUMENTALIZATION OF PROFESSIONAL SPORT

It is a question here of running counter to an *idée reçue*: the neutrality of sport. Contrary to the "clichés current in public opinion about the supposed neutrality of sport",[18] we show that professional sport has, ever since it first appeared, been instrumentalized by actors in the name of two sorts of logic: a political logic, with sporting victory thus reflecting the superiority of a mode of social organization; an economic logic, with professional sport subject to high financial stakes.

At the Service of Politics

The inter-war periods

During these periods, professional sport acquired the main characteristics that we know today. Two factors have to be taken into account: state intervention and the affirmation of ideological competition, arising as early as the nineteenth century around gymnastics and methods of military physical preparation, between rival political systems.

State intervention   After the First World War, politicians and those responsible for sport understood the benefits that could be drawn from developing sport. Sport started to be considered in the paradigm of international relations. As historians have shown, as a result there was a demand for state intervention to allow champions, whether professional or not, to become national ambassadors.[19] The state also had to build sports facilities in order to satisfy the passion of young people for sport. Many examples of state intervention in an affair deemed to be private, showed the diversity of visions of sport, depending on the country:

- In France, the debate was between the supporters of elite sport and those of mass sport; hence political choices were difficult to make. Léo Lagrange (Secretary of State for Sport and Leisure in the Front Populaire) was against building a 100 000-seater stadium to host the football World Cup in Paris. He preferred to finance "sport for all".
- In Italy and Germany, the Fascist and National-Socialist Parties controlled the sports movements and created sport and paramilitary organizations for young people.
- In Russia, sport was considered, after 1917, as a factor in emancipating the proletariat.

All this means that sport, whether professional or amateur, has been used to serve diverse ideologies. It has been used as a justifying argument for the superiority of one political system over another and has become the pointer to growing sources of tension between states.

Sport and ideology   The first examples of boycotting major international sporting events were seen after the end of the Great War. Sport did not manage to remove the resentment between victor and vanquished, or between supporters of opposing political systems. Patrick Clastres and Jean Saint-Martin[20] have reminded us of the following:

- Between 1919 and 1925, the Germans and their allies (as well as the USSR) were excluded from all major competitions: the Joint Allied Games (1919), the Antwerp Olympics (1920), the Paris Olympics (1924) and the Winter Olympics in Chamonix (1924).
- Until 1924, the French football team played only allied or neutral countries. Matches against Germany only started again in 1931, long after the country was admitted to the League of Nations (1926).
- The rise of communism prompted the emergence of the Workers' Olympic Games (the first in Frankfurt in 1925) and the Spartakiads hosted the sports festivals of the Communist Party in Moscow from 1928 onwards.

The idea that sport was apolitical and neutral was therefore over. Matches between democratic countries and dictatorships became major political issues. There are many examples. Let us take the example of Mussolini's fascist Italy, as was recently shown by Paul Dietschy and Stéphane Mourlane, where the instrumentalization of sport and football, in particular, went along with the euphoria following its two victories in the Football World Cup (1934 and 1938), which were attributed to the genius of Il Duce.[21] Other Italian champions also dedicated their victories to the dictator (Bottechia and Bartoli in cycling, and Carnera in boxing). There is no need to dwell on the Berlin Olympics of 1936, a propaganda triumph for the Nazi regime, as it has been highlighted by Jean-Marie Brohm (1983). "Hitler knew, during the XIth Olympiad, how to fool international opinion into one day being able to substitute the swastika for the Olympic rings".[22] On the eve of the Second World War, sport failed to achieve the Olympic ideal and became the real indicator of conflicts between states and political regimes. Tensions continued into the post-war period and grew with the Cold War between the two blocs (United States and the USSR).[23] Most top-level international sports matches became ideological issues with regard not only to the final tally of medals, but also to the decisions regularly taken since the 1980s concerning boycotts.

Post-war period
Here again, we find the same trends as in the inter-war period concerning state intervention and ideological conflicts.

State intervention: the French example   The Vichy government, with its conception of family and education, understood very well the use sport could be put to as part of youth training: discipline, health, virility and morale and so on. Hence the Charter of Sports (20 December 1940), which made the creation of sports associations subject to ministerial approval.

When the Liberation came, this state supervision was maintained. The regulation of 28 August 1945 instituted the regime of the delegation of power. The state delegated powers to the federations, as far as the organization and control of sport competitions were concerned.

This point is important for understanding the resolution of conflicts that, much later, pitted professional sports bodies against this state supervision. Sport in France has always been considered a public good, coming under the state. Federations had to respect this concept of sport, which later posed problems with the rise of sport as a spectacle and the advent of professional leagues.

The Cold War The Olympic Games started up again in 1948 in London, in itself a political choice by the International Olympic Committee (IOC), as the English capital was favoured because of the terrible damage it suffered during the war. These Games took place without Germany and Japan. As for the USSR, it did not return to the Olympic family bosom until 1952, on the occasion of the Helsinki Games. During these Games, Soviet athletes were ranked second behind the United States; this was the first serious challenge to US supremacy of the Games.[24] It was also the start of the systematic counting of medals – a complete distortion of the original purpose of the Games. Up till that date, involvement in the Games was purely individual, with the athlete only representing him or herself and financing the cost of participation with his or her own money. With the medal count, the results of the sporting competition were attributed to the effectiveness of the political regime behind it. Jean-Pierre Augustin and Pascal Gillon (2004, p. 83) have analysed it in an interesting way: "The race for medals during the Cold War replaced a military clash, which had become impossible with the nuclear deterrent. The medal tally, therefore, had to measure the performance of rival ideological systems."

This logic reached its peak at the Summer Olympics in Seoul (1988), where the Soviet Union headed the medals table, followed by East Germany. The United States was only third. The superiority of communism triumphed, whereas, in fact, it was question of state-sponsored doping!

Along with the medal tally, there are many examples that illustrate this political instrumentalization of the Olympics: the attitude of Tommy Smith and John Carlos in Mexico (1968), with the raised, black-gloved fist as a rallying sign of Black Power; and the attack on the Israeli delegation in Munich (1972), and so on. But the most blatant example, as in the inter-war period, is certainly the use of boycotts:

- Boycotts launched during the football World Cup in 1978 against the Argentinean dictatorship.
- The Moscow Olympics (1980) was boycotted by the United States because of the war in Afghanistan.[25]
- The Los Angeles Olympics (1984) was boycotted in return by the USSR.[26]
- Protest movements against all international competitions organized in South Africa, because of apartheid (from the 1960s to the end of the apartheid regime in 1991).

This head-on opposition declined with the fall of the Berlin Wall in 1992. Even if the choice of Beijing for the 2008 Olympics provoked some protest movements by defenders of human rights, the argument about the universality of sport and its contribution to world peace has again succeeded. The Olympic myth is still very much alive: "At a time when the great stories, dogmas and beliefs have lost some of their force, the Olympic myth and its ritual games can be considered as replicas of sacred ones . . .. Crowds gather in the concrete cathedrals that are the stadia to take part in celebrating the Games".[27]

Even if the myth is still effective, there is no choice but to note that the Olympic spirit is being subjected to pressures that are no longer just political, as we have just established, but that are increasingly economic. The false neutrality of professional sport with regard to politics has, in addition, to be coupled with an increasingly strong dependence, since the 1980s, on the economic logic of the market.

At the Service of Economics

The swing in the 1980s
From the 1980s onwards, sport became globalized and became progressively the subject of considerable financial stakes, linking various major actors: sponsors, broadcasters, manufacturers and marketing agencies (Bourg, 2004d). Pressure from these agents, following a financial logic exercised from outside the sporting sphere, considerably weakened the power of sports authorities (the IOC and International Federations [IFs]) to regulate the whole system.

A notable example is that of the Olympic Games. Two decisions made them turn to the world economic order; opening the competitions to professionals in 1981 and then authorizing the commercialization of the Olympic rings in 1986. Sport thus became an economic activity like any other; to such a point that one talked about the "sport industry". This signified reconstructing this field, based on market values. Hence the question of knowing what risks there are in organizing professional sport in an economic environment, in which financiers (sponsors, television and manufacturers, and so on) expect more of a return on their investment than the sporting performance itself.

In particular, the economic nature of professional sport has, over the last few years, profoundly changed under the influence of television. Two markets are concerned: sports programmes and broadcasting rights. The size that these two markets represent leads to a risk of "tele-dependence"[28] for a certain number of actors involved in the sporting spectacle (especially organizers, federations, leagues and clubs).

All this means that major sports events have become worldwide spectacles; but the size of them is now unequal, in terms of the number of countries or the number of television viewers concerned. From the economic point of view, this involves a turnover in the order of 3 per cent of world trade (Bourg and Gouguet, 2005), hence the name "media–sport complex", which is based on four pillars:

● major sports organizations (IOC, Fédération Internationale de Football Associations [FIFA], Union of European Football Association [UEFA] and IFs, and so on);
● worldwide communication companies (Eurosport, National Broadcasting Company [NBC] and Canal Plus, amongst others);
● multinationals (especially Nike and Adidas);
● marketing agencies.

Of course, the question is, who, amongst all the actors, holds the power? What is the balance of power? Is financial logic likely to overcome sporting logic?

If we add the nation states, which want to make national sporting success an indicator of their own status in the world, we move on from this "media–sport complex" to a "sport–industrial complex".[29] In the language of economics, that means:

● the fan becomes a consumer;
● the athlete becomes a worker;
● the club becomes a brand;
● and sport becomes merchandise.

In order to see the situation more clearly, two types of analysis are needed, so that the interaction between sport as a spectacle and economics can be better understood: an internal analysis of the sporting system applied to league–club–agent relationships, see (1) in Figure 1.1; an

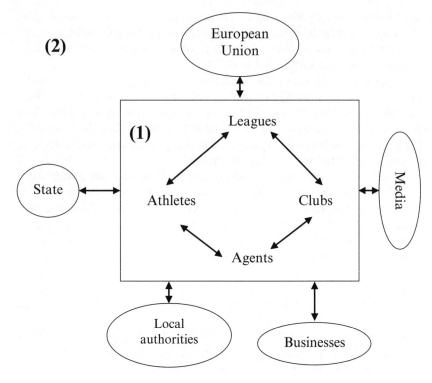

Figure 1.1   The interaction between sport and economics

external analysis relating to the socioeconomic environment of the previous system, see (2) in Figure 1.1.

Analysing the sporting system (1) poses the whole problem of the existence of sporting specificities, not to say, of a sporting exception. Analysing the socioeconomic environment (2) poses the problem of pressures exerted on the sporting system. We think that in order to understand fully the interactions between (1) and (2), it is necessary to be better aware of the real workings of the sporting system, from the inside. But, the greatest challenge for the analyst is to think of the balance between the two spheres, (1) and (2):

- Everybody agrees nowadays in recognizing that it is no longer possible to apply completely the total autonomy of the sporting exception.
- There also exists a relative consensus in admitting that (1) cannot be completely abandoned: to the domination of (2): there are sporting specificities that must be taken into account in the regulation of sport, so that it is not treated just as an ordinary economic activity.

Here again, we find the same problem in the theory of co-evolution applied to the interactions between economics and the environment (Passet, 1975). This theory sets out an optimum that must not be sought in one of the two spheres, if it is to the detriment of the optimum in the other. It is not legitimate to look for economic balance, if that has to be made at the expense of ecological balance – and vice versa.

This can be applied to the relationship between sport and economics. One of the best illustrations of this debate is formed by the development of the relationship between professional sport and the European Union. For a very long time, there has been a lack of understanding by the European authorities and sports authorities, with each defending its vision of sport: for the former, a wholly economic activity; for the latter, an activity apart. We will restrict ourselves to the example of the draft constitutional Treaty, which marked a considerable rapprochement between the two stated conceptions.

Article III-282 (2005)[30] stipulates:

> The Union contributes to the promotion of the European stakes in sport, whilst taking account of its specificities, its structures founded on voluntary service, as well as its social and educative function.
>
> The action of the Union aims to develop the European dimension of sport, by promoting equity and openness in sporting competitions and cooperation between those organisations responsible for sport, as well as protecting the physical and moral integrity of sportsmen, especially of young sportsmen.

These two points deserve comment.

Concerning the definition of sport, the Union does not go as far as a sporting exception, but it does recognize that sport is not just an economic activity like any other. We return here to a fundamental matter: how not to let economic logic alone be applied. This could involve serious attacks on sporting logic. The draft Treaty has responded to it in three ways:

- Sport presents specificities that are not set out explicitly in the text, but which could be the subject of greater or lesser interpretation that would make it possible for it to be protected from certain excesses. Everyone remembers, for example, the consequences on competitive balance of the Bosman Case.
- Sports organizations are completely different from other organizations and, in particular, sport works largely thanks to voluntary work. One of the issues here is to know whether one day, it would be possible to recognize voluntary activity further; that is, recognition of the total economic value, for example, through remuneration for a service done to society.

- Social and educative functions must be taken into account by the authorities, which is not easy, given that we are here in the field of externalities. However, these functions prove to be fundamental for saving the European model of organizing sport. In particular, taking them into account could be used to rethink the relationship between professional and amateur sport, which differentiates Europe radically from the United States (Arnaut, 2006).

Concerning the conception of a European sports policy, three factors make up the Union vision:

- Fairness and openness in competitions. Fairness refers to competitive balance, without which any sports competition loses the very heart of what are sporting ethics: the balance of forces together. Openness means not wanting closure, which is a powerful means of defending the European model. Indeed, one of the greatest dangers of challenging this lies in the attempts to set up closed leagues (the G14 is a good example, amongst others).
- Cooperation between responsible organizations is certainly a major issue for tomorrow. Too often, disputes can be seen between the actors involved in the world of professional sport, because of the financial stakes involved. Establishing the habit of talking to one another is therefore desirable. Traditionally, it has indeed been difficult to make the many sporting actors enter into a dialogue, as it is not really in their culture.
- Protecting the physical and moral integrity of sportspeople can have major repercussions for the denunciation of some of the reprehensible practices towards players: doping, trafficking, lack of training and exploitation, and so on.

Finally, the idea of sport in the European constitutional draft Treaty is a search for a completely acceptable compromise between economic logic and sporting logic. We are far from a total deregulation of the sector; and we are not in a situation where the sporting exception is recognized. In the elements retained, there is an interesting potential to promote a European model of organizing sport. That is the main thing.

The undesirable consequences of professional sport
We shall content ourselves with mentioning, in the tradition of work by Wladimir Andreff on funding sport (1999), the most important undesirable consequences. Let us remember with Andreff that two systems of sport finance have followed one another (Andreff, 2000): the SSSL model in the

1960s: Spectators – Subsidies – Sponsors – Local; the MMMMG model in the 1980s: Media – Magnates – Merchandising – Markets – Global. The operating procedures of these two models are radically different. But, above all, the risks of undesirable consequences with the second are much greater:

Subjecting sport to financial logic Imbalances can disturb the sporting spectacle when the financial interests of the media are involved. The results of that are modifications of times of events, according to television audience "prime time" – hence the possibility of times that do not respect the biological rhythms of sportspeople. It also results in the modification of sporting rules, in order to make the sporting spectacle more televisual; with all the risks that entails, despite the reassuring declarations of Jacques Rogge, the President of the IOC, at the 16th Sportel in Monaco: "If it doesn't want to disappear, sport must adapt even more to needs of television without losing its soul".[31] The list of sports involved is nonetheless a long one:

- tennis, with the tie-break and the colour of the balls, which became yellow from being white;
- judo, with discarding white kimonos for blue, which was a real sacrilege for the Japanese;
- rugby, with half-time and its commercials;
- athletics, with the second eliminatory false start and swimming, with the first eliminatory false start;
- volleyball, where the points counted were changed, thereby shortening the match time;
- table tennis, where victory is achieved after 11 points (and no longer 21), with a bigger ball and therefore has the virtue of being more "tele-visible".

All these examples are there to show that the sporting authorities had to look again at the competition formats, especially their duration, in order to conform to the injunctions of television. Broadcasting rights represent such a volume of funding that one more modification will not make any difference, and all that in the name of the modernization of sport. You cannot stop progress!

Various forms of cheating (Robert, 2006) Here again, the financial stakes are such that there is a great temptation to cheat to share out the "spoils": match fixing, slush funds, false passports, fictitious loans and transferring money to tax havens, and so on.

Doping   This point is so important that we devote an entire chapter to it.

Corruption and the Mafia (Arnaut, 2006)   Sport can be used to launder dirty money. In Europe, examples of corruption exist in most countries. Amongst the areas most affected are:

- Italy, with its system of illegal betting (*totonero*) on football matches, in which the risks and the gains are higher than in the official system (*totocalcio*). In this parallel market, corrupt practices by players, referees and managers have been noted.
- Russia, with the Mafia.
- Great Britain, with the purchase of major clubs like Chelsea, by Russian magnates, with money whose provenance has not been clearly established.
- The Internet, with its systems of rigged bets.

All these examples mean that the economic stakes in sport encourage some actors in guilty practices and the founding myth can no longer be believed. In fact, sport as a spectacle is destined to have the same problems as all other economic activities. This situation leads to a certain number of questions that are dealt with later in this work. In particular, it is a matter of wondering, because of the economic and political stakes represented by competition results, whether transforming the sporting spectacle into a circus can be avoided; and, also, of avoiding the need to use excessive scientific and technical ways to endlessly improve performance.

NOTES

1. Callois (1967b), pp. 102–3.
2. Callois (1967b).
3. Callois (1967b), pp. 102–3.
4. Ibid.
5. Ibid.
6. Callois (1967b), p. 212.
7. Queval (2004), p. 59.
8. Ibid., p. 193.
9. Ibid., p. 204.
10. Brohm (1976), p. 80.
11. Ibid., p. 240.
12. For two approaches to synthesis, see: Tétart (2007) and Clastres and Dietschy (2006).
13. Dockes and Rosier (1983), pp. 33–4.
14. For more about this story, see Wahl (1989).
15. On this point, the reader is referred to the pioneering work of Pierre Arnaud (1997).
16. Cf. Vigarello (1990).

17. *Union Royal Belges des Sociétés de Football Assn ASBL and others* v. *Jean-Marc Bosman*, Case C-415/93, ECR 1-4921.
18. Milza et al. (2004), p.24.
19. Concerning public policies and national stakes see: Callède (2000–2007). More widely, concerning international relations, see especially: Arnaud and Riordan (1993, 1998).
20. Clastres (2007) and Saint-Martin (2007).
21. See Chapters 4 and 8 in Dietschy et al. (2006).
22. Charpiot (2004), p.242.
23. Cf. Milza (2004).
24. See Niggli (2004).
25. Jérôme Gygax (2004a).
26. Gygax (2004b).
27. Augustin and Gillon (2004), p.9.
28. Bolotny (2005).
29. Maguire (2004).
30. *Traité établissant une Constitution pour l'Europe* (2005).
31. *Libération*, 28 October 2005.

2. Significance and measurement of the economic impact of professional sport

The economic impact of professional sport is not a subject on which economists agree, and it is a matter of debate amongst politicians and public opinion. One just has to see the number of articles dedicated to the 2012 Olympic Games bids, where the justification for competition between host cities was the size of the economic impact. We, therefore, find again in Europe the same passionate debate that has existed in the United States for some time between private consultancies on the one hand, and university academics on the other. The former find very important economic impacts to this type of event, whereas the latter usually find very minor effects.[1] Moreover, these controversies are usually stirred up before the organization of events and are forgotten afterwards – even if, in the case of the Olympic Games, for example, a few cities are continuing to pay back the loans for an event that did not hold up to its promises (this is, or was, the case for Montreal, Moscow and Athens). This all means that the debate on the economic impact of the sporting spectacle is often distorted by a lack of rigour and precision in the ideas used. From the point of view of economic theory, one must ask exactly what is understood by economic impact:

- Is it the measurement of the economic effects of a sporting spectacle on a given area (Gouguet and Nys, 1993) (that is, the Olympic Games on California or on Catalonia, and so on)? In this case, the problem is that of assessing the increase of value-added or of employment in the area hosting the event.
- Or is it rather the measurement of the total social utility created by such an event? In this case, the problem is the comparison with alternative projects: the Olympic Games bid for Paris, the renovation of the suburbs or the financing of research and universities.

The choice between both definitions is not neutral, for depending on the choice, neither the same theoretical paradigms nor the same measuring tools are used. Therefore, either tools are used that come from macroeconomics (circuits, multipliers and econometrics, and so forth), or, on the contrary, tools that come from microeconomics (cost/benefit analysis). In both cases, many methodological problems arise, which is why great caution is needed when using the results. Indeed, inconsistencies in economic analyses are too often found, which are more or less manipulated to political ends to back sporting spectacles.

1 THE IMPACT OF SPORTING SPECTACLE AS AN INCREASE IN VALUE-ADDED OR IN EMPLOYMENT

By analysing the literature dedicated to the impact of sporting spectacles (Barget, 2001), one realizes that two elements constantly characterize these works: on the one hand, the difficulty of measuring a complex phenomenon, with the particular problems of the time–space demarcation; and on the other, the ambiguity of the said measurement, as much in the great disparity of the obtained results as in their use.

The Difficulty of Measuring

The complexity of the flows

The first characteristic of the macroeconomic impact of a sporting spectacle on a given area is the complexity of the interactions between the many agents linked to the sporting spectacle, which give rise to values that are reasonably easily measurable.

Figure 2.1 shows the presentation by Holger Preuss (2000) for analysing the Olympic Games.

The left-hand side of the illustration represents the most currently used approach for the economic impact of sports events: it uses a typical Keynesian analysis. The sports spectacle generates an increase in effective demand (consumption and investment), which has positive induced effects on employment and income for the host area. However, crowding-out effects may occur (of consumption and investment) because of territorial saturation or of modification of the general level of prices. All this can be measured with the help of various tools, which we shall come back to later.

On the other hand, the right-hand side of the illustration poses serious problems of analysis. For this very reason, it is often neglected by many authors. The problem lies in measuring the change of image of the host territory, mainly caused by media coverage of sporting spectacles; along

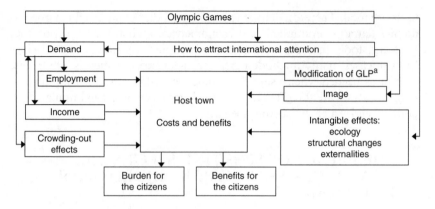

Note: a. General level of prices.

Source: Preuss (2000, p. 36).

*Figure 2.1   Macroeconomic impact of the Olympic Games on the host
            cities*

with measuring intangible, and in certain cases off-market, induced effects.
This enables one to understand that, in the end, it is the well-being of the
citizens of the host territory that is affected in a positive way for some and
in a negative way for others.

Such a comprehensive survey is rarely conducted in its totality. On
the one hand, there are many difficulties in measuring intangible effects
and existing externalities (cf. above); on the other, the partial nature of
the measurement, which is generally limited to positive induced effects,
often serves the interests of the project promoters. This should be open to
discussion.

Territorial delimitation
Defining the relevant area is fundamental for measuring the economic
impact of sporting spectacles. In fact, the area is not neutral. It has an
influence on the variables used in the models. Considering these characteristics, we have deemed it necessary to distinguish between areas hosting
sporting spectacles, according to their size:

- We do not deem the national area relevant in measuring the impact
  of big sporting spectacles, for two main reasons. First, the extent
  of subsequent effects is quite insignificant in percentage of national
  aggregates on this geographical scale. Second, the real understanding of such an impact can only make sense on a given geographical

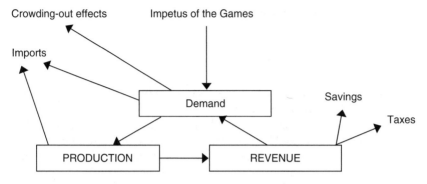

Source: Preuss (2000, p. 55).

Figure 2.2   Keynesian model on the impact of the Olympic Games

scale, especially when, as with the Football World Cup, the event is spread over several cities. Beyond the national territory one must therefore distinguish between geographical areas according to their size.

- For large territories such as California or Catalonia – for the Olympic Games – an integrated economic structure that possesses a relative autonomy of operation and relatively dense inter-industrial relations, and so on, can be considered. Macroeconomic tools and models may be used (input/output matrices and the Leontieff model, foreign trade multipliers and regional macroeconomic models, amongst others).
- For small territories, for example, an average town or city hosting a national elite team, the economic structure will not have the same level of integration as the first one; on the contrary, big sports events in such areas risk resulting in very large leakages (excluding the local circuit). The economic consequences are then very small, such as the Winter Olympic Games (1992) for Albertville and Savoy. But above all, more theoretical tools are necessary to understand such an impact (we suggest base theory).

The national area   Many studies have been dedicated to the macroeconomic impact of the Olympic Games (Preuss, 2000) or other mega-events such as the Football World Cup (Foucard and Torrenti, 1991). They are often based on a Keynesian approach, as shown by Holger Preuss in Figure 2.2.

Generally speaking, studies have shown a relatively small impact of the Olympic Games at a national level, which cannot constitute a significant exogenous stimulus on the economy. A few significant examples could be mentioned:

- The 2002 Silverstone Formula 1 Grand Prix.[2] This Grand Prix was held on 5–7 July 2002. It attracted 116 000 spectators. On the one hand, the economic impact seems to have been small and uncertain. It has been estimated at £17.2m and 11 148 full-time jobs. These figures do not reflect any significant impact, on a national scale. On the other hand, had the Grand Prix not been held, national consumers would have spent their income on something else, which results in the overall impact of spending being the same, save for foreign spectators being drawn to the event (3 per cent of the total spectators and 11 per cent of the total spending). By calculating the total sums spent by foreign teams and tourists (£7.2m), the Motorsport Industry Association (MIA) finds a net impact of £3.4m and 230 full-time jobs, which has little overall significance.
- The UEFA Euro 2008 held in Switzerland.[3] The point of this exercise lay in observing the impact that a sports mega-event would have on a small country of 7.4m inhabitants. In the present case, the impact included: stadia extension, spending by the organization committee, tourist spending, advertising and media activities, and actions by the telecommunications sector. The total impact on the national economy would be, in the best of cases, 316m Swiss francs and 3790 jobs, amongst which few new jobs would be created. Moreover, according to the authors who have examined the Euro 2008 project, it would only be a short-term impact, mainly related to tourist spending. There again, the macroeconomic impact is relatively small and it is better to analyse it on a regional scale, which has been done.
- Olympic Games Paris bid 2012[4] and Athens 2004. Without any demonstration or any kind of reference to the method of calculation, the Boston Consulting Group announced as early as 2004, a €35bn impact on the 2013–19 period for the 2012 Paris Olympics bid, as well as the potential creation of 42 000 jobs. Such affirmations do not appear legitimate to us, for they appear to be completely without foundation. Moreover, they do not result in a very large impact considering the investments agreed upon in principle. One would do better to remember the example of the Athens Olympic Games in 2004, which obliged the Greeks to pay a total bill of €9bn, which they will spend more than 30 years paying back. Nor have the economic effects been as high as predicted, due mainly to the cost of security (€1.5bn), which completely called into question

the profitability of the event. Considering the state of Greek public finances today, it is no longer possible to use the Olympic facilities and most facilities have been auctioned off to private investors. Here is a good example of the misappropriation of public funds for private purposes.

These few reminders are used here to show that the impact of mega-sports events, on a national scale, does not have the objective scale it is usually accorded. In addition, we refuse to enter into a discussion on the benefits of the good image a country can obtain from organizing such events. One can put forward nearly any kind of argument on the subject. For all these reasons, it seems desirable to analyse the economic impact of a sports spectacle on an appropriate geographical level.

Large territories   For subnational, but sufficiently large, areas to show productive integrated structures, it has also been estimated that it is possible to regionalize national macroeconomic models. Two types of models have been used: the Keynesian model and the input/output model.

The Keynesian model, in a more or less sophisticated way, results in the calculation of a multiplier – which, in itself, is more or less worked out according to the data available on various propensities (for consuming, for investing and for importing, and so on). The result is known – the multiplier rises: as the propensities for consuming and for investing rise; and as the taxes and the import leakages are small.

The input/output model is used much more in Anglo-Saxon countries (United States, Canada and Australia, for example) because of the existence of non-aggregated data on a regional level. Such necessary information for the construction of inter-industrial matrices is scarcely available in Europe, which helps explain the limited use of such a method. Once again, in practice, calculating the impact uses a Leontieff multiplier, thus enabling the repercussions of an exogenous variation of the final demand on a productive system to be determined.

In the sports world, such a multiplier has been used not only to measure the impact of the professional footballers' strike in Chicago (1988) and of the Los Angeles America's Cup (1985) and in San Diego (1987) (Barget, 2001), but also, in Australia, the impact of the Commonwealth Games on the urban area of Brisbane (1985), of the Australian Games (1985), and of the Adelaide Grand Prix (1986).

Small territories   The situation of small areas is radically different from the complexity of the previous cases. This does not, however, amount to a lack of difficulty in calculating the impact. The first problem concerns the choice of a theoretical base and, in that respect, it seems that base theory (Gouguet, 1979, 1981) may be suitable for small-size areas as an explanatory element for their economic development. Major sports events, as basic activities, can be considered as motors of economic growth in those areas. The second problem concerns the conditions of applying the theory. Although base theory is relatively simple in principle, it nevertheless presents many difficulties in its implementation, which may lead to errors, if ignored. Standardizing the method is therefore necessary, whether at the level of approach to the theory or at its application.

For small territories, the extent of the impact will depend on two elements:

- The scale of the project, which often determines the recourse to specialized external operators. Large projects in small territories also often benefit other areas.
- The territory's level of integration around its productive structure. The stronger the level of integration, the smaller the leakages.

We therefore come back to the following theory: the smaller, the less diversified, the less integrated is the region, the greater the leakages and the smaller the multiplier will be. One can, however, easily calculate the leakage rate, which cancels any effect of the multiplier inside the territory and we therefore return to the importance of geographical division. Y. Dion (1987) demonstrated the following:

Let

$$I_N = I_B - F = I_B - m^*I_B = I_B (1 - m^*)$$

with I_N: net injection
I_B: gross injection
F: leakages
m^*: rate of leakages.

It could be written:

$$\Delta Y_R = k_R I_N = k_R (1 - m^*) I_B$$

with YR: regional income
kR: regional multiplier

Let us calculate m^* so that one has $\Delta Y_R < I_B$

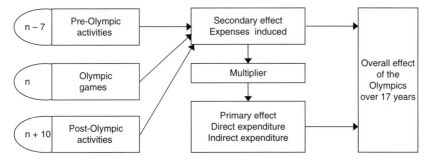

Source: Preuss (2000, p. 41).

Figure 2.3   Temporal breakdown of the multiplier

$$\Rightarrow k_R(1 - m^*)I_B < I_B$$

$$k_R(1 - m^*) < 1$$

$$m^* > 1 - \frac{1}{k_R}$$

It is the leakages rate that cancels any internal multiplier effect. The smaller the multiplier (therefore, the higher $1/k_R$ is) and the lower the rate of leakages cancel everything out. For example, if $k_R = 1.25 \Rightarrow m^* = 1 - 1/1.25 = 0.20$, all you need is 20 per cent of leakages for there to be no multiplier effect.

Temporal delimitation

Life-cycle of the event   The problem is simple in its formulation: in order to measure the economic impact of a sports event, is it necessary to take into account the whole lifetime of the event (preparation, procedure and ex post effects)? For the Olympics, studies most often measure the impact between the date of the bid being awarded and the date of the closing ceremony, that is, about seven years. Others sometimes include the time of the bid's candidature. Conversely, the problem is to know how far to go in long-term impacts that affect the very productive structure of the host region.

In the case of the Olympics and based on a multiplier calculation, Holger Preuss (2000) in Figure 2.3 suggests covering a period of 17 years. Moreover, from a qualitative point of view, the nature of the expenditure would not be the same, according to the period in which it is set, and therefore the multiplier would not be the same either. The pre-Olympic activities generate two types of expenditure: operating costs, and especially capital expenditure. These are massive investments for some Olympic sites, for example, which have the greatest indirect and induced effects. The proceedings of the Olympics, and the years that follow the event, mainly generate operating costs and costs linked to visits by external consumers (tourists and journalists, and so on).

Taking the long-term into account   It is worth noting that these long-term effects should not be ignored, in as much as they can be greater than short-term effects. Motorways, high-speed trains, airports, accommodation and the like, radically alter the operating conditions of a territory in terms of accessibility, mobility, image and, thus, attractiveness. The example of Barcelona is a good one: before the Olympics, the city experienced a generalized saturation that was overcome by the 1992 Olympiad and by the construction of new major roads, districts and accommodation.

From an analytical point of view, this taking the long-term into account in the economic calculation is, nevertheless, not without methodological problems. Indeed, it is necessary to know, in calculating a multiplier, what is going to remain stable and what is going to vary:

- the propensity to consume and the taste of consumers, and so on.
- governmental variables: expenditure, taxes and transfers, amongst others.
- structural variables: demography and technology, and so on.

It is necessary to try to identify the most unstable variables and, besides, use the multiplier cautiously to make long-term forecasts. Indeed, it is fairly tricky to assert, as many authors have done, that the multiplier always remains constant.

All these difficulties in calculating the impact of sporting events can only give rise to many questions about the validity of the results obtained, as well as about their use for political purposes.

The Ambiguity of Measurement

The scope of the results

Errors in calculating   Results from all impact studies appear extremely uneven (Barget and Gouguet, 2000). For example, the difference between assessing the impact of the Sydney Olympics and those of the

Barcelona Olympics ranges from 1 to over 1000! It could be thought that such differences could be explained not only by the differences in the nature and extent of the events, but also by the specificities of the organizing areas. And yet, it can be noticed that the estimates made by different authors about the same event are sometimes poles apart. Thus, for the Barcelona Olympics the impact varies from 1 to 3.4, depending on the author; and for the 1992 America's Cup in San Diego, from 1 to 1.5.

In the same way, Robert Baade (2005a) has often denounced the doubtful overestimation of many calculations of the economic impact of major sporting events. For example, he quotes the forecast of the American Tennis League, which estimated the impact of the Flushing Meadow tournament at 3 per cent of the total annual impact of tourism in New York. That means that 3.3 per cent of the tourists who come to New York, come to attend the Flushing Meadow tournament! It is the same for certain macroeconomic evaluations: the 2002 Football World Cup should have, by itself, increased the Japanese GNP by 0.6 per cent and the Korean GNP by 2.2 per cent. There has to be an end to this kind of pseudo-study, carried out very often by private consultancies that produce obliging results at the demand of various institutions. In most cases, these calculations are false and marred by glaring errors.

Therefore, all these differences in the impact studies that have been mentioned seem to us to come from a certain number of conceptual mix-ups and errors, distorting results in an uneven way. Let us mention the most common, before analysing them more precisely, through the example of investment expenditure:

- Not taking into account the substitution effect, which involves the expenditure of local agents. If the sporting event did not take place, they would spend (consumption or investment) on other types of economic activity anyway.
- The time switching in consumption or investment. Spending by external agents decided before the sporting event is simply displaced (moved forward or back).
- Omitting crowding-out effects, as far as consumption or investment is concerned. Spending could be discouraged, owing to the fear of the area being saturated or the various nuisances created by the sporting event.
- Omitting leakages from the area (consumption or investment) or, on the other hand, double accounting for the injection of funds (for example, ticket sales to outside spectators and spending by the organizing committee, partly financed by these same ticket sales).

- Shortcomings in justifying the multiplier, which can simply be transposed from a study about another area that supposedly shows similar characteristics; this is something that is not necessarily legitimate.

All these shortcomings point, in general, to an overvaluation of the impact. But they also largely explain, according to the rigour of the calculation, the differences between the studies in the amount of the impact.

To illustrate this type of methodological difficulty, we use the example of the investment expenditure during the Olympic Games. The investments made in the host area must be differentiated in two ways:

- With regard to the geographical origin of the investors (internal or external). Here again, we come across the problem of base theory.
- With regard to the aim of the investment: is it completely determined by the Olympic Games or not?

It is only by sorting out all the investments in such a way that one can select those that are truly generators of the economic impact of the Olympics. Holger Preuss (2000) suggests the classification presented in Figure 2.4.

According to these definitions, it will be noticed that A, B and I are "neutral" with regard to the impact of the Olympics. It remains to be seen if the sum of $D + E + F - G - C$ is positive; in which case, it can be deduced that there is a net injection of investment in the area. It can therefore be understood that in many studies, the investment supposedly linked to the Olympics is significantly overestimated. The same type of remark could be made about consumer spending.

Serious hypotheses   Even supposing that the net injection is correctly made in the host area, additional hypotheses must be postulated in order to calculate the impact generated by this spending – hypotheses that could possibly turn out to be rather daring:

- On the one hand, the not fully exploited production capacity of the area has to be accepted.
- On the other hand, it has to be assumed that the short-term impact is going to last in the long term to generate development for the area.

In the first case, an increase in demand in an area with saturated production capacity results in either leakages or inflation – or, indeed, both. The

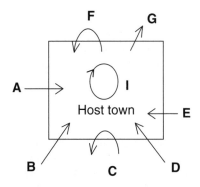

Source: Preuss (2000, p. 60).

Notes:
A. Investments by external agents that would anyway have been made even without the Olympics.
B. Investments by external agents that had already been planned but at another time.
C. Investments by external agents that will not be made, but that would have been made if the Olympics did not take place (crowding-out effect).
D. Investments by external agents that would have been made anyway, but that are greater because of the Olympics.
E. Investments by external agents solely because of the Olympics (private sector, organizing committee and the state).
F. Investments by local agents that were planned for elsewhere, but that are now made in the host city.
G. Investments by local agents that are not made in the city because of the Olympics (crowding-out effect).
I. Investments by local agents that are made in the city independently of holding the games.

Figure 2.4   Origin and aim of investments in the host city

impact of a major sporting event on an area as a result of an increase in external demand is therefore not automatic: everything depends on the capacity of the area to respond to the supply. In the second case, several scenarios can be envisaged:

- Sporting events have a limited localized impact over time. Once the event is finished, the host area finds itself in the same situation as before.
- Sporting events, because of capital spending, generate a continuous level of activity through the use of these facilities by tourists and external visitors, and so on.
- Sporting events, through their induced effects, can give a boost to territorial development of a new type.

In these conditions, it is dangerous to extrapolate over the long term, the short-term consequences of the sporting spectacle. All these approximations in calculating the economic impact thus make the systematic use of results for political or commercial purposes all the more suspect and without credible theoretical justification.

Using results

The reasons cited   In all cases, calculating the economic impact of sporting events serves to justify the project. Two main categories of economic agents are at the origin of such a use: public authorities that host the event or are partners of it, and the sports authorities that organize the event.

As far as public authorities are concerned, one is faced with a mainly political issue. It is a question, in fact, of making public opinion accept the legitimacy of hosting a large-scale sporting event, which, in that opinion, is going to generate increased expenditure, taxes and, possibly constraints and nuisances, and the like. To do this, two arguments have been put forward:

- The economic effects for the area: job creation and increased revenues, and so forth. This point is systematically highlighted, because, of course, it appears to be the most convincing to public opinion, which is not necessarily aware of what happens in sport. On the contrary, it is difficult to remain impervious to job creation and territorial development in general.
- The fiscal multiplier is the second argument, though less often used than the first. It consists of maintaining that the support given by a public authority to organizing sporting spectacles will benefit from a positive fiscal return. The reasoning is simplistic as shown in Figure 2.5:

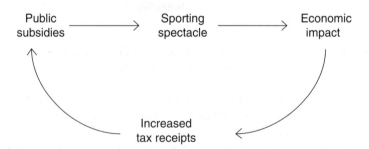

Figure 2.5   The fiscal multiplier

The argument put forward here is that the extra activity generated by the sporting spectacle leads to additional tax receipts, which make it possible to cover the public subsidy granted. Organizing the event would therefore cost the local authority nothing, or could even bring a net gain.

As far as sports organizations are concerned, the economic effects argument is used in the competition for the candidature for hosting the event. Two interlocutors are targeted:

- The public authorities, from which the subsidies will be requested. Indeed, despite the fact that most major sports events are economically profitable, there is always a call to the public authorities for funds. This is partly to support the construction of the necessary large facilities. Here again, the same arguments can be found for requesting such aid: job creation, revenue and tax returns.
- The international bodies that attribute the organization of the event can be made more aware by the results of an economic impact study. They are supposed to indeed show the dynamism of an area, its ability to organize and its expertise, and so forth. It is worth noting, nonetheless, that this condition is perhaps necessary, but it is not enough. All we need to do is remember the examples of the candidatures of Sion for the 2006 Winter Olympics or Quebec for the 2002 Winter Olympics, cities where the impact studies were, however, of good quality (Barget, 2001).

In the end, despite the apparent validity of the argument for economic effects in justifying organizing sporting spectacles, one is persuaded that, on the one hand, these arguments are often false and, on the other, that they are not legitimate.

The inadmissibility of the argument for economic effects   Even supposing that calculating the economic impact has been correctly done (which is not always the case), it would appear that manipulating the results to show the legitimacy of the project lays itself open to two major criticisms.

The first concerns the arguments used by public authorities and sports organizations to justify or ask for subsidies, because they are generally false. Here again, the substitution effect plays a role in relation to job creation or fiscal multiplier: one can perfectly imagine that in the absence of a sporting spectacle, public funds would be used to develop activities that already exist or new activities generating the same volume of employment and tax receipts. The question that must be asked is, in the name of what, why is such or such a project selected? For that, it is not an impact calculation that is needed, but rather a calculation of profitability.

Thus we come to the second criticism. It is the most fundamental criticism that can be made about the improper use of the results of economic impact studies of sporting spectacles. The legitimacy of a project (for example, a large stadium or the organization of the Olympic Games) should be assessed, at the risk of leading to absurdities, with regard to the social utility that it generates and not with regard to the extent of the economic effects. Yvon Stringer[5] has provided convincing illustrations (we recommend the case of the plane accident[6]), from which we have adapted the following example: a local authority has the choice of building a large stadium or a hospital; for reasons to do with the economic structure of the area, the large stadium can be mainly built with local resources (employment and capital, and so on), whereas the hospital has to call on external specialized companies, with imported materials; owing to this fact, the economic effects of the first project are very large, unlike those of the second. Does one, for all that, have to build the large stadium?

It can clearly be seen that this reasoning does not hold. Choosing between the two depends on the extent of unsatisfied needs, as far as sport or health is concerned. If the hospital is part of the deficient facilities in the territory, the health of the whole population weighs more heavily in a cost/benefit analysis than the simple entertainment of some of the inhabitants. There are many more deliberately grotesque examples and one could raise again the problem of the suburbs, of research and universities and the like. France, today, certainly has a greater need for massive support for its research policy than for organizing the Olympic Games!

This means that even when the calculation of the economic effects is correct, these effects must not be likened to the social return of the project. This return is the difference between the benefits that a population derives from the project and the costs that it must bear. The conclusion is clear; it is not enough to calculate the economic impact of a project without assessing its utility for the population.

In other words, calculating the economic effects cannot, by definition, demonstrate the return of a project. It tells us simply that the project in question generates a certain volume of economic activity, and that is all. It does not tell us if the project deserves to be pursued or not. On this matter, we give a very educational example sent to us by our Canadian colleague, Professor Fernand Martin. Let us suppose that a stone is thrown into a lake. As it falls, it makes circles, the number and amplitude of which can be calculated. This is the calculation of the effects (of the stone). But before doing such a calculation, Professor Martin told us that it is necessary to ask a basic question: was it necessary to throw the stone? The parable seems to us to be illuminating and it is this question that we are going to try to answer through the problems posed by calculating the economic profitability of sporting spectacles.

2   THE IMPACT OF THE SPORTING SPECTACLE AS AN INCREASE IN TOTAL VALUE-ADDED

If the extent of the economic effects of a project cannot in itself be a criterion for deciding, this element can nevertheless possibly be included in calculating the total economic value of the sporting spectacle. The first difficulty in doing this comes from measuring the social utility of the projects, particularly evaluating externalities. It is in this context that the economic effects can be brought in, since they are synonyms for social cohesion, job creation, reducing delinquency and the like, which are all things that are comparable to positive externalities or to avoidable social disutility. Nevertheless, as for the economic impact, such a measure of created total social utility encounters formidable methodological obstacles that, once again, could be the origin of manipulating economic assessments for partisan purposes.

Taking Externalities into Account

Typology of externalities linked to sporting spectacles
An externality can be defined as the impact of actions of an individual on the well-being of other people, without this impact being taken into account by the market. If this impact is negative, one speaks of a negative externality or of external diseconomy; if the impact is positive, of positive externality or external economy. In the sporting field, there are also many cases of externalities:

- Among the most significant negative external effects, one could cite: the damage caused by sporting practices or major sports events to sensitive natural environments (noise, erosion, sound and pollution, and so on);[7] certain consequences of intensive sporting practice (especially, doping, accidents and illnesses); nuisance linked to the presence of large sports facilities (for example, noise and visual pollution, and urban integration) and sports goods industries (pollution, etc.).[8]
- Among the most representative positive external effects could be certain human and social consequences of sporting practice (improved health, extending life expectancy, reducing absenteeism and sick leave at work, social integration, reduced social

pathologies, and so forth), as well as of sporting spectacles (national identity, social links and territorial brand image, amongst others).

From a theoretical point of view, taking externalities into account leads to the results of welfare economics; these have important repercussions as far as economic politics is concerned. Indeed, without governmental intervention, the price and quantity exchanged for a good on the market is set at the intersection of the supply curve and the demand curve of this good. In the absence of externalities, this market balance is socially optimal, reflects the value given by the buyers and sellers to the good concerned and it maximizes the sum of the consumer surplus.

On the other hand, in the presence of externalities (positive or negative), there is a gap between social cost and private cost, or (and) between social advantage and private advantage, the result of which is that the equilibrium is not optimal. It is necessary, therefore, to internalize the external effects in order to re-establish equality between social cost and private cost. But to do that, one must be capable of quantifying such a social cost.

Total economic value of sporting spectacles

New definitions of the value   Traditionally, economic theory is in the habit of putting use value and exchange value in opposition:

- Use value is the subjective utility attributed by an individual to a certain good and the satisfaction that he or she gets from it. It is a value that does not necessarily require the existence of a market and that is valid for an individual isolated from his or her fellow creatures.
- Exchange value is the objective measure of the capacity of a good to be exchanged for other goods on a market. This is a social value. The price is an expression of the exchange value.

From there, we find again the paradox of the value when these two elements are compared: certain goods could have a very high use value and no exchange value (and conversely). This paradox is known in economic literature as "the paradox of water and diamonds". If the first has a high use value (water is life), it has a very low exchange value. For the second, their very high exchange value does not justify their utility.

This paradox was resolved in the history of economic analysis by simultaneously taking into account the utility and scarcity of the goods. Nonetheless, the fact remains that economic theory is interested, first and foremost, in the exchange value. The objectivity that governs its determination fits in well with a research programme that claims to be scientific; but it is at this level that one of its main weaknesses can be found.

That is why, over the last few years, with the awareness of environmental problems on a global scale, economists have been trying to reconsider the problem of value. This has given rise to new concepts that are starting to change economic calculations:

- The intrinsic value or value in itself of a good, that is, its non-use value. How much is such and such a good worth, if it is not used (a tree or an animal, and so on)? It is a value that has led to much debate, since the subjective dimension is essential here.
- The option value. Even if individuals do not exploit a given resource at the present time, they may wish to keep an option for the future. Thus it is that goods that do not have a high use value today may acquire a high option value tomorrow, in view of scientific progress (the option value of tropical forests today as a reservoir of materials for the medicine of tomorrow).
- Asset value or legacy value: what value do I attribute to the fact of relinquishing the immediate use of a good in order that future generations can benefit from it?

The total economic value of a good is the sum of all these values (Figure 2.6). It is that which should be used for economic calculations. The problem lies, of course, in measuring that total value and in the choice of methods available that are best adapted to the specificities of sporting spectacles.

Application to sporting spectacles　Based on previous definitions that come under environmental economics, it could be said that the total economic value of sporting spectacles is the measurement of the total utility that individuals in the host area derive from it. It is a question, therefore, of knowing whether one can use Figure 2.6 to describe sporting spectacles. Eric Barget (2001) analysed the following proposals in his doctoral thesis:

- Use value: it corresponds to the utility indeed felt by the consumer of sporting spectacles. The willingness to pay is partially revealed by spending on entry to the spectacle (tickets) or on various purchases. By recreating the demand curve of the spectacle, it is then possible to calculate the consumer surplus.
- Option value: this is the amount of utility felt by individuals for the possibility of benefiting in the future from a sporting spectacle. It is

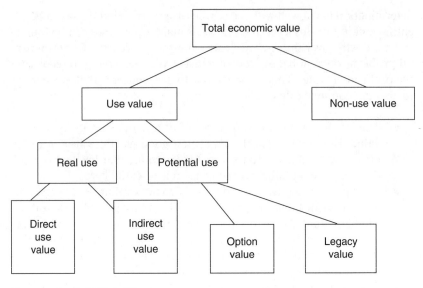

Source: Barde (1992, p. 74).

Figure 2.6   Components of the total economic value

a matter of keeping the option of organizing such a spectacle, and avoiding its disappearance.

- Legacy value: this is the satisfaction felt by the fact of transmitting a sporting spectacle to future generations. It mainly measures all the value that can be given to sports culture as a heritage of humanity (see Chapter 7).
- Existence value (non-use value): this is the utility drawn by an individual from the fact of knowing that this spectacle exists, with all that could represent from the economic, social, symbolic and cultural point of view . . . even if he or she does not attend it.

The sum of all these values gives the total economic value of sporting spectacles. As many of these values are off-market, economists have tried for the last 30 years to experiment with various methods to reveal the willingness to pay of agents; which is not without a certain number of difficulties. Nevertheless, this makes it possible to lead to another typology for sporting spectacles, these events not being all of the same nature and not presenting the same characteristics, as far as economic impact and created social utility are concerned. For example, in the case of occasional events, two types of event can be distinguished:

- Events for the general public that are close to being more pure spectacle than sporting performance. The analysis will be the same as any other economic activity that wants to yield a profit.
- More media-grabbing events that attract an informed public and that are closer to general interest events. It has to be asked, what is the value of the social utility thus created that can possibly justify the payment of public subsidies?

A new typology of occasional sporting events could thus appear: some will have important economic effects, but a relatively low, or even negative, social utility (the Dakar Rally); others will present a high degree of social utility, in spite of insignificant economic effects. The problem is that a number of constituent elements of this social utility belong to the category of external effects, which inevitably complicates the measurement.

The Dangers of Manipulation

Methods of assessment

General presentation Economists have devised different methods of revealing and assessing individuals' preferences:

- Substitution markets: as far as the environment is concerned, individual preferences are evaluated by examining their behaviour on three markets linked to environment: travel (costs), protection (expenses) and housing (hedonist prices).
- Hypothetical markets: also called the "contingent evaluation method" (CEM), it is increasingly used to estimate the intrinsic value or potential value of environmental goods. It is spoken of as the direct method, since one tries to know directly the preferences of individuals and their willingness to pay, using questionnaires and interviews.
- Indirect methods: the aim is to calculate a dose–effect relationship, then to carry out a monetary evaluation of the physical effects. These methods are possible only with difficulty in the specific case of sport.

Some of these methods come from the field of environmental economics and are used in the field of sport; mainly the travel costs method or the CEM: the travel costs method has been used to assess rock-climbing in the Briançonnais (Bourdeau and Rotillon, 1999); the CEM was tried out by Eric Barget to determine the value of a Davis Cup semi-final (Barget,

2001). In both cases, it was found that the costs linked to these operations were largely outweighed by the profits. Nevertheless, as for calculating the consequences, these methods are difficult to use and involve many biases.

Difficulties of application

The travel costs method is relatively simple in principle but has been subjected to much criticism (Bonnieux and Desaigues, 1998), as it requires the difficult and costly collection of information: the option value of the travelling time and the characteristics of the consumers (income, education and preferences, and so on). In the absence of quality information, the results obtained can be controversial.

In the same way, the CEM presents a certain number of biases. Jean-Philippe Barde (1992) has listed six of them: the strategic bias, the initial bias, the informational bias, the instrumental bias, the hypothetical bias and the operational bias. It is therefore necessary to take many precautions when using the CEM, which is what Eric Barget (2001; Barget and Gouguet, 2007) and Hervé Gilliard (2001) suggest in their doctoral theses. For Gilliard in particular, the problem is to know whether the CEM makes it possible to result in a monetary measurement that truly reflects the preferences of individuals. Many procedures have thus been tested out in order to try to neutralize the different biases inherent in the system.

Beyond these commendable proposals for methodological improvements, it nevertheless seems that the problem is other than in a simple technique of economic calculation. It is all the decision-making that is at stake here and that calls into question the prior assessments, while showing the need for negotiation.

The need for a voting democracy

The limits of the assessment   The evaluation methods that we have just presented remain dominated by a neoclassical toolbox (cost/benefit analysis). That presupposes two strong hypotheses:

- The individual is the best judge of his or her utility and his or her preferences can be disclosed through his or her willingness to pay.
- One can move from individual utility to social utility by aggregation of individual preferences.

Faced with the difficulties of these methods to internalize external effects correctly, new analyses have been developed (fuzzy mathematics multi-criteria analyses). It is no longer a matter of finding the best solution, but of clarifying the choices; which is why we have progressively focused on assisting negotiations.

From a theoretical point of view, we again find the influence of the criticisms of the concept of rationality and to its use in economics. Since the work of Herbert Simon and his recognition with a Nobel Prize for Economics, the principle of limited rationality has been slowly accepted, which makes it possible to understand that the optimum, or "the one best way" (Taylor), is a utopia. Indeed, the experience shows that decision-makers are happy with the first satisfactory solution that comes along rather than the best, which they will perhaps never reach.

Impact studies have not escaped such a general development of ideas and, at the present time, the problem is not so much to measure the consequences of a project, but rather to start negotiations. It is not a matter of imposing a technocratic or scientific study led by experts, but, through a wide participative process, to bring forth a compromise that takes into account the preferences of all the parties involved. The traditional economic calculation, which necessarily involves more or less arbitrary elements, must not be used directly in decision-making, but must be put at the service of looking for a compromise between actors with diverging rationalities. That is the whole issue of good governance.

Towards a participative democracy   The intended goal is an increased participation of all actors in decision-making processes. In particular, decision-making could proceed in a context of conflicts of powers and interests. For example, organizing the Olympic Games can have positive repercussions for some actors and negative ones for others (see below). It is desirable, faced with such situations, to lead to compromises between actors, if one does not want to see the systematic domination of the strongest turning things to their own advantage. That is why the real problem is not so much to perfect a more or less reliable method of evaluation, but to have deliberative institutional procedures in place in order to take decisions.

Many instruments of governance have, at the present time (Lagadec, 2000; Van den Hove, 2000), been tested and seem to give satisfactory results (citizens' juries, focus groups, consensus conferences and mediation). From a methodological point of view, the origin of these proposals is the rejection of the cost/benefit analysis that is based on the monetarization of all the assets. The refusal to reveal a willingness to pay in the CEM is thus the result of, from the individuals asked, an inability to attribute a monetary value to common goods. From this perspective, they do not act like consumers (of private goods), but rather as citizens.

Therefore, for these citizen values, the deliberative approach is more appropriate than the cost/benefit method and its monetary evaluation.

This is particularly true for the citizens' juries. The panels have the possibility of having recourse to experts' hearings and to interest groups and they finalize their verdicts by written recommendations.

For Hervé Gilliard (2001), the deliberative approach, such as a citizens' jury, favours the expression of citizen motives, whilst the CEM encourages the individual to behave like a consumer. Nevertheless, the former method presents a certain number of methodological difficulties that could call into question the general validity of the results obtained: how to select a citizens' jury? What sort of representativeness does it have? What credibility should be given to the proposals put forward?

Completely different evaluations of sporting spectacles will be obtained, depending on the instrument used. The choice between the two methods comes close to a true political option, according to the emphasis one wishes to put on the economic stakes or, on the other hand, on ethical problems in the widest sense. It is a question, therefore, of wondering whether these two points of view cannot complement each other. For Hervé Gilliard, there are two possible ways of doing this:

- In the contingent study, collect both quantitative (willingness to pay) and qualitative information in order to put the former into perspective.
- Systematically use a deliberative approach as a complement to cost/benefit analyses; there again, to put the results into perspective, as well as to include the citizen in decision-making.

It is, once again, mainly in the field of the environment that these instruments are used. It is to be regretted, therefore, that as far as sport is concerned, decision-making about the organization of sporting spectacles or the construction of large facilities are always subject to a rather technocratic approach. You only have to see the committed discussion over the choice of the host city for the 2012 Olympics. Citizens have scarcely been listened to and when, occasionally, criticisms have been made, their authors have been quickly treated as traitors to the country for being against the Games! A major national debate deserved, however, to be organized so that the costs and advantages of holding the Olympic Games could be honestly presented – but it did not happen.

NOTES

1. Baade and Matheson (2000); Baade (1996); Noll and Zimbalist (1997); Coates and Humphreys (1999).

2. Motorsport Industry Association (MIA) (2003).
3. Heinz Rütter et al. (2004).
4. The Boston Consulting Group (2004).
5. Stringer (1980).
6. If a plane crashes in a desert, there will be much less economic impact than if it crashes in a city. So, should you wish for all plane crashes to occur in cities, just to have a strong economic impact?
7. Proceedings of CDES-CRIDEAU symposium (2000).
8. Regional Economic Sports Observatory (1998).

3. Economic development and sporting performance on a worldwide scale

The purpose here is to propose an analysis of the relationships between economic and sporting development, in order to characterize the great imbalance in world sport from the point of view of amateur or professional participation, performances and spectacles. This study also shows the diversity of Third World countries on the international sporting scene (Andreff, 1988; Bourg, 1993; Fates, 1994).

With such disparities between developing countries, the framework of Third World identity breaks down. Therefore, is there a problem common to this heterogeneous group?[1] What role do multinational firms play? Is the even more exaggerated price paid by certain countries in the global competitive sphere reasonable? Is sport not a costly way of having access to "modernity"? Is it necessary to suggest disengagement from this highly productivist sporting order, for the least developed countries? In other words, is not sport as a spectacle an obstacle, rather than a lever, to economic development in most of these countries? Lastly, is it necessary to escape from this particular sporting underdevelopment?

An assessment of the vicious circle of sporting underdevelopment should be drawn up and its persistence analysed.[2] Studying the spatial distribution of those participating in sport, performances and competitions reveals a limited, although unequal, international spread in areas where economic development makes facilities and supervision possible. This encourages extending leisure time and floods the middle classes with money and behaviour patterns.

1 THE FIELD OF ANALYSIS

Such an approach is in line with development economics, a branch of economics that appeared after the Second World War, and that was recently rehabilitated after two decades of being ignored by dominant theories (Treillet, 2005). In fact, major international institutions such as the World

Bank or the United Nations are readdressing the massive phenomenon of poverty and the mechanisms that perpetuate it.

Studying the relationship between economic development and sporting performance requires, beforehand, a critical identification of the criteria and terminology of "underdevelopment". As soon as poverty is concerned, two sets of questions arise: measuring poverty gives rise immediately to fundamental questions about the definition and objectives of development (Assidon, 2004).

According to the World Bank classification, all countries are divided up every year according to the gross national product (GNP) per inhabitant.[3] In 2006, the World Bank report distinguishes between, according to the 2004 figures:

- low-revenue economies or the least developed countries (LDCs), bringing together about 60 countries whose GNP per capita was $765 per year or less (40 countries in sub-Saharan Africa, 15 Asian countries, some countries in Eastern Europe, Central Asia, the Middle East and Latin America);
- countries with lower middle-income economies (LMICs), bringing together 40 countries whose GNP per capita was between $765 and $3035 per year (15 Eastern European countries and Central Asia, a dozen countries from the Middle East and the Maghreb, as well as several African countries);
- countries with upper middle-income economies (UMICs) or emerging market economies (EMEs), bringing together about 40 countries whose GNP per capita was between $3036 and $9385 per year (15 Latin American countries, a dozen central and Eastern European countries and a dozen sub-Saharan African countries and Asia);
- higher-income economies or developed countries bringing together 50 countries whose GNP per capita was higher than or equal to $9386 per year (24 OECD countries and 30 countries from outside the OECD).

According to the World Bank, lower-income and middle-income economies are developing countries and represent more than 80 per cent of the world population and about 20 per cent of the production of goods and services. However, the quantitative and monetary criteria that, for a long time, have been the only ones used by the International Monetary Fund (IMF) and the World Bank, do not properly show underdevelopment. Admittedly, they convey the differences in revenue between the countries and their development. But they overestimate the monetary dimension, while the non-monetized part of the economy is all the greater when poverty is greater.[4] Moreover, these indicators do not show the level of welfare reached and do not reflect the relative differences of success between countries classed in the same per capita income groups. That is why, during the 1990s, the United Nations Development Programme (UNDP) put in place composite development indicators, in order to provide an overall assessment of the level reached by each country in different domains of human development. Amongst them, the human development indicator (HDI) measured the development of a country according to three basic criteria of human development: health and longevity (life expectancy at birth), knowledge (adult literacy rate and gross school enrolment ratio for young people) and standard of living (GNP per capita in purchasing power parity [PPP] in US dollars to compare the standard of living between countries by neutralizing price differences). The HDI is the arithmetical mean of the sum of these three indicators. The annual calculation of the HDI makes it possible to produce a ranking of all countries in three categories, graduating from 0 to 1:

- high human development (equal to or higher than 0.800);
- average human development (0.500–0.799);
- low human development (lower than 0.500).

The difference compared with this theoretical maximum measures the "human development deficit". In 2003, the highest HDI, that of Norway, was 0.963, which represented a human development deficit of 3 per cent; the lowest, that of Niger, was 0.281, which represented a deficit of 71 per cent.[5]

The HDI marks a significant advance in measuring human welfare, because it takes account of the specificities of underdevelopment; unlike the GNP per capita, which is an indicator that is linked only to revenues. Actually, a discrepancy frequently appears with Third World countries, between classification according to per capita income and classification according to the HDI: in 2004, 100 countries had a better ranking according to the HDI than to their GNP per capita.

Admittedly, like all synthetic indicators looking to take account of a complex reality, the HDI has its own limits. First, it only gives a national average, which conceals the inequalities of human development within the country. Second, it provides data over the long term and does not include the deterioration of the situation due, for example, to economic crises.[6]

This chapter considers countries according to the two ways of classification: according to the level of human development, as well as revenue, by large groups on a global scale. However, and insofar as human development consists in the first place of allowing individuals to lead the way of life that they wish and to give them the tools and opportunities to make that choice, the HDI seems to be more pertinent than per capita income in analysing the relationship between economic development and sporting performance. Indeed, and in Amartya Sen's perspective of human development, the increase in individual rights and abilities must be an integral part of that of the availability of goods (Sen, 2000).

Access to sport played competitively or as leisure, as a direct or indirect spectacle, is indeed determined by such criteria. But this exercise in measuring the level of development leads to basic problems. The choice of terms is a theoretical issue. The notion of underdevelopment presupposes a delay to be made up for, compared with a standard to be attained according to a linear and standardized process.[7] In addition, that of developing countries implies that the situation of all countries improves in a continuous way. The North–South divide is the result of a geographical, or even naturalist, conception, even if there is a certain unity to these two groups. The term "poor country" ignores the existence of significant inequalities and that of "Third World" does not reflect the diversity of the countries concerned. Is it legitimate to lump together countries as different as Brazil (EME), China (LMIC) and Niger (LDC) under the same name?

On the other hand, are the common characteristics of massive poverty, recurrent inequality and multidimensional dependence of some countries, not superior to the elements of differentiation of the economies?[8] Therefore, and without underestimating their many disadvantages or implicit grounds, we will also use these terms both for convenience and, because in our opinion, stylized facts are identical in these countries and represent major elements of continuity that span decades, even centuries (Braudel, 1967–79).

2   THE LOW LEVEL OF SPORTING SUPPLY AND DEMAND IN DEVELOPING COUNTRIES

Sporting underdevelopment is first of all characterized by weak or non-existent supply and demand, which can be identified through the following indicators:

- A very low rate of licensed practice compared with the population. In 2005, in most LDCs in Africa, there were only 1.2 members per 1000 inhabitants on average, that is, a rate of practice of 0.12 per cent. In Europe, between 200 and 250 per 1000 inhabitants were counted, that is, a rate of 20–25 per cent.

*Table 3.1   Playing a sport in the world: the example of 15 countries
             qualifying for the final stages of the 2002 Football World Cup*

Continent, Country	Number of Licensed Members per Inhabitant
Africa	
Tunisia	1 per 255
Ivory Coast	1 per 680
Angola	1 per 2500
South America	
Argentina	1 per 75
Brazil	1 per 119
Mexico	1 per 442
Asia	
South Korea	1 per 96
Japan	1 per 128
Iran	1 per 156
Central & Eastern Europe	
Czech Republic	1 per 20
Poland	1 per 56
Ukraine	1 per 106
Western Europe	
Germany	1 per 21
France	1 per 28
Italy	1 per 49

Source: France Football (30 May, 2006).

- A concentration of the vast majority of the members in a small number of sports (particularly, football, volleyball, basketball, wrestling, boxing and athletics). Frequently, football by itself represents 50 per cent of the licensed members in these countries. But even for football, which is nonetheless the most complete example of the globalization of competing in sport (250 million licensed members in 204 national federations in 2006), a marked differentiation in the rate of practice appears – and this, even if the situation within the elite is compared (see Table 3.1).
- A virtually non-existent participation in sports in the LDCs, above all when advanced technology or expensive equipment is used (cars, motorbikes or bicycles), or specific facilities (swimming pools, golf courses or ski slopes) or even slightly developed sports equipment (pole-vaulting, the hammer and the hurdles) (Souchaud, 1995; Andreff, 2001a). That is how several dozen disciplines (motor

sports, skiing, horse-riding, fencing, rowing, swimming, tennis, golf and sailing, and so on) have rates that are practically non-existent in three-quarters of countries in the world.

- A very low presence of physical and sporting education at school, linked to a low level of schooling (fewer than 30 per cent enrolment in primary education for the LDCs), and a shortage of teachers and facilities. The number of adolescents playing a sport in the Third World fluctuates between 0.2 per cent and 1 per cent, whilst in developed countries it is between 20 per cent and 50 per cent (*Sport et Vie*, 2004).

- A weak ratio of availability per inhabitant of a club or facilities. The associative supply in the Third World is very inadequate. The "sporting sociability" index, measured by the ratio between the number of inhabitants or licensed sportspeople and the number of clubs, shows major differences between countries: one football club per 130 000 inhabitants in Egypt, one per 77 000 inhabitants in Morocco, one per 18 000 inhabitants in Tunisia and one per 3000 inhabitants in France. The existence of a local club, as well as its carrying capacity, has an influence on the number of licensed players: one football club per 652 licensed players in Morocco, one football club per 445 in Egypt, one football club per 153 in Tunisia and one football club per 100 in France.

- The shortage or absence of facilities and material slows or prevents the development of sport in most nations in the South. Nearly 70 per cent of countries on the planet do not have appropriate facilities for teaching physical education. In 2003, more than half of the 160 000 schools in Brazil did not have sports facilities. Two-thirds of the African continent (29 countries) did not have athletics tracks (2004). The ratios of availability of facilities per inhabitant are enlightening: in the 16 African LDCs studied by UNESCO in 1995, there were no boxing gymnasia, no courses for horse-riding, no lakes for watersports, one football pitch per 106 000 inhabitants, one swimming pool per 2.35m inhabitants and one gymnasium per 8.6m inhabitants (Souchaud, 1995). India has only 20 athletics tracks, that is, one per 50 million inhabitants and Africa is equipped with a single dojo that meets international standards (in Morocco).

Frequently, in countries of the South that are tourist areas, sports facilities are relatively numerous. Golf courses, tennis courts and swimming pools are managed by groups of private hoteliers. These facilities are, de facto, only accessible to foreign tourists or to a wealthy minority of nationals. It is the same thing when the supply emanates from commercial businesses: for example, in Argentina, the annual subscription to play tennis in a private club in Buenos Aires is equivalent to 50 per cent of the minimum wage. The lack of public or national intervention also penalizes judo, which requires both a judo mat and kimonos that have a cost beyond the budget of African towns and inhabitants (where a kimono is worth the equivalent to two months' minimum wage). The share of sales by Puma – €44.5m, that is, 3 per cent of its turnover in 2004 – shows the narrowness of the sports items market on this continent.

The Third World represents roughly 80 per cent of the world population, 55 per cent of footballers, 10 per cent of tennis players, 1 per cent of golfers and 20 per cent of organized sportspeople.

3   INSUFFICIENT DOMESTIC AND EXTERNAL FUNDING IN THE THIRD WORLD

In the Third World, public budgets allocated to sport are limited, or even non-existent. Voluntary work is even more thinly spread and can, therefore, only partially compensate for the shortcomings of the state and local authorities. However, it so happens that the public sector is omnipresent in producing the national sporting supply. But its intervention is selective (football in Africa) and often ineffective, because of a bureaucratization of the sporting institutions, of confiscation by the state and of embezzlement by political and sporting managers of the funds raised (Kenno Keimbou, 2000).

Indeed, having always to decide between the fight against famine, poverty, major epidemics, or illiteracy and physical education (PE), Third World countries, especially the LDCs, cannot favour sport to the detriment of the major problems with which they are faced. This sporting underdevelopment correlated with economic underdevelopment aggravated by the demographic growth of the nations of the South, has lowered the ratios of availability of human, material and financial resources per capita (Chappelet, 2005).

Many Third World countries have a GNP that is lower than the total sporting expenditure of a developed country, that is, the sporting expenditure of households, the state and local authorities, business and the media. This aggregate is the most convenient for assessing the monetary weight of sports markets and has been estimated at 1.73 per cent of the GNP of France in 2003, that is, €27.5bn, of which €11.1bn is from public spending and €16.4bn from households (€14.2bn) and business sponsors and broadcasters (€2.2bn).[9] The total spending on sport in France is comparable to the combined annual GNP of 23 African LDCs, bringing together 102 million inhabitants (Benin, Burundi, Liberia, Somalia, Rwanda, Chad and Togo, amongst others). French public spending on sport by itself is equivalent to the combined GNP of 18 of these LDCs (56 million inhabitants). In these conditions, it goes without saying that the proportion of spending on sport in the national wealth is clearly lower at 0.5 per cent in the LDCs, while it is 1.5–2 per cent in developed countries.

The shortage of public money is even more of a handicap for the development of sport in that, most of the time, governments concentrate their credits on those disciplines that bring medals (Cuba with judo, volleyball and baseball; Kenya with long- and middle-distance running) or on hosting a prestigious event; but the facilities required by the standard specifications are oversized, compared with the needs of the country and are located in the capitals of the developing countries.

From this point of view, the example of Mali, the co-organizer of the football African Cup of Nations (ANC) in 2002, is revealing. Having one of the lowest income per capita in the world (197th GNP, $360 per year), Mali devoted €52m to the construction of five stadia, which did not in any way correspond to the demands of clubs and the national championship, and the operating and maintenance costs of which were higher than what they could afford. This windfall could have been used to finance many local PE projects. Football became a political priority, while the majority of the population lived without roads, water, gas or electricity. Incapable of ensuring televised coverage of the event, because of the precariousness of the technical facilities of its national operator, the Malian government had to call on a foreign company at a cost of €4.3m.

What has to be added to this technological dependence in relation to the outside world, is a kind of privatization of a public good, in that the African Cup of Nations does not belong to the organizing and investing country, but to the African Football Confederation (AFC) – which put the European group Sportfive in charge of running it. This group sold the broadcasting rights to African television and radio, amongst which more than six LDCs (Gambia, Guinea-Bissau and Malawi, amongst others) limited their purchases to certain matches, or even gave up the final stages of the 2004 and 2006 ANC.

Development aid for Third World countries is another method of funding. The total public aid given by industrialized countries in 2003 represented €57bn, but it would be necessary to have €40bn extra every year in order to fulfil the "objectives for the millennium".[10] As far as sport is concerned, the Olympafrica Foundation, financed by the IOC and Daimler Chrysler, built and financed basic sports facilities in eight African LDCs to favour playing sport, mainly athletics. The international football, basketball and volleyball federations have acted in the same way, to do up courts and pitches in Southern Asia and the Caribbean. Since 1999, FIFA has supported the Goal programme (grounds and technical centres) and it devoted €65m from 2003–06 to help 20 Third World countries to equip themselves. The IOC and the IAAF (the International Association of Athletics Federations) have taken charge of the construction of 30 athletics tracks in Africa. It is difficult to establish, a priori, a positive or a negative relationship between this windfall and sustainable development in those countries receiving aid, as foreign aid can lead to dependence effects, depending on the nature of the projects implemented, waste and embezzlement.

Can the investments made by foreign companies compensate for the insufficient public funding of sport and foreign development aid, especially by the international sporting movement? Admittedly, and on the whole, foreign direct investment (FDI) has strongly increased: $59bn in 1982, $648bn in 2004. But its destination is unequally distributed: EU (33 per cent), developing Asia (22 per cent, including 9 per cent for China), the United States (15 per cent), Latin America (10 per cent) and Africa (2.7 per cent).

Actually, football is the only sport that attracts significant foreign capital in the Third World. However, the interest of foreign companies concerns only clubs and national teams involved in international competitions that are the focus of media attention throughout the world. But, even this Third World elite does not manage to obtain comparable sums to those of the elite in developed countries (Table 3.2). That means that the less prestigious teams of the developing countries have difficulty attracting foreign commercial partners.

Once teams start getting bad international results, many multinational companies can no longer be depended on. Hence the Algerian team, which has not made the major grade for a decade, receives only €100000 p.a. from Coca-Cola, that is, 40 times less than the French team.

The German equipment-maker, Puma, sponsors nine of the 16 national teams that took part in the African Cup of Nations in 2006, including the five teams that qualified for the 2006 World Cup (Angola, Ivory Coast, Ghana, Togo and Tunisia). The media coverage of the 2006 ANC (4 billion television viewers) explains the support that it received from six multinational sponsors (Canon, Toyota, LG Electronics, Tamoil, Pepsi-Cola and Western Union). The Japanese company, Canon, the world leader in image processing and printing, thus intended to strengthen its presence in emerging countries, by developing its reputation with professionals, as well as the general public. The US company, Western Union, is number one in the world market for money transfers and can be found in 200 countries. Its partnership with the ANC from 2002 to 2008 was

Table 3.2   The unequal economic development of professional football

Revenue	Clubs, National Teams, Events (Country)	Annual Sums (in €m)	Year
Sponsorship			
Shirt			
Tamoil	Juventus Turin (Ita.)	24	2005–10
Pepsi-Cola	Corinthians São Paulo (Braz.)	4	2003/04
Official sponsor			
Coca-Cola	French team	4	2006–10
Coca-Cola	Algerian team	0.1	2004/05
Equipment manufacturer			
Puma	Italian team	16	2007–14
Puma	Ghanaian team	3	2006–08
Broadcasting	World Cup (Germ.)	970	2006
rights TV	African Cup of Nations (Egy.)	2	2006
Turnover	Real Madrid (Sp.)	306	2004/05
	Flamengo de Rio (Braz.)	12	2004/05
	European Champions League	580	2004/05
	African Champions League	3	2003/04

Source: Press.

founded on the emotional ties between the expatriates who sent the money and those who received it. From the same point of view, Western Union also sponsors the young players' championship in Togo. The telephone operator, Orange, a subsidiary of France Telecom, sponsors the championship in the Ivory Coast. Renault, the car-maker, supports the Moroccan championship in order to increase its market share.

Most Latin American football clubs are bankrupt as a result – more than the general economic crisis – of an irrational organization of championships, bad management of clubs, bribery and financial embezzlement by directors. For example, the 20 Argentinian, first division clubs had an accumulated deficit of €362m in 2002, despite a surplus balance from player transfers of €533m for 1997–2002.[11] For its part, the national team received €17m per season from its commercial partners (amongst others: Adidas, Coca-Cola, Carrefour and Visa). Brazil suffers from the same difficulties, despite an enormous potential for its football industry, not only because its national team is ranked first in the world, but also because of the huge amount of talent and popular success of the sport (30 million players). Despite the Zico (1993) and Pelé (1998) laws, which were intended

*Table 3.3   Foreign investment in sport in a developing country: the
example of Brazilian football clubs*

Partner Companies (Countries)	Clubs (Cities)	Total Investment in € Millions	Term	Proportion of Receipts Deducted (%)
Hicks, Muse, Tate & Furst (US)	Cruzeiro (Belo Horizonte)	156	10 years	49
UFA Nations Bank (US)	Vasco de Gama (Rio)	117	10 years	60
	Fluminense (Rio)	27	5 years	NR
Media Sports Investments (UK)	Corinthians (São Paulo)	35	10 years	51
Exxel (US)	Vitoria (Salvador Bahia)	20	15 years	33
International Sport and Leisure (Switz.)[a]	Flamengo (Rio)	664	15 years	75
	Gremio (Porto Alegre)	32	15 years	60

Note: a. ISL bankruptcy in 2001.

Sources: Sport, Finance and Marketing, 21 February 2002 and *Revue juridique et
économique du sport*, July–August supplement 2005.

to professionalize football organizations, the spirit of the 1941 law remains,
with top-level sport considered as amateur sport coming under unpaid
"associative patriotic work". Thus, well-paid activities (for example, the
transfer of Brazilian players and sponsorship of the national team) coexist
with a lack of economic and institutional viability in the championships:
clubs in debt, overstaffed professional teams, stacking of competitions, best
players exiled and low attendance rates in stadia (16 per cent in 2004).[12]

Since the mid-1990s, an alternative to internal private funding has
appeared with the *parceria*, a system of external economic partnership that
allows a company to invest in a club over a reasonably long time (10–15
years), with, in return, the right to take a share of club receipts and transfer
fees (see Table 3.3). Thus, the Brazilian Series A football championship
has become an economic space for competition between US and European
firms evolving in the financial sector: Hicks, Muse, Tate & Furst (HMTF),
US pension funds; Media Sports Investments, British investment funds;
and Exxel, US investment funds.

HMTF, already the owner of two franchises in North America (the Texas Rangers in Major League Baseball and the Dallas Stars in the National Hockey League), has created investment funds to attract capital and clients, of which a $963m fund has been invested in sport since 1999, mainly in Latin American football.

Such investments in football compensate partly for the shortage of internal resources (national broadcasting fees of only $100m and international broadcasting fees of $36m in 2004), owing to the low subscription rate of Brazilians for pay television (10 per cent of those possessing a television in 2001) and to a "rent economy" by clubs, some of which are interested in selling players abroad, which is the main source of club receipts (15–25 per cent).[13] This unequal exchange, which is the expression of a dominated economy, has the effect of money leaking away from the economic circuit of football in favour of players' agents, shell companies based in tax havens, or in the form of deductions by the partner. Clubs have sold a large part of their future assets with a view to short-term sporting and financial survival, which they have given up according to the *parceria* model.

In the absence of FDI, football has become professionalized with the assistance of national private or public companies in Cameroon (since 1987) and in Algeria (since 1989). The same happened in Angola, where the major clubs are supported by the Petro Luanda and Petro Huambo oil companies and the ASA airline. This "dual" economic system can be found again in Senegal, whose national team was brilliant during the 2002 World Cup and has 14 Senegalese sponsors, while the championship takes place on dirt pitches, with the exception of one club in Dakar.

The central place of football in Africa or in Asia could explain the following paradox. Zambia belongs to the category of heavily indebted poor countries (HIPCs). Even so, the club of Mufulira Wanderers was listed on the Lusaka stock exchange in 1997, which had only ever listed six other companies since its creation in 1994. Until that date, the club had been financed by a Zambian mining group. The development of football in the south of the African continent is such that the club owners reckoned that it would be profitable to call on public savings. In Thailand, the Prime Minister's plan to create a special lottery of €230m intended to finance the acquisition by a national company of 30 per cent of the capital of the British team, Liverpool, only just failed because of a campaign of opposition to the government in June 2004.

On a global scale, only football can manage to call on real private funding, albeit at a very unequal level, which can offer, despite everything, an alternative to ineffective state funding.

Table 3.4   Proportion of developing countries in organizing global main sporting events

Sporting Events (Dates)	Number of Events Attributed	Total Number of Events	Proportion of Developing Countries (in %)
Football World Cup (1930–2014)	8	20	40
Formula 1 Grand Prix (2006)	4	18	22
Motorcycling Grand Prix (2006)	4	18	22
Tennis ATP/WTA (2006)	26	128	20
Summer Olympics (1896–2012)	3	27	11
Winter Olympics (1924–2010)	0	21	0

Source: Press.

4   THE GEOGRAPHICAL CONCENTRATION OF EVENTS IN DEVELOPED COUNTRIES

It is necessary to put the process of globalization into perspective, for the competitiveness of host countries is clearly limited to restricted geographical areas (see Table 3.4). Whether it is a question of the choice of organizing sites or the origin of the flow of money, the EU–North America–Asia triangle is the leading pole. Few cities in developing countries apply to host the Summer Olympics: between 1896 and 2012, only 20 applications out of 140, and they came from a dozen cities in the Southern Hemisphere (notably, Rio, Buenos Aires, Cape Town, Havana, Alexandria, Istanbul and Brasilia). The number is even lower, if the awarding of the Olympics is taken into account: only three cities out of 27 (Mexico in 1968, Seoul in 1988 and Beijing in 2008). The global area for the Winter Olympics is even narrower; out of 21 locations, not one involved a Third World country. Underdevelopment and climate explain this absence. Indeed, the EU (15 Summer and 13 Winter Olympics) and North America (four Summer and six Winter Olympics) together account for nearly 80 per cent of Olympic sites. These two areas are the most attractive, as sporting practice there has been long established and widespread. It is also where economic development, political will and influence make holding expensive events possible, by being able to call upon a wealthy public and large-scale sponsors.

The choice of city is often dictated by economic considerations: first, the level of development demanded by the IOC specifications (sports, transport and communication facilities, and so on); second, the preference of

Olympic commercial partners (the choice of Atlanta in 1996 and Beijing in 2008 was influenced by Coca-Cola, as part of its policy of capturing strategic or emerging markets).

It is true that the major part of the Olympic organizing committee's receipts comes from these companies of the triad. They intervene as broadcasters (NBC for the United States, EBU for Europe and NHK for Japan), as sponsors (nine US and two Asian multinationals make up The Olympic Partner Programme) or as equipment-makers (the US Nike and the European Adidas–Reebok and Puma). No company from a developing country plays a significant role, as far as funding the Olympics is concerned.

In hosting a world event in a single sport (football, motorbike, Formula 1 and tennis), the connection between developed and developing countries is more balanced. This is the case with the Football World Cup: out of 20 attributions, eight favoured a developing country: Uruguay in 1930, Brazil in 1950 and 2014, Chile in 1962, Mexico in 1970 and 1986 and South Africa in 2010.

The spatial confidentiality of world events located in the Third World (nine countries for the ATP/WTA tennis tournaments, six countries for the Football World Cup and four countries for the Formula 1 and Motorbike Grands Prix) is explained by the giant scale of these events. The investment and facilities are such that few developing countries (a dozen) could organize them (Table 3.5).

Even if the costs of investment for hosting international competitions are strongly hierarchical (see Table 3.6) and, in certain cases, exceed the annual GNP of many LDCs, it is necessary to identify their common characteristic, that is, the socialization of the cost – in other words, the state taking responsibility for most of it. Historically, the emergent economic powers – such as Japan (Tokyo Olympics in 1964), South Korea (Seoul Olympics in 1988), China (Beijing Olympics in 2008), South Africa (Football World Cup in 2010) and Brazil (Football World Cup in 2014) – have adopted a public policy of organizing major events.

Beyond this essential rite of passage to join the group of developed countries, these nations want to stimulate the growth of sports markets (playing, equipment and events) and associated markets (building and public works, and tourism, and so on). According to the Grant Thornton organization, the expected effects of the 2010 Football World Cup in South Africa represent a contribution of $3bn to the GNP, coming from 300 000 tourists. As a comparison, with the creation of 160 000 jobs and a gain in growth of 1.5 points, the 1995 Rugby World Cup had attracted 27 000 tourists and the 2003 Cricket World Cup, 18 500.

Methodological problems (no cost/benefit analyses or opportunity costs

Table 3.5 *The main world sporting events in developing countries 1950–2014 (organized or attributed during the period and known on 1 July 2006)*

Country	Events (Dates)
South Africa	Rugby World Cup (1995), World Athletics Championships (1999), Cricket World Cup (2003), Football World Cup (2010)
Argentina	Football World Cup (1978), World Volleyball Championships (2002)
Brazil	Football World Cup (1950, 2014), Motorcycling Grand Prix (year unknown), Formula 1 Grand Prix (year unknown)
Chile	Football World Cup (1962)
China	Formula 1 Grand Prix (since 2004), Motorcycling Grand Prix (since 2004), Summer Olympics (2008)
Colombia	World Cycling Championships (1995)
South Korea	Summer Olympics (1988)
Cuba	World Fencing Championships (1969, 2003), Athletics World Cup (1992), Baseball World Cup (2003)
Egypt	World Handball Championships (1999), World Judo Championships (2005)
Malaysia	Motorcycling Grand Prix (since 1995), Golf World Cup (1999), Formula 1 Grand Prix (since 1999), World Table-tennis Championships (2000)
Mexico	Summer Olympics (1968), Football World Cup (1970, 1986), Formula 1 Grand Prix (up to 1992 and since 2007)
Tunisia	World Handball Championships (2005)
Turkey	Formula 1 Grand Prix (since 2005), Motorcycling Grand Prix (since 2006)

Source: Press.

Table 3.6 *Investment costs of hosting international sports competitions*

Events, Dates (Places)	Costs (€)
Summer Olympics 2008 (Beijing, China)	36 billion
Football World Cup 2006 (Germany)	6 billion
Euro 2004 Football (Portugal)	1 billion
Pan African Games 2003 (Nigeria)	430 million
Formula 1 Grand Prix 2004 (Shanghai, China)	270 million
African Cup of Nations 2002 (Mali)	190 million
Mediterranean Games 2001 (Tunisia)	150 million

Sources: *L'Equipe; Les Echos: Sport, Finance et Marketing; La Tribune.*

Table 3.7   Budgets for organizing international sports events

Events, Dates (Places)	Budgets (€)
Football World Cup 2006 (Germany)	1.7 billion
Summer Olympics 2004 (Athens, Greece)	1.5 billion
Euro 2004 Football (Portugal)	828 million
International tennis at Roland-Garros 2004 (France)	103 million
Tour de France cycling 2005 (France)	90 million
Formula 1 Grand Prix 2005 in Shanghai (China)	29 million
African Cup of Nations 2004 (Tunisia)	8 million
Tour du Faso cycling 2003 (Burkina Faso)	650 000

Sources: L'Equipe; Les Echos: Sport, Finance et Marketing; La Tribune.

or ex post studies), as often happens, distort this type of approach (see Chapter 2). But if the economic rationality of hosting these competitions and the well-being that the population gets from them are questionable, the worldwide prestige associated with organizing an international sports event is supposed to generate a favourable climate for attracting FDI and mobilizing public opinion around a unifying project. Such was the ambition of Morocco, which, despite the failure of its candidature in 1994, 1998, 2002 and 2006 for the Football World Cup, declared itself ready to invest €2.15bn between 2003 and 2010 to equip itself with the necessary facilities in 2010, which was finally attributed to South Africa.

The budget for organizing sports events has neither the same volume nor the same nature as the investment budget (Table 3.7). Their funding is very largely secured by television chains, sponsors and spectators, and the share that falls to the host country can be marginal. What's more, several of them are partially or totally financed from foreign sources (the Paris-Dakar Rally, and the Formula 1 and Motorcycling Grands Prix in Brazil, China, Malaysia and Turkey). Relocated competitions in the Third World are, very often, only one stage in an international circuit and demand few resources because of the technical features of the discipline or its weak influence: the Foil and Epee World Cup in Havana (Cuba), the IAAF Athletics Grand Prix in Belem (Brazil), the Table-tennis Internationals in China, the Colombian Coffee Cycling Grand Prix, the ATP/WTA Tennis tournaments in China (four), Indonesia, Morocco and Thailand (three), India and Mexico (two), Colombia and Turkey (one) and the golf tournament in Agadir, and so on.

Indeed, many nations are content with hosting regional games, replicating the Olympic Games imagined by Pierre de Coubertin in the 1920s, on a different scale (see Table 3.8). These events help to spread sporting

Table 3.8   *"Regional" international sports events in developing countries*
              1950–2008 (organized or attributed during the period and
              known on 1 July 2006)

Country	Events (Dates)
South Africa	African Athletics Championship (1993), African Cup of Nations (1996), African Games (1999)
Algeria	African Games (1978), African Cup of Nations (1990)
Brazil	Pan-American Games (2007)
Burkina Faso	Tour du Faso cycling (since 1986), African Cup of Nations (1998)
Cameroon	African Cup of Nations (1972)
China	Asian Games (1990)
Congo	African Games (1965)
Ivory Coast	African Cup of Nations (1984)
Cuba	Pan-American Games (1991)
Egypt	African Games (1951, 1991), Mediterranean Games (1953), African Cup of Nations (1959, 1974, 1986, 2006)
Ethiopia	African Cup of Nations (1959, 1962, 1968, 1976)
Ghana	African Cup of Nations (1963, 1978, 2000, 2008)
India	Asian Games (1951, 1982)
Kenya	African Games (1987)
Libya	African Cup of Nations (1982)
Mali	African Cup of Nations (2002)
Morocco	Mediterranean Games (1983), Pan-Arab Games (1984), African Athletics Championships (1985), African Cup of Nations (1988), Francophone Games (1989)
Mexico	Central American Games (1990)
Nigeria	African Games (1973), African Cup of Nations (1980, 2000), Pan-African (2003)
Senegal	African Cup of Nations (1992)
South Korea	Winter Asian Games (1995)
Sudan	African Cup of Nations (1957, 1970)
Syria	Mediterranean Games (1987)
Thailand	Asian Games (1998)
Tunisia	Mediterranean Games (1967, 2001), African Cup of Nations (1965, 1994, 2004)
Zimbabwe	African Games (1995), Cricket World Cup (2003)

Source: Press.

practice, while taking part in relocating top-level competitions: the Asian
Games, Mediterranean Games and Pan-American Games (1951), the
African Cup of Nations (1957), the African Games (1965) and the Central
American Games (1973), and so forth.

Even by adopting a strategy of specialization that results in a concentration of their resources on one or several events, many countries cannot meet their specifications. Only aid from the International Fencing Federation (220 000 Swiss francs) made it possible for Cuba to host the World Championships in 2003. Anti-smoking and anti-alcohol laws in force in Europe have contributed to the relocation of Formula 1 and Motorcycling Grands Prix to several emerging countries, where such legislation does not exist (China, Malaysia and Turkey) and that therefore profited from the receipts from cigarette and alcohol brands that are omnipresent in these two disciplines. Car manufacturers also take part in this commercial policy, which is intended to canvass, and then conquer, new markets in countries where the rising middle classes are growing.

For want of external commercial support, the cycling tours of Morocco, Nigeria and Tunisia were cancelled in 2005, because of the cost of the equipment for the cyclists and their team supervisory staff. Since this disappearance, Africa has had only one top-level event in the international cycling calendar (the Tour du Faso). Created in 1987 and recognized by the International Cycling Union in 1996, it was taken over by the French Group, Amaury Sport Organization (ASO) in 2001, after having nearly disappeared for financial reasons. ASO provides 50 per cent of the budget, with the assistance of the Tour de France, with the rest coming from public and private companies in Burkina Faso. Comparing the turnover of the Tour de France (€90m) and the Tour du Faso (€650 000) very clearly shows the difference in the market and sporting value of these events.

Even more than participation, international sporting spectacles do concern a small number of countries: 40 developed countries alone were responsible for 90 per cent of competitions organized in 2005. The rest of the world, that is, 160 countries, nearly all belonging to the Third World, hosted 100 events out of a total of the 1000 that made up the international calendar. Indeed, the history of sport in the Third World shows that 19 countries organized at least one international event and 13 countries at least one global event (all coming under the category of emerging market economies: South Africa, Argentina, Brazil and Mexico, amongst others) in half a century. In other words, 150 countries have not organized any global competition for over half a century. It is necessary to qualify this exclusion of three-quarters of the world by the fact that it is often a case of very small, underpopulated countries, but it is not always so (for example, Vietnam and Burma). However, four geographical groups are badly served: South-east Asia, Central America, the Arabian peninsula and, above all, Africa, which apart from South Africa and Egypt, has hosted no event. The African continent is not included in international sport, as it is made up of poor and recently created nations, where sports facilities and practice are few or undeveloped,

5 THE MUSCLE-DRAIN FROM THE SOUTH TO THE NORTH

Is it possible to measure the extent of the migration of sportspeople between different countries in the world? What are the main countries exporting and importing talent? Despite a lack of a thorough count, several indications are witness to the growing mobility over the last few years on the one hand, and the direction of the flow mainly from the South to the North on the other.

This migratory process is in line with a general movement that has become significantly widespread. According to the Global Commission on International Migration (GCIM), migrants represented nearly 200 million people in 2005, that is, 3 per cent of the world population.[14] Their number has multiplied by 2.5 in 25 years and it constitutes nearly 8 per cent of the European population (56 million) and 13 per cent of the North American population (41 million). This mobility is destined to grow. The appearance of and broadcasting by modern media (television, telephone and the Internet) in developing countries have highlighted the inequality of living conditions depending on the country, while the decrease in transport costs helps the movement of persons. There are many reasons for emigrating: differences in income and unemployment rates, differences in life expectancy and level of education.

Before being strictly sporting ones, the determining factors in deciding to emigrate come under the specificities of the environment for the departure of migrants. In 2004, 800 million people in the world did not eat enough, 900 million lived in shanty towns, 1 billion did not know how to read and write and 1.2 billion people lived on less than one $1 a day in income ($80 a day on average in Western Europe in 2004). This threshold for the state of absolute poverty affects one out of two Africans.

Even more than the general causes, several very strong incentives magnify the vague desires of sportspeople to leave: wage differentials (1–50 between Africa and Europe and 1–20 between South America and Europe for the football elite), the shortage of material and human resources for training, the prospect of limited careers, the lack of top-level professionalism and the low level of turnover in national sports markets.

The mobility of sportspeople coming from the Third World has also been favoured by the development of European Community law since the mid-1990s. The Bosman Ruling in 1995 by the European Court of Justice

(ECJ) (see Chapter 1) put an end to quotas for professional sportspeople from the European Union. This liberalization of the market was increased by the Malaja Ruling from the French Council of State (2002) and by the decision of the ECJ in the Kolpak Case (2003), which also removed quotas for sportspeople from outside countries having signed an association and cooperation agreement with the EU. Sportspeople from 23 new countries (in Central and Eastern Europe and the Maghreb) could from that time on join any club of their choice in Europe, without limitation. Since the coming into force of the Cotonou Agreement between the EU and countries in Africa, the Caribbean and the Pacific in April 2003, sportspeople from 76 extra countries are no longer, in their turn, considered as extra-Community. In total, professionals from more than 120 countries are treated the same as Community nationals, and who can from now on be recruited without restriction by European clubs.

Measuring Migration

Between 1976 and 2001, 5482 footballers left Argentina for foreign clubs, essentially European. Between 1989 and 1997, 2004 Brazilian players emigrated to 63 countries, including Portugal (532) and Japan (232), for a fee of €230m paid to the Brazilian clubs who trained them and that themselves were heavily in debt.

Argentinian basketball players (200 in 2004) play in Europe. Baseball players from the Dominican Republic emigrate in great numbers to the United States, in the major and minor leagues (1300 over the last few years). The best African and Mexican boxers make their professional careers in Europe or in North America. As far as the "brain-drain" is concerned, the opposite appears true: among the 16 national teams qualified for the African Cup of Nations in 2006, eight had a foreign coach, mainly European, with salaries matching the market price in Europe (for example, €25000–50000 per month for the Democratic Republic of Congo or Morocco).

This series of examples illustrates some of the chronic handicaps of sport in the Third World: a situation of economic subordination and an unequal exchange.[15] Clubs are obliged to sell their talent in order to survive financially. These transfer fees are frequently the main source of receipts for African and South American clubs: 31 per cent in 2000 for Argentinian first division clubs, ahead of ticket sales (27 per cent), sponsorship and advertising (22 per cent) and broadcasting fees (20 per cent). The economic and social crisis in Argentina in the early 2000s (devaluation of the peso, increase in external debt, strikes, violence and insecurity) accentuated the structural difficulties of Argentinean football (a decrease in ticket revenue, shortage of sponsors and broadcasting rights, low-quality matches and spectacle).

Beyond the fact that clubs are not encouraged to look for other medium- or long-term levers for development, unequal exchange characterizes every economy influenced by, and dependent on, wealthy countries and international markets. In this instance, poor countries export young talent at relatively low prices and import qualified and experienced coaches with financial conditions that have no relation to the practices of the national market. The average cost of importing an African footballer in France was €0.43m and that of a Western European footballer was €1.84m (2005/06 season). African players are victims of a purely speculative system, for they are a raw material that is imported in the hope of being developed in order to sell more expensively. To increase their value, a vast majority of players pass through third-level championships (Romania, Cyprus or Malta), then second-level (Switzerland, Belgium and the Netherlands), before being sold on to major European clubs. An African player who confirms his talent will be resold for 10–20 times more, once established in Europe.

In addition, the market value of South American players must not conceal the strong "evaporation" of the transfer money: out of the €25m paid by Real Madrid to FC Santos in 2005 for the transfer of Robinho, 40 per cent went to the player and his agents, and 30 per cent to the commercial partner of the Brazilian club.

The proportion of foreign footballers in the five major European League 1 championships rose very appreciably between 1995 and 2005: from 14 per cent to 31 per cent in Italy, from 20 per cent to 28 per cent in Spain, from 18 per cent to 36 per cent in France, from 19 per cent to 50 per cent in Germany and 34 per cent to 56 per cent in England. As soon as their performances reach an international level, Third World sportspeople leave their home countries for European (football, rugby and basketball) and North American (basketball) professional leagues (see Table 3.9).

In 2005, African footballers represented 20 per cent of the 5000 foreign players playing in professional European clubs, especially in Germany, England, Spain, France and Italy. In the North American basketball championship, as in the major European football championships, professionals from developing countries constitute, every year, a substantial proportion of the professional workforce and a majority proportion of the foreign workforce. Over an extended period of time, Africa's contribution to the French football championship rose from 6.7 per cent of the workforce in 1955 to 21.6 per cent in 2006 (Table 3.10).

In effect, the championships in developed countries mainly drain from those much less developed countries to top up their numbers (see Table 3.11).

Table 3.9   Participation in three sports by professional sportspeople from developing countries in North American and European championships

Championships, Sports, Country (Dates)	In % of Total Number of Professional Players	In % of Total Number of Foreign Players
Premier League football, England (2003–04)	3.3	33.5
National Basketball Association, North America (2005–06)	14.4	79.3
Serie A football, Italy (2003–04)	21.0	68.0
Top 14 rugby, France (2005–06)	22.9	64.0
Liga football, Spain (2003–04)	27.6	74.7
Ligue 1 football, France (2005–06)	31.4	87.2
Bundesliga football, Germany (2003–04)	38.5	65.2

Sources: France Football; L'Equipe.

Table 3.10   Progression of the proportion of African players on the professional roll of the French Division 1 (1955–2006, in percentage of the number of players)

Year	1955	1960	1970	1980	1990	2000	2006
Percentage	6.7	12.0	2.2	5.5	10.5	13.9	21.6

Source: France Football.

Table 3.11   Geographical origins of foreign professional footballers playing in the five main European championships (Germany, England, Spain, France and Italy) in 2003–04

Geographical areas	Percentage
Asia and Oceania	3.0
Central and Eastern Europe	16.0
Africa	19.3
Central and South America	28.8
Western Europe	32.9
Total	100.0

Source: France Football, 16 January 2004.

Change of nationality has to then be added to these growing migratory movements. However tempting it was for team sports to naturalize players by opening the borders, the Bosman Case (1995) made it possible for them to resist. This decision thus protected national teams. From then on, it was no longer necessary for sportspeople to change nationality to progress abroad and develop their talent. On the other hand, mainly in individual disciplines and especially those that figure in the Olympic programme, the pace of naturalizations has accelerated before every Summer Olympics since 1996. Naturalization is a fundamental right that brooks no absolute ban and it allows national teams of developed countries to act in the same manner as European or North American professional clubs in strengthening their potential. Admittedly, the Olympic Charter states that the IOC, an International Federation or a National Olympic Committee (NOC) can forbid a sportsperson, who has been naturalized for less than three years, if he or she has already been selected for international competitions by his or her home country. But, a new form of skewed globalization is developing. For example, the French delegation to the Sydney Olympics was made of 5 per cent naturalized citizens; Germany was represented by table-tennis players who were originally Chinese; the United States by potential medallists from the USSR, Central America and Africa. Such a phenomenon ensured not only the economic and social promotion of naturalized citizens, but also their sporting development. And the host country received more titles. For its part, the Olympic movement benefited from media, sporting and market promotion of its competitions.

The Impact of the Muscle-drain

The consequences of young talent leaving for their home countries are starting to be understood:[16]

- A degeneration of national championships linked to the drain of talent, the bad quality of the game and the absence of both sponsors and spectators.
- The institutionalization of a black economy in transfers to developed countries (racketeering in Africa, laxity and by-passing rules with the agreement of federations and clubs, and so on).
- An exploitation of the market for Third World sportspeople by companies from developed countries. For example, the Africa Football Management Company (Ita) is the owner of four training centres in Africa and manages the careers of 100 African footballers in Europe.[17]

- A consolidation of the domination by clubs from rich countries with an acquisition of, or participation in, clubs from developing countries: for example, Ajax of Amsterdam in Ghana and Manchester United in South Africa.

The increase in these agreements leads to price dumping. Indeed, many European clubs benefit from a priority in recruiting young players belonging to African or South American clubs at a very low purchase price that does not cover the agreed costs of training by the original clubs:

- A reduction in the competitivity of Third World national teams, due to a lack of team homogeneity, whose players have been playing in various foreign championships and who have still not been released by their club or who have not considered their national team a priority. For example, 90 per cent of Nigerian players, 95 per cent of Senegalese players and 100 per cent of Cameroon players during the 2002 Football World Cup were under contract to a foreign club.
- A dilution of "international" quality. For example, the Brazilian Football Confederation (CBF) increases the numbers selected, in order to put up the value of its exports.
- A growing subsidization of rich countries by poor countries (especially, Europe and Africa), insofar as the latter invest money in training players, while the former import the qualified players at a nearly non-existent cost. These migrations thus deprive the home countries of income from their investments. In effect, there is a sort of indirect transfer of prosperity from the Third World to rich countries.[18] This loss of the elite deprives countries of the South of a factor for economic growth and sporting development. Moreover, globalization has accelerated this muscle-drain, as those who have talent do not stay and those who should return do not come back.
- The participation of the African continent in the migratory flows to the North has greatly increased over the last few years, although it has been going on at a high level for several decades.
- The project by international federations to establish compensation for professional clubs by national federations, for making internationals available during official matches, appears incompatible with the financial resources of African federations. For example, the salaries of some players (the Ivorian Drogba at Chelsea and the Cameroonian Eto'o at Barcelona) are higher than the annual budget of their national federations. On the other hand, FIFA, which is both the owner and the administrator of the World Cup, could make funds available to compensate the clubs. Indeed, the market

value of the event is the result of the contribution of 32 qualified national teams, and FIFA stored up €102m in profit from a turnover of €478m in 2005.

If a wide consensus appeared on the negative effects of the talent drain during the 1970s, the assessment seems to be more shaded in the 2000s:

- The desired performance of sporting human capital is likely to make the number of sportspeople who embark on high-level sports training grow significantly. The result of it will be an increase in the potential of talented players from poor countries. The prospect of migrating could also, therefore, create an incentive to be trained.
- The financial transfer of migrants (including several thousand wealthy sportspeople) plays a growing role, as far as reducing poverty is concerned. In 2005, such transfer fees through official channels represented a total of $225bn and about $400bn informally. The transfer of official funds by themselves is three times the value of public development aid. Taking this stagnation into account, along with the concentration of FDI in several emerging countries, the transfer of migrant funds towards the South has increasingly important and positive effects:
  - They help reduce poverty in very many countries (500 million people depend totally or partially on these cash dispatches; Ozden and Schiff, 2006).
  - They increase the revenue of families from the home countries.
  - They represent a real alternative in terms of social protection (illness and unemployment, and so on) in the countries that have none.
  - They often allow access to essential services such as health and education.
  - They strengthen the balance of payments of the collector states and improve, de facto, their credit rating, which makes their access to international money markets easier.

However, the impact of the flow of funds from emigration can be negative in development terms:

- It can result in inflationary pressure.
- A proportion of consumption can be diverted towards imported products.
- The country's competitiveness can be weakened.
- It can encourage people not to work.

- The vicious circle of dependence can be reinforced.
- These flows deal more with a need for subsistence, than with the productive investment towards which they are directed.

In effect, assessing the economic and social consequences of the muscle-drain depends on, first of all, from what point of view the question is considered. From the migrant sportspeople's point of view, some manage to optimize both the monetary and non-monetary advantages of their mobility. For the home countries and the destinations, the assessment is obviously more uneven.

Regulating the Transfer Market

Can the appropriation of sporting talent from low-income countries by rich countries be remedied, while international migration is destined to grow? What regulations for the movement of sportspeople from the Third World should be implemented? How can trained sports talent be retained or how can low-income countries benefit if the players emigrate? Obviously, only a high level of economic development can make it possible to offer Third World sportspeople a way of life and career prospects to match up to their talent.

The search for new terms of funding international solidarity requires a technical study of the mechanisms that make it possible to raise funds in a consistent and predictable way over the long term. From the 1970s onwards, various worldwide taxations were envisaged. In 1972, the US economist James Tobin, who won the Nobel Prize in 1981, devised a tax on short-term financial transactions in the field of exchange rates. Tobin's idea, presented in 1978, was to discourage purely speculative movements by taxing the sum exchanged during each operation, in order to reduce short-term fluctuations that are too violent, so that the effectiveness of macroeconomic policy could be improved and so that tax receipts for development aid could be allocated (Tobin, 1978).

In 1983, the Indian economist Jagdish Bhagwati proposed compensating the subsidizing of rich countries by poor countries that was generated by the brain-drain. To do this, Bhagwati envisaged a tax on migration, payable by migrants themselves to their home countries or levied by governments of the host countries to be transferred to the home countries in the Third World (Bhagwati, 1983).

The principle was outlined in 2001 and developed in 2002, and then the technical and financial aspects were studied in depth in 2004, when a "Coubertobin" tax on the muscle-drain was conceived by Wladimir Andreff (Andreff, 2001a, 2002, 2004b). It concerned slowing down the flight of young talent from developing countries, to release more funds for the Third World to ensure a real development of sport and to strengthen the universal character of competitions, in accordance with the philosophy of Pierre de Coubertin, the modernizer of the Olympic Games. The increasing number of transfers of young sportspeople under 18 years old from Africa and Latin America to Europe (football) and to the United States (basketball and baseball) from the 1990s onwards raised moral, legal and economic problems, engendered by practices that were frequently illegal.[19]

The continual liberalization and unification of the labour market made it easier for clubs in rich countries to call on cheaper, but good-quality, sportspeople. Removing most of the restrictions on the workings of a free market caused a constant increase in wages and a surge in the amount of transfer fees. To curb the development of wage costs, resorting to Third World talent en masse therefore developed.

Therefore, regulating the international mobility of talent by a tax raises many questions, and as many obstacles to its implementation. What are the main objectives set for this tax? What transactions and what type of economic actors should be subject to it? What geographical area does the taxation cover? To what sport disciplines should this measure be extended? What could be the tax rate? What international organization would collect the income from this tax? How should the receipts, thus deducted, be redistributed? Who would be the beneficiaries of it and what would they do with it? Is such a tax viable? Are there not counterproductive effects to this idea of tax?

For Wladimir Andreff, its promoter, the Coubertobin tax would have four objectives:

- to cover, at least, the cost of training paid by the host developing company of any sportsperson transferred abroad;
- to constitute a negative incentive to transfer a sportsperson from a developing country, which would be even stronger if the sportsperson is younger at the time of the transfer;
- to slow down the muscle-drain from developing countries to the labour markets of developed countries;
- to replenish a sports development fund in the original developing countries, thanks to deducting this tax on every transfer of a sportsperson, whatever the discipline.[20]

Wladimir Andreff proposes a tax of 1 per cent on all transfer allowances and salaries, stipulated in the first contract of employment signed by sportspeople from developing countries with foreign clubs and agents.

Thus, not only could the muscle-drain be slowed down, but also the differences in labour costs between markets in developing countries would be slightly lessened – this would, in fact, lessen a little the temptation of sportspeople to leave their home countries.

As far as the transfer of sportspeople under 15 from Africa and Latin America is concerned, differentiated taxation could be instituted, for a surcharge based on the amount of the transfer fee and first annual salary with rates of 48 per cent for under-16s, 240 per cent for under-12s, 300 per cent for ten-year-olds and 1000 per cent for under-tens.[21]

The host club or the sportsperson's agent would be responsible for this tax, the collection of which could be carried out by the national sports federation, under the control of an ad hoc international organization created for the purpose and that would be placed under the dual supervision of the UN and the IOC. For the home developing countries, the revenue from this tax would finance, as a priority, the building of sports facilities and their upkeep, as well as implementing PE programmes and promoting sport for all.

Difficulties in Applying a Tax

However, the feasibility and effectiveness of the Coubertobin tax are uncertain, because of the many obstacles to be overcome:

- So that it can be both implemented and respected, the Coubertobin tax has to be accepted by all contributors (sportspeople and their families if they are under 15, clubs and national federations from home countries, clubs and national federations from host countries and agents, and so on). If not, some actors will adopt the behaviour of a free rider, by continuing to transfer sportspeople without paying the tax, which would deprive the developing countries concerned of the expected income.
- To be effective, this charge has to be general to all disciplines having a professional sector, and to be applied throughout the world.
- For its imposition, as well as for its control and possible sanctions in case of circumvention, the tax would involve transaction costs, as there would be the risk of bargaining and corruption in developing countries.
- For its creation, as for its application, the Coubertobin tax needs active cooperation between the sports movement, states and international organizations. This would assume a common will to act and restrictive international legislation.[22]

As for all taxation of this type, the Coubertobin tax is based on two appealing, but inconsistent, ideas: on the one hand, reduce speculative transfers of sportspeople from developing countries, but on the other, collect significant revenue based on these operations. Indeed, profit from the double dividend is impossible to obtain. The higher the income from the tax, the more it would mean that the tax has missed its aim, since it would mean that speculative migrations were continuing.

This taxation coming into force also raises another contradiction and an uncertainty:

- Only a low-level tax could make support easier for all contributors in the labour market. But in this case, would the tax act as a deterrent on the volume of the muscle-drain and what level of resources could be expected from such a limited debiting?
- Assessing the income engendered by a tax presupposes an agreement between all parties involved to define the tax rate and to define the tax base. It also implies knowledge of the elasticity of the volume of sporting transfers from developing countries to rich countries.

Although limited in impact and ambition, but having the advantage of being applied since 2001, FIFA's rules wanted to reform the trade in young talent. Like the Coubertobin tax, FIFA's restrictions concern compensating training clubs when a player leaves for a developed country and protecting young sportspeople; but differ from it, however, by forbidding the transfer of young players unless the player's family leaves its country for reasons unrelated to football.[23]

Within the EU and the EEA, such mobility of young sportspeople depends on the commitment of host clubs to provide both schooling and sports training. FIFA rules have created a mechanism for compensating for the costs of training sportspeople between the age of 12 and 21, paid to the original club at the time of signing the first professional contract, and then at each transfer up till the age of 23 (5 per cent of the total of all transfer fees). Thus, the increase in value of each transfer is redistributed, including to the first club in developing countries.

But even if they are a first step as far as regulating the players market is concerned, the FIFA rules do have some drawbacks:[24]

- risks of avoidance by certain clubs and agents, as well as by certain young sportspeople and their families (naturalization of a player brought in from a developing country, the international mobility of the family linked to football but presented officially as due to non-sporting motives, and the false declaration about the age of players, and so on);

- an attack on two fundamental rights: the economic right of free trade and the right of free movement, since these rules totally block the market mechanism by forbidding the mobility of adolescent footballers from the Third World;
- a limited financial yield and a slight impact on aid for sporting development from the Third World.

Obviously, only sustainable economic and sporting development can reduce the temptation of sportspeople from developing countries to leave in order to find better working and living conditions. The muscle-drain can, however, be cleaned up and become more balanced in its specific details, if taxation in all professional sports is implemented on a global scale.

6 UNEQUAL ACCESS TO PERFORMANCES

Western European and North American countries have been the cultural and institutional originators of contemporary sport and, up to the mid-twentieth century, made up the majority of delegations involved in major global events. They also were the exclusive areas for sporting success.

Statistical Assessment of the Distribution of Performances

The example of the Summer Olympics, from 1984 onwards, leads to this first assessment being modified. In fact, the number of National Olympic Committees (NOCs) present at the Athens Olympics in 2004 corresponds to the IOC strategy of universal participation. The total number of NOCs present at the Olympics strongly increased from 1984 (140) to 2004 (201). This increase is basically due to a nearly general participation from developing countries.

However, 30 countries reached the Olympics only because of dispensations from sports rules: engagement clauses for two athletes not having the minimum qualifications in athletics and swimming, continental criteria reserving several places and invitations in some disciplines (gymnastics, weight-lifting, judo, shooting and archery, amongst others) (Augustin and Gillon, 2004). The very unequal size of the delegations shows, in another way, the imbalance of the groups present.

During the Sydney Olympics (2000), Australia had as many athletes (635) as the 114 smallest delegations.[25] Half of the NOCs taking part

Table 3.12   Participation and results of countries at the Summer Olympics (1976–2004)

Olympics	Number of Medal-winning Countries	Number of Countries Without Medals	Number of Participating Countries	Percentage of Countries Without Medals
1976	41	51	92	55
1980	36	44	80	55
1984	47	93	140	66
1988	52	107	159	67
1992	64	105	169	62
1996	79	118	197	60
2000	80	119	199	60
2004	74	127	201	63

Source: IOC.

brought together 4 per cent of all the athletes involved, whilst nearly half of them came from 8 per cent of the NOCs present.

Moreover, only a very small elite from developed countries was present in nearly all sports in the Olympic programme (28 sports).[26] Conversely, a quarter of NOCs took part in two sports and a half in four sports. More than 50 per cent of African countries took part in only two disciplines and three-quarters in four (Chamerois, 2002). During the Athens Olympics (2004), 120 of the 121 participating countries were not represented in more than five of the 28 disciplines on the Olympic programme. All the others were too costly.

Admittedly, between 1984 and 2004, the number of medal-winning countries rose from 47 to 74 (Table 3.12). But the percentage of NCOs without medals has remained stable (60–66 per cent). If more restrictive criteria were used, Olympic "productivity" is reserved for an even smaller number of countries: 20 NCOs won at least one gold medal and 57 NOCs gained at least ten medals.

In reality, the medals obtained by developing countries at the Olympic Games are concentrated in a small number of sports: 80 per cent of the medals from Africa in 2004 were in athletics and more particularly in disciplines where technical demands are less important, such as middle- and long-distance running (Table 3.13). Mounting the podium was also limited to a small number of countries: mainly Ethiopia, Kenya, Morocco and Egypt.

Over a short period (1984–2004), and concerning solely the Summer Olympics, the percentage of medals from developing countries appreciably

Table 3.13   Number of medals and sports with medals at the 2004 Summer Olympics

Countries/Continents	Number of Medals	Number of Sports with Medals
United States	102	22
Central and South America (12 countries)	64	18
China	63	20
Africa (nine countries)	35	6
General total	903	28

Source: IOC.

progressed: 13 per cent in 1984, 6 per cent in 1988, 11 per cent in 1992, 22 per cent in 1996 and 2000 and 21 per cent in 2004. This improvement was mainly due to several countries (China, Cuba, Ethiopia, South Africa and Morocco), members, for the most part, of EMEs. This assessment must also be put into perspective, for the number of developing countries present at the Olympic Games has increased by 50 per cent in 20 years, hence a higher theoretical potential for candidates to obtain medals (70 per cent of the NOCs present are from the Third World).

As far as the Winter Olympics are concerned, participation and mounting the podium remains very concentrated. Nearly 60 per cent of NOCs did not send any sportspeople and more than 87 per cent did not obtain any medals in the Turin Games in 2006, an event that, however, registered record levels of representation (Table 3.14). The climate, geography and state of underdevelopment of the South on the one hand and the high cost of practising winter sports and the very restrictive conditions for qualifying for these Olympics on the other, actually prohibit most Third World countries from taking part in these Games.

As an example, Central and South America were represented by ten countries at the 2002 Winter Olympics (Salt Lake City), while 40 were counted at the 2000 Summer Olympics (Sydney). Africa had three in 2002 and 53 in 2000.

It is therefore not surprising that, in the whole history of the Winter Olympics (1924–2006), only 94 countries have taken part, that 40 NOCs have been rewarded with medals and that 16 countries have shared 91 per cent of the medals. With the exception of China (4 per cent of the medals in 2006), the Third World plays virtually no role in the Winter Olympics.

A historical and geographical reading of Olympic performances confirms the weak influence of developing countries. Admittedly, 126 countries won medals in the Summer Olympics (1896–2004) and the Winter

Table 3.14   *Participation and results of countries in the Winter Olympics*
              (1980–2006)

Olympics	Number of Medal-winning Countries	Number of Countries Without Medals	Number of Participating Countries	Percentage of Countries Without Medals
1980	19	18	37	49
1984	17	32	49	65
1988	17	40	57	70
1992	20	44	64	69
1994	22	45	67	67
1998	24	48	72	67
2002	24	53	77	69
2006	26	56	78	68

Source: IOC.

Olympics (1924–2006). Winning a gold medal noticeably reduces the perimeter of success to 86 countries. But if, in order to avoid the vagaries of small numbers, we consider the number of countries having won at least ten medals, we then have 69 countries winning 99 per cent of the medals. In other words, the 57 countries having fewer than ten medals only represent 1 per cent of all Olympic medals (169 medals out of a total of 15 357). It must also be said that 75 countries that have taken part in the Summer and Winter Olympics have never won a single medal.

A long-term analysis (1896–2006) shows that developing countries (World Bank definition) have an average Olympic "productivity" four times lower than that of developed countries: 58 medals/246 medals (Table 3.15). This ratio of the concentration of medals is calculated by dividing the number of medals obtained by the number of medal-winning countries. Within developing countries, this average varies from 11 for the LDCs, to 97 for the EMEs.

Table 3.15 highlights the relationship between economic development and sporting performance, so as to account for the results from developed countries and those from developing countries. It also explains the relative degree of success of the three categories of developing countries.[27] This conclusion can be applied as much to the distribution of medal-winning countries according to the criterion of GNP per capita (World Bank), as to that according to the HDI (UNDP). A strong connection can be noticed between the average GNP and the average number of medals: $1046 in 2003 PPP, and ten medals for countries with a low human development index; $4474 and 58 medals for countries with an average human

Table 3.15   Distribution of medals according to GNP per capita of countries in the Summer (1896–2004) and Winter Olympics (1924–2006)

Classification of Medal-winning Countries According to World Bank criteria	Number of Medals	Share of Medals in %	Number of Medal-winning Countries	Average Number of Medals per Country
Developed countries	10 573	68.9	43	246
Developing countries	4 784	31.1	83	58
Emerging market economies	3 890	25.3	40	97
Middle income countries	665	4.3	22	30
Least developed countries	229	1.5	21	11
Total	15 357	100.0	126	122

Sources: IOC; author's calculations.

Table 3.16   Distribution of medals according to the human development index of countries at the Summer (1896–2004) and Winter Olympics (1924–2006)

Classification of Medal-winning Countries According to UNDP Criterion	Number of Medals	Share of Medals in %	Number of Medal-winning Countries	Average Number of Medals by Country	Average HDI Value (2003)	Average GNP per Capita (in $, in PPP, 2003)
High human development	12 003	78.2	53	226	0.895	25 665
Average human development	3 169	20.6	55	58	0.718	4 474
Low human development	185	1.2	18	10	0.486	1 046
Total	15 357	100.0	126	122	0.741	8 229

Sources: IOC; *World Report on Human Development 2005*, UNDP, p. 234; author's calculations.

development index; $25 665 and 226 medals for countries with a high human development index (Table 3.16).

In reality, 100 developing countries take part symbolically in the Summer Olympics and do not reach the Olympic finals. Only 40 Third World countries have reached the podium, that is, less than 30 per cent of these countries. A deep, double fracture has appeared between developed countries (69 per cent of the medals) and developing countries (31 per cent), on the one hand, and inside the Third World between the EMEs (25 per cent of the medals) and the lower and middle-income countries (6 per cent), on the other. If taking part in the Olympics strives for universality, that is not the case for competitiveness, which is very far from complete globalization. Some EMEs appear in the Olympic medals table, where the results give the impression that sport is taking off in the Third World.

The stigma of such underdevelopment results in, and also accompanies, an under-representation of Third World sportspeople during other international competitions. Of the 540 riders in the first division of professional cycling, four come from developing countries (South Africa, Brazil, Colombia and Venezuela), that is, less than 1 per cent of the elite pack (2006). Western Europe is very much the major geographical origin. The nationality of Formula 1 drivers (two Brazilians and one Colombian) and motorcyclists (one Argentinian and one Colombian out of 84 riders active in the Motorcycling GP, 125 and 250 cc) confirms the marginal role of the Third World on the circuits (2006). The final women's and men's table of Grand Slam tennis tournaments (Australian Open, Roland Garros, US Open and Wimbledon) includes fewer than 10 per cent of players from the Southern Hemisphere, and those mostly from Latin America. Africa and Asia are scarcely represented at all.

Indeed, only football escapes from the distinctly circumspect nature of the spatial dividing up of the world elite, with more than half the professional players, and with nearly every country represented in the eliminatory phases of the World Cup. Therefore, why should anyone be astonished that since its creation in 1903, the Tour de France has never had a winner from the Third World in any of its 92 editions? It is the same for the major events of the tennis calendar. Players from only six countries shared out 20 per cent of victories in secondary tournaments: Russia (16), Argentina (ten), Chile (three), China (two), South Africa and India (one).

The results of the 2005 World Athletics Championships confirm the concentration of medals in a small number of nations. In fact, out of nearly 150 Third World countries taking part, only 11 developing countries obtained at least one medal, that is, 28 per cent of the total of medalwinners: Ethiopia (nine), Jamaica (eight), Kenya (seven), Cuba (six), Morocco (three), China, Equador, Ghana, Mexico, Uganda and Tanzania (one). On the other hand, nearly one developed country out of two won at least one medal, that is, 72 per cent of the medals for these 29 countries. In other words, 92 per cent of developing countries left the championships without a single medal, as opposed to 42 per cent of developed countries. However, Africa played a more important part in such a championship (with 16 per cent of the medals), thanks to specializing in certain disciplines that are inexpensive to enter (middle- and long-distance running), than in multi-sport competitions such as the Olympic Games (4 per cent of the medals in 2004) or in a competition for which the conditions of training, preparation and practice constitute a real barrier (2 per cent of the medals at the World Judo Championships in 2001).

But even in an event such as the Football World Cup, where the Third World is very widely represented, only three EMEs have won it since its creation in 1930: Brazil (three), Argentina and Uruguay (two). Apart from these events, developing countries have never, or only exceptionally, reached the heights of the world hierarchy in swimming, basketball, handball, fencing, golf, horse-riding or rowing and the like, and have rarely taken part in the qualifying rounds.

Explanatory Variables of Sporting Success

Literature concerning the determining factors of Olympic performance is quite old (from the 1950s onwards) and multidisciplinary.[28] Historians, geographers, doctors, sociologists, demographers, jurists and economists have all called upon their different tools and concepts to explain them: the age of the sports, their social and spatial distribution, climate, diet, race, population, political system and per capita income. It is accepted that sporting culture and tradition, the wealth and standard of living of a country, as well as national political will, largely explain Olympic success. But these variables can be combined in a complex way (Augustin and Gillon, 2004).

Several studies have established a correlation between the level of economic development and the number of wins at the Olympic Games. Econometric estimates about the 1996 and 2000 Summer Olympics, as well as the 1924–98 Winter Olympics, show that the level of GNP per capita and the population are very significant determining factors in the winning of medals (Andreff, 2001b, 2006). However, from tests carried out on the Summer Olympics between 1960 and 1996, the hypothesis of proportionality beween the number of medals and the population can be rejected. On the other hand, GNP per capita is the main explaining variable in this model used to analyse the production function of medals (Bernard and Busse, 2003).

An elevated standard of living makes it possible for a country to have many varied and quality facilities. Important purchasing power also facilitates access of the greatest number to all sports. The wealth of a country can offer better conditions of preparation (trainers, researchers and doctors, and so forth). The existence of markets in sport with substantial turnover (spectators, broadcasting fees and sponsors, amongst others) is necessary for the professionalization of sportspeople. Such a status enables them to reach a high level, since they can devote themselves exclusively to it.[29]

But a high GNP per capita does not guarantee a large haul of medals at the Olympics. Norway (six medals in 2004), Switzerland (five medals) and Luxembourg (no medals) all figure amongst the wealthiest countries, but all occupy a marginal position in sporting success. On the other hand, Russia (2nd place in 2004 with 92 medals), China (3rd place with 63 medals) and Cuba (11th place with 27 medals) obtained an excellent sports ranking, while these countries have an average or low GNP per capita. In order to have an elite, a country must have at least 1 million inhabitants. And yet, a quarter of NOCs have a demographic size below this threshold. Whilst being a limiting factor for small countries, population is only a potential to be exploited for others. A large population does not constitute a sufficient condition for obtaining results. India, Pakistan, Bangladesh and Vietnam together represent 25 per cent of the world population, yet won only 0.1 per cent of the medals at the 2004 Olympics. And China, which is certainly an emerging sporting power, won only 7 per cent of the medals in 2004, whilst representing 20 per cent of the world population.

It is blatantly obvious that a country that, all other things being equal, has a large population, is going to benefit from a huge reservoir of potential talent. This would improve the level of its elite. Moreover, a densely populated country can spread its fixed costs (facilities, personnel and the like) in a more "profitable" way (see the example of China).

As with GNP per capita, population is a necessary, but insufficient, condition for winning medals. However, econometric tests show that the two variables are extremely significant in explaining the distribution of medals in 1996 and 2000. Small countries with fewer than 2 million inhabitants and medium-sized countries (2–29 million inhabitants) with a GNP per capita of less than €2000 p.a., have infinitely less possibility of winning medals than large countries (more than 29 million inhabitants) or very large countries (more than 100 million inhabitants) with a GNP per capita of over $9000 (Andreff, 2001b).

Such a conclusion was confirmed by the results of a predictive model designed to predict ex ante the distribution of medals in the Olympic Games (Johnson and Ali, 2000). A strong correlation between the economic and demographic variables and Olympic success was confirmed ex post. GNP per capita seems to have the greatest influence. If not, how can the fact that China and India recorded 7 per cent of the medals, whilst having 38 per cent of the world population, be explained?

In addition, given the same rate of development, a distinct advantage appears in favour of planned economies, such as the ex-USSR or Cuba with a single-party political system, compared with capitalist developed countries with a politically democratic regime. More generally, when sport is used as a vehicle for national unity and social integration, or as a tool for promoting or affirming its power in foreign policy, the public will modifies the distribution of medals. On the contrary, India, which has an immense demographic potential, a high rate of economic development, despite strong inequalities and a venerable sporting tradition linked to British influence, sent a delegation to the Olympic Games in 2000 that was limited both quantatively (66 athletes in 13 sports) and qualitatively (three finalists' places and one bronze medal). The lack of a public sports policy (funding, incentives, preparation and training facilities) explains such sporting results.

The state and national institutions have a positive or negative influence on the level of Olympic success, according to the means implemented, objectives pursued and arbitration made between the other sectors of social life and sport; and on, within sport itself, sport at school and top-level sport, sport for all and hosting major events (Bernard and Busse, 2003; Moonjoong, 2004). In other words, it is very much a question of the model for the organization of sport that is suggested. What should be in this notion of "sustainable sporting development",[30] especially in Third World countries where many fundamental needs have to be met?

NOTES

1. On the new configuration of North–South relationships and the persistence of underdevelopment, see Adda (2006).
2. The lack of statistics on sport (whether organized or unorganized, or public or private financed, and so on) characterizes, with particular acuteness, however, Third World countries. Generally, information is scanty, lacking detail and not always reliable, especially in the least developed countries. Moreover, these figures suffer from a lack of homogeneity, which makes comparing different countries difficult, because of either the differences in definitions used or the will to retain information or because of confidentiality. The absence or insufficiency of organizations specializing in the collection and compilation of international data explains this shortage, which does make the development of specific statistical indicators difficult. In many fields, it is better to apply internationally harmonized standards and procedures, in order to make a comparison as exhaustive as possible between countries. The IOC and International Federations intend to become producers of these statistics, in collaboration with national federations of all disciplines.
3. See Treillet (2005), pp. 18ff.
4. More than two-thirds of real economic activity of the African continent is not counted in official statistics. See Treillet (2005), pp. 20ff.
5. See UNDP (2005).
6. See Treillet (2005), p. 22.
7. See Treillet (2005), pp. 13ff.
8. Despite the break-up of the Third World engendered by the accelerated industrialization by certain developing countries, all the characteristics of underdevelopment are

present: the extent of poverty and underemployment, the low salaries, the high levels of fertility and infant mortality, the fragility of political structures, the diffusion of ethnic or religious violence, the marginalization in international exchanges and the insufficiency of private capital. See Adda (2006).

9. According to the "Mission statistique du ministère de la Jeunesse, des Sports et de la Vie associative".

10. The UN, IMF, OECD and World Bank decided on eight objectives in 2000, broken down into 18 targets and 48 indicators. This costed commitment from all the international organizations constitutes an obligation to have a result by 2015 (especially, reduce extreme poverty and hunger, and ensure primary education for all).

11. It is a question of a surplus economy and self-maintaining and accepted economy. See Adda (2006).

12. According to the Brazilian Central Bank, footballer transfers brought in €840m between 1994 and 2005. In 2005, Brazil exported €133m worth of players, generated by 804 transfers abroad (€25m for Robinho to Real Madrid and €18m for Fred to Lyon, and so on).

13. It is possible to compare this situation to the fact that those countries with oil revenues are technologically dependent on developed countries because they have no national heavy industry. See Adda (2006), pp. 136–7.

14. The UN considers a migrant to be any person who lives outside his or her country for more than a year.

15. The abundant supply of talent has not given rise to a real development of sport in these countries (of Africa and South America) but, on the contrary, has fuelled waste and corruption.

16. A recent comprehensive study of the impact of these departures on the home countries presents the first really significant database concerning the brain-drain and discusses different aspects of it. See Ozden and Schiff (2006); www-wds.worldbank.org.

17. Another example: out of 534 agents authorized by FIFA, only one is African.

18. The career of Ronaldo is a good example. The Brazilian footballer left the club that trained him in 1992 for PSV Eindhoven for compensation worth €50000. Since that date, he has been transferred three times, for a total sum of €90m (FC Barcelona, Inter Milan and Real Madrid).

19. See Andreff (2004b), pp. 804ff for a description of the unlawful market for footballers, in which no legislation or administrative rules protect the players. In fact, neither predatory agents, who are very often not authorized by FIFA, nor clubs, which are often not affiliated to their national federations, are under the control of sports or state authorities. In 1998, a report handed to the Senate assessed the number of non-European players under the age of 16 employed by amateur clubs, which were most of the time hidden subsidiaries of the main clubs in the first division, as being 5282. Out of these 5282 players, only 23 had an employment contract.

20. Ibid., p. 808.

21. Ibid., p. 809 for the method of calculation.

22. Ibid., pp. 810–11.

23. See Andreff (2002), pp. 57–63.

24. See Andreff (2004b), pp. 812ff.

25. Interpreting the medals table is not enough to understand the strategies of the countries at the Olympics. The analysis must also apply to participation, through the composition of the delegations, and then to the finalists (the first eight). Thus, the statistical field is bigger and therefore more reliable. See, in this sense, Chamerois (2002).

26. Apart from China, which actively prepared for the 2008 Olympics (Beijing) by massively investing in most Olympic sports.

27. One finds comparable international differences in different domaines: the United States, Europe and Japan control 65 per cent of world exports – the proportion of developing countries in world wealth is lower than 21 per cent; Africa has 13 per cent of the world population, yet represents 2 per cent of world trade and 3.5 per cent of medals (2000

Olympics). Europe has 12 per cent of the population and 55 per cent of the medals (2000 Olympics).
28. See, especially, Grimes et al. (1974); Johnson and Ali (2000); Moonjoong (2004).
29. See Augustin and Gillon (2004), p. 113.
30. That is, projects avoiding setting up structures that do not respect local cultural models or constructing facilities that are too big compared with local needs.

4. What is at stake in the new economic relationships between professional sport and television?

History has shown that sport and television have, for a long time, maintained a mutually interested relationship (Andreff et al., 1987; Bourg and Gouguet, 1998; Fort, 2006; Bolotny and Bourg, 2006). For half a century indeed, sport and television have developed side by side, benefiting from the convergence and complementarity of their interests: sport is a reservoir for programmes and audiences for television, which is in itself a financial reservoir and a vehicle for the promotion of sport.

As it is subject both to administrative deregulation (especially in Europe, with the abandonment of the public monopoly of broadcasting) and technological revolution (the emergence of cable, satellite, digital and subscription TV), television can no longer be considered as a pure public good, since the creation of subscription channels and pay-per-view.[1] The increase in the number of channels increases the supply of programmes, while the competition they provide for getting broadcasting fees increases the income for sport. Owing to the high level of the broadcasting fees paid by the channels that want to win him or her over, the television viewer has indirectly supplanted the spectator as financier of major world sports events. The world market for television rights was estimated to be €60bn in 2006.[2] According to the Carat Sport Agency, sport represented 5 per cent on average of general European terrestrial channels, but 15 per cent of programme costs.

Therefore, understanding the financial relationship between sport and television requires linking the sports programmes market and the sports broadcasting rights market. Downstream, the primary market for sports programmes is a place of exchange between broadcasters (the supply side) and viewers (the demand side). Upstream, the secondary market for sports broadcasting rights brings into play the same broadcasters, here the demand side, and the sports organizers (clubs, leagues and federations) or sports marketing companies, which are the supply side for the rights they hold. The ability of sport to create large audiences in the broadcasting market represents a major source of revenue – either directly by the sale of programmes (subscription channels), or indirectly by the commercialization of advertising slots (free or subscription channels).

This situation generated intense pressure on the broadcasting market during the 1990s, which was, moreover, characterized by an explosion in numbers on the demand side, because of the increase in subscription channels. In view of a generally monopolistic (or cartel) supply of rights for a given competition or event, the adjustment was generally made by price – that is, by an increase, as a result of the cost of acquiring sports programmes.

Bringing together a theoretical analysis and an empirical approach, we here use the concepts of the standard view of markets in competition and that of administrated markets, in order to describe the relationships that are established between the different actors in these two markets. More especially, we will try to explain the pricing on the secondary market, that is, determining the amount for sports broadcasting rights. Then, we will examine the consequences of the development of the structures of the rights market on the well-being of the television viewer and the profit of sporting organizers, as well as on the "glorious" uncertainty of sport.

1 THE IMPERFECT BROADCASTING RIGHTS MARKET

In the broadcasting rights market, one is faced with a demand for the acquisition of broadcasting rights for events by networks and a supply of these same rights by sporting organizations (clubs, leagues, national and international federations and the IOC). It is there that broadcasting prices are set, even if many interactions resulting from the twists and turns of other markets affect the contents of the negotiations (Andreff et al., 1987) (Figure 4.1).

Over time, the development of the legal framework has modified the way of determining the supply and demand, and reorganized the broadcasting rights market by strengthening the power of sports organizers with regard to the networks. At the time of the first sports broadcasts in the United States in the 1930s, and in Europe in the 1950s, sport either received no fees or very few. From the 1960s onwards in the United States, and the 1980s in Europe, television had to pay fees that were thereafter increasingly high.[3] It is true that these transactions were chronologically included in different configurations that reflect the divergent organizations of supply and demand. Among the main market structures, four forms are analysed: monopoly, supply-side monopoly, bilateral monopoly and monopsony (buyer's monopoly). The first three convey a monopoly supply situation,

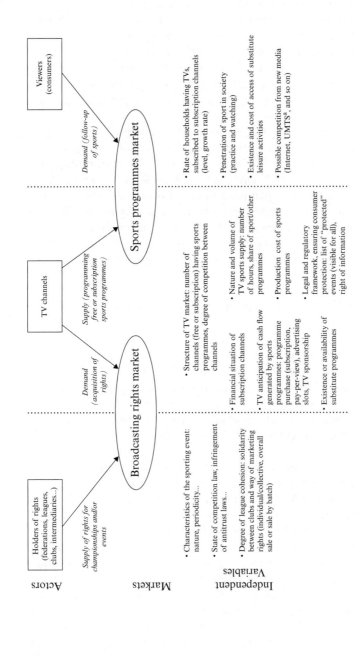

Actors

Holders of rights (federations, leagues, clubs, intermediaries...)

TV channels

Viewers (consumers)

Supply of rights for championships and/or events

Demand (acquisition of rights)

Supply (programming free or subscription sports programmes)

Demand (follow-up of sports)

Markets

Broadcasting rights market

Sports programmes market

Independent Variables

• Characteristics of the sporting event: nature, periodicity...

• State of competition law, infringement of antitrust laws...

• Degree of league cohesion: solidarity between clubs and way of marketing rights (individual/collective, overall sale or sale by batch)

• Structure of TV market: number of channels (free or subscription) having sports programmes, degree of competition between channels

• Financial situation of subscription channels

• TV anticipation of cash flow generated by sports programmes: programme purchase (subscription, pay-per-view), advertising slots, TV sponsorship

• Existence or availability of substitute programmes

• Nature and volume of TV sports supply: number of hours, share of sport/other programmes

• Production cost of sports programmes

• Legal and regulatory framework, ensuring consumer protection: list of "protected" events (visible for all), right of information

• Rate of households having TVs, subscribed to subscription channels (level, growth rate)

• Penetration of sport in society (practice and watching)

• Existence and cost of access of substitute leisure activities

• Possible competition from new media (Internet, UMTS[a], and so on)

Note: a. Universal Mobile Telecommunications System.

Source: Bolotny and Bourg (2006).

Figure 4.1 The two markets for sport and television (independent variables of the total sum of broadcasting rights)

102

whereas the fourth shows a monopoly demand position. The dual movement of cartelization of the supply – that is, the sports organizers – and of the demand – that is, television companies – will determine the structure of the reflections made.

A cartel is usually defined as a horizontal agreement between companies having the same activity, concerning minimum sale (supply cartel) or maximum purchase (demand cartel) prices and concerning the quantities exchanged. It is a question of organizing a monopoly through a specific market in order to control and charge prices without competition. In this instance, there is a cartel of the supply side when a sporting group (leagues and federations) is the only holder of the negotiating rights for selling broadcasting to television channels. In principle, this agreement tends to reduce the quantity offered in order to raise prices and make large profits. There is a cartel of the demand side when TV channels group together within the same organization – a public company on the national level, the European Broadcasting Union on the international level – which is responsible for negotiating with sports organizers for the purchase of broadcasting rights. The aim of this agreement is to influence purchase prices and to limit the volume of the demand.

Thus, broadcasting rights markets are going to be imperfect, since the agents on both sides try to group together to modify the free play of competition. Several scenarios concerning perfect competition are not respected.[4] For example, a major concentration of the market is opposed, in reality, to the atomicity of economic theory: the monopoly of the leagues in the broadcasting rights market generally meets with the oligopoly of television channels, or even the monopoly of subscription channels on the broadcasting market.[5] Because of this, the "strategic isolation" of agents is not guaranteed, in that there are conscious interactions between the choices decided by them (Gabszewicz, 2003).

The Cartelization of the Demand for TV Rights

The first forms of cartel appeared on the TV networks side, either because of a public broadcasting monopoly or because of a voluntary grouping of channels. Two market structures result from this: monopsony and bilateral monopoly.

Monopsony: a rare and favourable form of market for the buyer

Monopsony is a rare form of market in which there is only one purchaser of a very specific product facing a large number of sellers. Just as a monopolist has power in its product market, a monopsonist has power in the market where there are one or more factors of production. In this scenario, the prices paid, as well as the volume bought, will be weaker than in a competitive regime.

Between the 1950s and the 1970s, relationships between sport and television in Europe followed this configuration. From the beginnings of television to the disappearance of the public broadcasting monopoly, a single buyer was faced by clubs that negotiated in an isolated and individual way. Sports were not structured in leagues, or when leagues did exist, they left freedom of negotiation to their members. For example, in football, fees paid by public television hardly existed, if at all (€80 000 in 1973/74 in France) and the number of hours broadcast was also very limited: about 30 hours per year in the case of France.

There have since been very few examples in the world of this situation, even if the pressure exerted by some major clubs in line with an individualized marketing of rights could, in a general context of decreasing numbers of customer channels, make this particular form of market reappear.

Bilateral monopoly: the example of the European Broadcasting Union (EBU) faced with international events

Strictly speaking, there is a bilateral monopoly where a single seller of a very specific product has only one customer. Contrary to the monopolist trying to maximize its profit by reducing production and raising prices, the monopsonist tries to maximize its profit by reducing its demand in order to lower prices. This practice of compensatory power, an anti-cartel cartel, operated on a European level for about 30 years from the 1950s onwards.

Indeed, the EBU was created in 1950 by national, monopolistic, public networks in order to be a place of exchange for programmes. It has become a real cartel for purchasing and currently brings together 71 active members in 50 European countries. This collective bargaining strengthens its power in the market. Only members of the EBU are allowed to have exclusive broadcasting rights.

To fight against higher bids, the action of this group responds to the cartelization of sporting supply (for example, IOC, FIFA, UEFA and IAAF) by making its aim to control demand by strict rules (the free rider strategy is forbidden), in order to push down prices. In this encounter between two monopolies (for example, UEFA-EBU), the many possible price–quantity combinations depend on many variables (balance of power, coalition stability), which are difficult to formalize. Determining the amount of TV fees takes place inside an area delimited by the price that would eliminate any profit for the television coalition, and the price that would eliminate any profit for the sports organizer. The modest nature of the fees paid by the EBU for the 1984 European Football Championship brings this setting closer to the second limit (see Table 4.1).

Table 4.1   *Forms of market for sports broadcasting rights and cost of images (in € or $)*

Markets	Events (Area of Exclusive Rights)	Supply	Demand	Total Fees (Broadcaster)
Monopoly	2010 Winter and 2012 Summer Olympics (US)	IOC	ABC, CBS, FOX, NBC, ESPN, TBS, CNN Sport, HBO, Direct TV, Newsport, Showtime	$2.004 billion (NBC)
	2006 Football World Cup (world)	FIFA	ABC, Cable TV, UER, Team AG, Kirch-ISL, IMG-UFA, CWL	€1.09 billion (Kirch-ISL)
Supply-side monopoly	2004 European Football Championship (Europe)	UEFA	UER, Kirch, Team AG, Octagon	€514 million (UER)
	2004/05 French Football Championship (France)	League	France Télévisions, TF1, Canal Plus, TPS, M6	€600 million (Canal Plus, TPS)
Bilateral monopoly	1984 European Football Championship (Europe)	UEFA	UER	€2 million
Oligopsony	1960 Baseball Championship (MLB, US)	Professional clubs	ABC, CBS, NBC	$16 million
Monopsony	1973/74 French Football Championship (France)	Professional clubs	ORTF	€80 000

Sources: IOC; FIFA; Ligue de Football Professionnel.

However, a double threat is weakening the EBU in its encounters with the sports movement and is channelling the broadcasting price towards the first limit. First of all, the increase in the number of private networks and agencies that are not members of the EBU is reducing its power – for example, the German group Kirch, Team AG and Octagon during the negotiations over rights for the 2004 European Football Championship. Under this pressure, the EBU had to pay €514m to UEFA, while it only paid €84m in 2000; that is, a fee increase of 512 per cent. However, the EBU has kept its advantages: a complete cover of the territory of its European members, free programmes and a complete broadcasting of the event. This exposure, in terms of audience (nearly 700 million potential viewers) and number of hours, greatly encourages the public and the advertizers. That is why the EBU, despite lower offers than its private competitors, still gets the contracts: so it was that the IOC preferred to sign with the EBU for the 2000, 2004 and 2008 Olympics, despite an offer $200 million lower than that of the Murdoch Group.

The result of negotiations is not always favourable. Although possessing the rights to the 1990, 1994 and 1998 Football World Cup, the EBU could not match the higher bids of its private competitors for the 2002 and 2006 events.

A second uncertainty is affecting the very existence of the EBU as a collective purchasing group and is weakening the market power of the demand side for rights. A suit lodged with the Court of Justice of the European Communities by the non-member private networks led to a decision being given in 1996, which considered the membership conditions of the EBU system networks to be discriminatory. Since 1989, European authorities have considered that the joint purchase of TV rights, as well as the rules relating to negotiating and sharing these rights, infringed Community rules on free competition. Similarly, the term, and the impact, of the exclusive rights of the EBU negatively affect competition. Thus, it was that Court of First Instance of the European Communities cancelled the exemption from competition rules in favour of the EBU for a term lasting from 1993 to 2005. In fact, this bilateral monopoly already no longer exists. It was temporary, as is the case for this form of market.

The Cartelization of the Supply of Rights by Sports Organizations

It was in the United States, at the beginning of the 1960s, that an excess of competition on the broadcasting supply side caused a strong drop in revenues (minus 50 per cent for baseball in 1959). In order to remedy this situation, some authors developed a theory on the beneficial effects of a cartelization of supply in a league, so that club profits and turnover could be maximized – and this would take the economic particularities of sport into account.[6] This was a paradoxically contradictory proposal, with their model of reference (perfect competition) supposedly achieving the best allocation of resources, with the production of optimum volumes and the market-clearing prices satisfying both the supply side and the demand side.

However, US antitrust legislation (1890 Sherman Act) was infringed by the setting up of an authority responsible for selling TV rights – for example, the American Football League in 1959. The law of 30th September 1961 (87-331), based on the idea that a centralized sale of rights made it possible to keep the balance and interest of competitions and therefore, in the end, the consumer utility of sporting events, resolved this incompatibility.[7] In fact, it created a special regime of common law that allowed clubs to negotiate as a cartel with TV networks that, themselves, are still subject to antitrust law, making the oligopsony situation from which TV networks benefited actually disappear. In this case, the confrontation of many on the supply side (clubs and leagues) with some broadcasters marginalized the volume of fees and their weight in the club budgets: 9 per cent in American football and 17 per cent in baseball (1956). That is why a supply monopoly was put in place.

Monopoly or the power of leagues and sports organizers
This is the situation of a market that comprises a single seller faced with a large number of potential purchasers. Depending on the geographical area of activity, here it has two forms: the league, on the national level, and the IOC or International Federations, on the international level.

The league cartel   With the increased power of the leagues, more or less pure forms of monopoly appeared in the United States in the 1970s.[8] By creating a cartel, the supply side (National Football League, Major League Baseball and the National Basketball Association) eliminated all competition on their side. This collective bargaining brings higher bid mechanisms into play, which are all the more effective since the demand expands and splits. To the three "free" access networks (ABC, CBS and NBC), were added the thematic cable (ESPN) and subscriber (HBO and Showtime) channels, along with local stations, all wanting to capture or secure the loyalty of an audience. In such a configuration, the monopolist (the league) – having all the demand – will choose the price (TV fees) and the quantity (the volume of broadcasting) and therefore maximize its profit.

However, the monopolist will fear the loss of its privilege in a scenario where high profits attract one or several rival leagues (a common situation in the United States). If one is in the presence of a temporary monopoly, two strategies are possible:

- A policy of penetration with reasonable broadcasting fees, a large volume of broadcasting and small profits. This strategy is intended to establish itself in the market, while discouraging possible imitators (leagues and federations).
- A policy of prestige with high broadcasting fees, a low volume of broadcasting and high unitary profits. This strategy is intended to collect large profits as quickly as possible, with the minimum of financial risks.

Owing to this cartelization of supply, the fees cashed by sports organizers have increased strongly. Thus, the annual share of receipts from television received by every American football club has risen from $45000 in 1960 to $39m in 1994 to $73m in 2004. The overall amount of fees cashed by the NBA developed thus: from $188m in 1990 to $660m in 2002. In relative value also, the average share of TV fees in club revenues for the four major US leagues (NFL, NBA, MLB and NHL) developed appreciably: less than 15 per cent in the 1950s, 39 per cent in 1997. The cohesion of the league even caused a rise of 100 per cent of the annual amount of fees at the time of the National Football League contract renewal for the 1998–2005 period.

Like every cartel, the league generally shares out its receipts from television on an equal basis between clubs. In addition to the beneficial effects of a more equal distribution on competitive balance, negotiating as a cartel makes it possible to impose longer-term contracts on channels, compared with what would have been possible selling rights individually. Therefore, clubs have a guaranteed income independent of how their sporting results progress. Moreover, the league aims to maintain broadcasting fees received by clubs at the highest level (Horowitz, 1974; Andreff and Bourg, 2006).[9]

The monopoly of the IOC and FIFA   The International Olympic Committee is more stable than a league (a cartel of clubs that can be possibly weakened or competed with) and holds the property rights for the Summer and Winter Olympics, as well as for their by-products.[10] This absolute monopoly reinforces its bargaining power and is a source of very high increases in fees. For $0.5m, CBS had obtained the exclusive rights to the Rome Olympics in 1960. ABC had to pay $225m in 1984. NBC bought the 2000–08 Olympics rights for a sum of $2392bn – that is, an average of $800m for each. It is interesting to compare the fees paid by the US networks and those paid by the EBU. The amount paid by the former for the 2000–08 Olympics is twice as high as that paid by the latter ($1187bn). This difference was one to three times for the Summer Olympics from 1988 to 1996. And yet, the potential audience, the effective audience and the public interest are comparable. The explanation lies in the form of the US market, which is a monopoly that brings together a supplier (the IOC) with a large number of channels; this is the opposite of the European market, which was a bilateral monopoly for a long period, opposing two cartels: the IOC and the EBU. The way of determining the prices actually differs significantly.

The Fédération Internationale de Football Association (FIFA) has the same power as the IOC. As with the Olympic Games, the World Cup is a unique event, which is likely to get exceptional audiences. It is a de facto supply monopoly, since there is no rival or substitute competition. Therefore, why should one be surprised by the higher bids for the broadcasting rights for this event: €15m in 1978, €84m in 1998, €853m in 2002 and €1.09bn in 2006? It is true that the balance of power is particularly favourable to FIFA, which faced alone the seven accepted candidates to negotiate for the 2002 and 2006 events: ABC (United States), Cable TV (Hong Kong), CWL (Switzerland), Team (Switzerland), IMG (United States)–UFA (Germany), Kirch (Germany)–Sporis (Switzerland) and UER (Europe).

Supply-side monopoly: the dominant model in the European markets   There is a supply-side monopoly when there is always one seller facing several purchasers. This has been the dominant situation of the last 20 years, which has lasted, in a certain way, in every national arena for most main sports in Europe. Thus, in football for example, every national league invites three or four media groups to tender. Unlike the former monopsony (clubs–public network) or bilateral monopoly (league–public network) context, which are not very remunerative for sporting organizations, the current system brings together a greater number of TV channels, as well as, more importantly, a greater number of broadcasting slots via a system of selling by the lot. There is, in fact, no longer just one broadcasting demand, but several. Until the middle of the 1980s, negotiations were concerned exclusively with broadcasting a live match on terrestrial, unscrambled channels, that is, on a free channel. Since then, the market has fragmented and the demand for broadcasting covers several forms of exploitation: live, recorded, in its entirety, shortened versions, unscrambled, scrambled, terrestrial, cable, satellite and pay-per-view. The rights that are sold concern the exclusive rights for a type of broadcasting and no longer just geographical exclusive rights. These media rights windows – the new possibility to negotiate, over the same period with alternative supports, for the same programme two or three times – therefore increase, in

*Table 4.2　Football broadcasting fees (1991–92, 2007–08, in national first
division championships) in €m*

Country	1991/92	2007/08	Growth
England	21	830	× 39
France	21	650[a]	× 31
Italy	55	550[a]	× 10
Germany	36	420	× 12
Spain	30	310[a]	× 10

Note:　a.　2005/06.

Sources:　Andreff and Bourg (2006).

a way, competition on the demand side and increase the profitability of the product in exceptional conditions. In 16 years, this diversity of rights has triggered sharp rises in revenue for the leagues (see Table 4.2). Television has actually been the main source of football club revenue in all European countries since the mid-1990s (35 per cent), becoming the majority source from the beginning of the 2000s (50–55 per cent). In the early 1970s, this percentage was less than 5 per cent.

Contrasting prospects: the unequal growth of rights

A dual conflicting movement of the cartelization of sports organizers and the decartelization of TV channels has had positive consequences for the funding and development of professional sport, and has done this in a continuously increasing way since the 1960s. Now, at the beginning of the twenty-first century, the market structure is tending to be reversed, especially in Europe. First of all, the leagues' monopoly of the ownership and, above all, the sale of TV rights has been questioned. According to the annual UEFA survey of 2003, 43 per cent of European football clubs partly or totally manage their own TV rights. This new order is likely to create favourable competition between clubs for the purchasers of rights. Indeed, economic theory, like experience, shows that united strategies are more effective than individual strategies. A centralized sale brings in more, overall, than club-by-club negotiation (Andreff and Bourg, 2006).

The cartelization of clubs has been called into question in Europe over the last few years, with legal action (Italy, Spain, Germany, England and the Netherlands) or with action before national and European competition authorities (France). This was all in order to give clubs back the complete use of their rights. Major clubs exert often-effective pressure to take back broadcasting rights individually, by threatening the leagues to bring a claim before competition judges for a restriction of their free development. It is true that sporting sanctions encourage them in this opportunistic behaviour, when what is at stake is taken into account: access to the market (European Cup tournaments and national championships) based on sporting criteria (Bourg, 2003a). Indeed, the major clubs cannot take this sporting risk or its economic consequences. They also consider that the share they receive is lower than what they would receive if they marketed their rights themselves.

Nevertheless, the European Commission is concerned with promoting economic and sporting balance; in 2002, it recognized the beneficial effects of a centralized sale for the Champions League – which would normally be prejudicial to the principle of free competition. It did, however, add this recognition to a certain number of conditions, aimed at re-injecting competition in different national markets: three-year maximum contracts; selling in lots, making it possible for several channels to acquire a share of the rights; and the possibility of clubs themselves selling some rights from the 2003/04 season onwards (live matches, summaries, recordings, Internet and mobile telephones), if UEFA's agency did not do it. Without this development, UEFA could have been described as having an anti-competitive agreement and of being an association of companies that have put aside their individual negotiations for the benefit of a single entity. That is why it asked for, and obtained, an exemption from competition rules until 2009 from the European Commission, provided that the terms stated above are respected. Similarly, in France, the principle of pooling the sale of TV rights is written down in sports law.

The reduction in the number of potential buyers, following the mergers of cable and satellite networks (Stream and Telepiù in Italy, Via Digital and Canal Satellite in Spain, and the current merger between Canal Satellite and TPS in France) or bankruptcies (Kirch in Germany and ITV Digital in Britain) has tended to make competition disappear by causing reduced demand. And in this new market form, it will be the demand side (the TV channels) and not the supply side (the leagues or the clubs) that will direct prices, which will certainly be lower. Moreover, the private and public free terrestrial channels do not appear to have either the means to compete with scrambled subscriber channels or to have the appropriate mode of operation (subscription that pays them directly). That is why the contraction of TV rights can be seen mainly on a national level, because of the concentration of subscriber channels or the lack of real competition for purchasing rights (Table 4.3). Conversely, the increase is continuing in continental or world fees, because competition is still fierce: +33 per cent for the 2010 Winter Olympics and 2012 Summer Olympics compared with those for 2006 and 2008, +512 per cent for the football Euro 2004

*Table 4.3   Global progression of sports broadcasting fees (from the two
              last contracts signed)*

Sporting Event (Area of Rights)	Broadcasting Fees	Progression in %
Football World Cup (world)		
1994 and 1998	€157 million	+ 1140
2002 and 2006	€1.950 billion	
European Football Championship (Europe)		
2000	€84 million	+ 512
2004	€514 million	
National Football League (US)		
1994–97	$4.4 billion	+ 100
1998–2005	$17.6 billion	
English Football Championship (UK)		
2004–07	€1.457 billion	+ 65
2007–10	€2.500 billion	
PGA international golf circuit (US)		
1999–2002	$586 million	+ 45
2003–06	$850 million	
Olympic Games (US)		
2006 (Winter) and 2008 (Summer)	$1.507 billion	+ 33
2010 (Winter) and 2012 (Summer)	$2.004 billion	
National Basketball Association (US)		
1998–2002	$2.456 billion	+ 25
2002–08	$4.600 billion	
National Hockey League (North America)		
2003–05	$240 million	− 44
2005–07	$135 million	
Champions League Football (France)		
1999–2002	€330 million	− 46
2003–06	€179 million	
Formula 1 Grand Prix (France)		
1999–2002	€95 million	− 50
2003–2006	€48 million	

Sources: IOC; FIFA; UEFA; Premier League; Fort (2006); press.

compared with 2000, and +1140 per cent for the 2002 and 2006 football
World Cups compared with those for 1994 and 1998.

Faced with the dual threat of a return to a monopoly of demand for
rights, and with the pernicious effects of individual negotiation, the

creation of a TV package by clubs and leagues directly selling and produc-ing images offers a real alternative for solving the problems of the market reversal (a study concerning this was carried out in Italy, the United Kingdom and France).[11] This strategy could in future be implemented, since digital technology has reduced broadcasting costs and has also made it possible for the viewer to pay directly. Clubs could therefore amortize their costs. Moreover, these plans by TV channels are a means of pressure when it comes to renegotiating contracts.

We are entering a mature phase of the "televised sport" product. The first years of the twenty-first century have marked a new phase, character-ized by: shrinking advertising investment; a merger strategy for subscrip-tion television networks; a slow-down in the rate of growth of households taking out subscriptions; a levelling-out or drop in audiences; the financial difficulties of intermediate agencies; and the major clubs calling into ques-tion the centralization of rights. All these trends converge to curb the devel-opment of broadcasting rights. They will put an end to the economic model of sport, which has been based for several decades on a continual growth of fees. Even more so, since the large increase in the cost of these rights is weakening the economic profitability of subscription channels. Thus, the recent movement of broadcaster mergers and takeovers should be inter-preted as the wish to amortize the acquisition of rights and technical costs, with a better optimization of the means of production and profits.

Therefore, will the increase in broadcasting fees reach a limit? An uneven progression is probable. The dual nature of the broadcasting rights market will grow, with competitions and clubs segmenting according to the single criterion of value creation (audiences, market shares and adver-tisers). The higher bids of the channels will apply only to the most lucrative of the major events, that is, those that have an international impact. But the golden age of televised sport, which developed between 1985 and 2005, is seemingly being called into question by a reversal of the market. Indeed, minor sports and second-order events will have less and less access to channels and to broadcasting fees. On the other hand, there is no known limit for telegenic sports and federal events (Table 4.4).

2   THE CONSEQUENCES OF THE STRUCTURE OF THE BROADCASTING RIGHTS MARKET

A Growing Supply of Images, but Where the Viewer Has to Pay for Access

From 1968 to 2005 in France, the 400-fold increase in the supply of televised sport over 37 years came about thanks to the development of

*Table 4.4   The diversity of broadcasting fees according to the event,
              discipline and the area of rights*[a]

Events (Geographical Area of Rights)	Totals in €m
2010 Football World Cup (world)[b]	3000
National Football League 2007 (USA)	2850
2010 Winter Olympics and 2012 Summer Olympics (world)	2700
Football Premier League 2007/08 (UK)	830
2008 Summer Olympics (USA)	745
2007 National Basketball Association (USA)	660
Football Champions League 2005/06 (Europe)	650
Football National Championships European Nations 2004 (Europe)	514
2006 Winter Olympics (USA)	510
NASCAR 2007 (production models, USA)	460
Major League Baseball 2006 (USA)	420
2008 Summer Olympics (Europe)	380
PGA Tour 2007 (golf, USA)	130
National Hockey League 2007 (North America)	55
Super 14 & Tri-Nations 2007 (rugby, Southern Hemisphere)	50

Notes:
a.   Broadcasting fees in dollars have been converted to euros (1 euro = 1.3 dollars, June
     2006).
b.   Estimation.

pay television[12] (see Table 4.5). 2005 was an odd-numbered year and the
sporting events calendar included the usual annual competitions, but no
very large-scale events such as the Football World Cup and the Olympic
Games that lead to an especially high volume of sports programmes in the
years when they are organized. The rise in power of sports programmes on
cable and satellite is at the origin of this structural development, which is
manifested by the fact that, since then, all growth in sporting supply for
the public has come from subscription channels. From 1988, two-thirds
of the hourly volume of sports programmes were subject to the payment
of a subscription. This share reached 99 per cent in 2005. The increase in
the number of channels (two in 1968, 20 in 2005), as well as their diversity, generated the totally new possibility of selection for the television
viewer, who could choose his or her programme and who would be billed
individually. This made it possible for the channel to be paid directly.

Extending the air-time of sport, diversifying access methods, differ-
entiating the products (direct, pre-recorded and highlights, and so on),
based on the variety of viewer preferences and their revenue, have been

Table 4.5 The supply of televised sport on French channels 1968–2005 (in hourly volume and in %)

Type of Channel (Date of Creation)	1968	1980	1984	1988	1999	2005
Total number of hours (number of broadcasters)	232 h (2)	793 h (3)	989 h (4)	5622 h (7)	32640 h (11)	90998 h (20)
"Free" channels TF1 (1949), France 2 (1964), France 3 (1972), La 5 (1986), M6 (1986)	232 h (100%)	793 h (100%)	939 h (95%)	1886 h (33.5%)	1168 h (3.6%)	998 h (1%)
Subscription channels Canal Plus (1984), TV Sport (1988), Eurosport (1989), France Supervision (1991), Canal Satellite/Kiosque (1996), TPS/Multivision (1996), ABSports – Pathé Sport – Sport Plus (1996), Canal Plus Vert-Canal Plus Sport (1998), L'Equipe TV (1998), Infosport (1998), OM TV (1998), Equidia (1999), Motors TV (2000), AB Moteurs (2004), OL TV (2005), ESPN Classics (2005), Extreme Sports Channel (2005)	–	–	50 h (5%)	3736 h (66.5%)	31472 h (96.4%)	90000h[a] (99%)

Note: a. Estimation.

Sources: *La Lettre du CSA*, No. 193, March 2006; Bourg and Gouguet (1998, 2005).

accompanied by an increase in the price of sports programmes. In 2006, 10 million out of the 23 million households having a television in France, had access to Hertzian subscription channels, on cable or satellite: Canal Plus, CanalSatellite or TPS. Sport is the main reason for subscription: for 40 per cent of viewers of TPS and 73 per cent for those of Canal Plus.

After strong growth in the late 1990s, this market seems to have arrived at maturity. It is true that, in Europe, the television viewer who wanted to follow all the football matches in their national championship in 2005–06, had to pay €27 per month in France (Canal Plus), €38 in Germany (Première), €45 in Spain (Digital +), and €49 in the United Kingdom (BSkyB) and Italy (Sky Italia). To these sums, could be added, for example, a subscription to the clubs' channels for the demanding viewer: €5 per month for those in Barcelona, Lyon and Marseille; €6 for those of AC Milan and AS Rome; and €9 for those of Chelsea and Manchester United. Therefore, it is not surprising that such receipts for the channels result in significant broadcasting fees paid to sporting organizations.

In the United States, which was the pioneering country for pay-per-view in 1975, a single world boxing championship can attract completely new cash flows. Thus, the fight between Mike Tyson and Lennox Lewis on 8 June 2002 gave €106m to the broadcasters (HBO and Showtime), from 1.8 million subscribers who paid €59 each. The television receipts constituted 81 per cent of the whole budget for the event.

The viewer does, indeed, suffer the consequences of the increase in costs of sports programmes. Admittedly, most events broadcast by subscriber channels would not have been on a free general channel, but this development in subscription TV presents the risk of a progressive shift of major events, which are currently available on the major "free" national networks, towards scrambled channels. Concerned about moderating the harmful effects of exacerbated competition between broadcasters (exclusivity and subscription), the European Parliament adopted in 1997 the directive "Television without Frontiers", the sporting section of which asked Member States to draw up a list of events that had to be accessible, unencrypted and free to the majority of viewers. According to the European Commission, these protected events have to meet at least two of the four following criteria: bring together a wide public, contribute to the national cultural identity, involve the national team within the framework of a substantial event and be traditionally the subject of a large televised audience.

Sport has Unequal Access to TV Rights and to Broadcasting

Owing to cost inflation, the proliferation of private channels and marketing agencies, as well as the pernicious effects of competition, programming

Table 4.6   Hierarchy of broadcasting fees and air-time for four team sports in France

Sport	TV Fees in Division 1 (2005–06)	Air-time (2005)	Main Broadcaster
Football	€550 m	549 h 32m	Canal Plus
Rugby	€20 m	185 h 15m	Canal Plus
Basketball	€1.6 m	183 h 08m	Canal Plus[a]
Handball	€0.7 m	1 h 57m	Eurosport
General total	€800 m[b]	1796 h[c]	–

Notes:
a. Canal Plus is the main broadcaster of basketball matches, but these matches concern the NBA (177h 19m). The Pro A championship is partially broadcast by TPS (regularly eight matches per season).
b. Assessment of all broadcasting fees paid during 2005 for all sports and all competitions in France.
c. Air-time for sport on five terrestrial channels: TF1, France 2, France 3, Canal Plus and M6.

Sources: CSA, *La Lettre de l'économie du sport.*

could only be regulated by the relationship between cost and audience. Indications are building up already that confirm this development, which has been governed by criteria of profitability. Thus, the range of the supply of sports programmes has been reduced to just several disciplines that attract the best audiences (football and Formula 1 for the biggest general commercial channel in France, TF1). Admittedly, the number of sports shown on public channels underlines a greater willingness to offer a pluralist supply, as provided for in their specifications: 14 disciplines for France 2 and 23 disciplines for France 3. But in France, most sports do not have access to broadcasting for more than an hour a year. The expansion of a discipline, however, is based on growing media coverage; a source of financial receipts that comes both from the networks and the sponsors, which widens the audience for those who play sport, spectators and television viewers. Undeniably, television establishes a hierarchy of disciplines by differentiated treatment, a source of promotion or decline (Table 4.6). Football alone concentrates 68 per cent of broadcasting fees and 31 per cent of air-time in France.[13]

It is no longer surprising that the choice of broadcasting matches is governed exclusively by a logic of maximizing the audience and not by equality of exposure for clubs; nor even according to the sporting stake of the matches. Of the accumulated number of French Ligue 1 matches broadcast between 2000 and 2005, 151 concerned Olympique de Marseille (OM), 120 Paris Saint-Germain, three Le Mans and zero for Nancy. Although not being at the top of the table over the last few years, the Marseille club is, every season, the leader in the number of televised matches. It is true that OM, by itself, brings together more than 20 per cent of the paying audience. This assessment is a testimony to the competition between channels that, having paid a great deal, have an obligation to produce results as far as paying connections are concerned. This depends more on the fame of the clubs than on the sporting interest of the matches.

The function of programming is, therefore, to offer those programmes preferred by the public, at times when the potential audience is maximal. With this greater interactivity between supply and demand, the supply being henceforth chosen and football being the viewers' preference, this sport has seen its air-time increase in both hourly volume and percentage of programming everywhere in Europe: from 10 per cent in 1982 to 30 per cent in 2005 in most European countries.

TV Rights and Fair Competition

Under pressure from the demands of the major clubs, a decline in the pooling of broadcasting fees can be seen everywhere in Europe. In reality, as it is possible to measure accurately the commercial appeal of every club, as a priority the networks buy and broadcast matches played by the most prestigious teams. In fact, solidarity is the strongest when the league is owner and administrator of the television rights (France). It does not exist at all when the league has no role at all in the matter (Spain) or is very weak when the league holds only limited power (Italy).

The criteria for distributing broadcasting fees have all developed according to a liberal principle, which desires that there is a greater proportionality between the lists of winners and the ability to attract the audience of clubs and the television revenue that they receive. In France, for example, the proportion distributed in an equal way between clubs represented 91 per cent of fees in 1998–99, as opposed to 50 per cent in 2006–07. In the championships where clubs are the owners and sellers of individual rights, the richest teams are not so because of their sporting results. The revenue paid annually by encoded channels to Italian or Spanish clubs is connected exclusively to their commercial appeal and are guaranteed for four or five years.

On the other hand, in countries where the ownership and/or negotiations are collective and centralized, the club that receives the most television receipts is always the winner of the national championship: €20–40m in France, Germany and England. It is the same for small clubs: the club that is the least wealthy in Italy (€7m), is so because it attracts the lowest number of season tickets, and it receives a sum that is half that of its English or French counterparts.

A priori, clubs do not have the same financial resources within national championships as within the Champions League. Juventus received €90m in 2005–06, that is, 12 times more than Treviso.[14] The three teams with the best share-out in the Italian championship – Juventus, AC Milan and Inter Milan – received 50 per cent of all the broadcasting fees of all the 20 clubs in Serie A; the three least remunerated only cashed 5 per cent.[15]

There are also significant inequalities between countries, even amongst the best remunerated: €16m for Bayern Munich, €44m for Lyon, €78m for Real Madrid and €90m for Juventus. Yet all these clubs take part, every year, in the same European competition. The revenue distributed by UEFA to the clubs qualifying for the Champions League strongly contributes to reinforcing the major clubs, both in their national championships[16] (collecting revenue that their national rivals do not have access to) and in European competitions (a difference of 1–8 in 2004–05 between the richest, Liverpool, with €30m and the poorest, Sparta Prague, with €4m.[17]) Taking the method of distributing television receipts into account, the two clubs that received the most collected 22 per cent of the total and the two clubs that received the least collected 3 per cent of the total. A distribution based on a principle of solidarity would have produced a share of 3.1 per cent for each of the 32 qualified clubs.

The unequal amounts of these fees, their stability or otherwise over time, their autonomy or not with regard to the vagaries of the competition, have the effect of a more or less great uncertainty of results in the championships. Juventus and Real Madrid, which each hold 28 national titles, have shown their sporting domination over a long period. This has been supported by the financial hegemony that has given them the means to invest in talent and thereby maintain their sporting supremacy.

The open and linked (national/European) system of championships complicates implementing these regulatory procedures. In fact, an optimal distribution at a national level, which is the case of the French first division, will not necessarily be so for the degree of competitiveness of those of its clubs involved in European Cup tournaments: French clubs twice reached the quarter finals of the Champions League between 1997 and 2003, as opposed to 15 times for Spanish clubs. According to the UEFA performance index of clubs in European Cup tournaments, France is ranked fifth while Spain and Italy are the best placed. Admittedly, the economic homogeneity of the French championship helps the access of a large number of different clubs to the title, but the strong regulation of the Ligue handicaps its European clubs, insofar as they do not have the means to invest massively in talent. This compromises their chances of victory in European competitions.

That is why the Ligue, anxious to ensure a "fairer" return for the main clubs on their contribution to turnover and to avoid the consequences of their actions before national and European courts "to impede their free development and despoliation", has relaxed its criteria: 50 per cent of fees distributed in an equal way, with 30 per cent according to performance and 20 per cent pro-rata of the number of televised matches.[18] Those most shown on the media, and therefore the most telegenic, will be the best remunerated: up to €32m, if they finish in one of the top three places in the championship, that is, an increase of 33 per cent of their allocation. On the other hand, the small clubs will have to content themselves with €11m, that is, 35 per cent less than before.

The concept of competitive balance – a statistical indicator of the degree of competition within a championship – makes it possible to compare the degrees of uncertainty in the five biggest European championships. The hierarchy, going from the most to the least uncertain, that is, the championships of France, Germany, England (collective bargaining of rights and a high degree of revenue pooling), to those of Spain and Italy (individual bargaining and a low distribution of revenue in the league) is not a surprise.

What helps to explain the position of each of these countries is the economic organization, which shows more or less solidarity, mainly through the regulatory function of the broadcasting rights. Hence the difficulty of reconciling implementing national economic solidarity with the major clubs involved in European Cup tournaments, with "liberal" criteria for distribution that ensure them a "fair" return for their contribution to creating value (the number of matches broadcast and the number of paying connections created, and so forth).

This is why we have set out several recommendations (Andreff and Bourg, 2006). It very much seems that pooling revenue equal to, or higher than, 50 per cent – which is the situation in France – is counterproductive for those clubs taking part in European Cup tournaments, especially when some distortions of competition establish an equal hierarchy of the clubs: the weight of social and fiscal costs, an unequal turnover and forbidden from accessing the financial markets and such like. The French regulatory system is relevant at the national level. It is the fairest of all the European championships, even coming close to the model of the North American leagues, especially that of the National Football League. That said, it is the one that, a priori, best ensures competitive balance and promotion of uncertainty. On the other hand, the differences in budgets (from 1–10 or 1–20), in Italy and Spain and between television fees (from 1–8 or 1–12) do not make it possible for real economic solidarity to be created. The French model is a reference in the case of a closed league, with clubs only taking part at a single level of competition. For its part, the Italian-Spanish model is effective in endowing major clubs with considerable resources, in order to be competitive on the European level. The difficulty, therefore, lies in the fact that these two models are only effective at a single level (national or European).

Therefore, what would be the best synthesis of the two aims of a regulatory function for broadcasting rights? What is the intermediary level between Italy and France that is likely to regulate the championship correctly, without penalizing the clubs involved in the two levels of competition?

At this stage, it is a question of specifying that neither theoretical analysis, nor any empirical approach, has determined the effective level of competitive balance, with regard to the expectations of fans, the media or sponsors (Bourg, 2004c). From a statistical point of view, in a perfectly balanced competition – a hypothesis that is, admittedly, unrealistic – all teams would have equivalent strength and every match would finish with an equal score. It would be impossible to draw up a classification and the interest of such a championship would be debatable. The divergent developments of competitive balance in the five championships studied do not, in the short term, seem to have affected the well-being of fans who, independently of the variations of this indicator, are increasingly numerous in the stadia.

One should also recommend a minimum of distribution of television fees by the league – without which, the national championships would not be viable. It is true that the sporting results of a club correlate with its financial capacity. The positive relationship between the distortion of the balance of the competition and the dispersal of the financial capacities of clubs makes the liberal tendency that dominates Europe rather worrying. Indeed, in the debate about the distribution of television fees, one should favour the most egalitarian division possible. The legal possibility of a collective sale is certainly useful, but it is not enough. Only a redistribution of these fees could lead to a homogeneous competition and not lead to distribution according to sporting ranking, media exposure of teams and paying connections. For it is in this latter case that the major clubs would be encouraged to behave in a more individualist way.

This question illustrates the classic debate between fairness and effectiveness. To be effective, it is necessary to concentrate the resources between just some clubs, at the risk of harming the competitive balance. This was the choice of most European championships that favoured, even anticipated, European performance, but that broke with national balance.

To be fair – and this was the case of France, for historical and cultural reasons – one takes the risk of not being effective. And that is, indeed, the situation of French clubs, which encounter difficulties qualifying at European competition level.

The debate that has been going on these last few years represents significant stakes for the structure and efficiency of the sporting system in Europe, as well as for supporting its principles – which distinguish it from the US model.

NOTES

1. Following Paul Samuelson, economists make the distinction between public goods and private goods: see Samuelson (1964). A pure public good must respond to the principle of non-competition: consumption of a good by an agent does not decrease the quantity available of this same good to other agents. It must also satisfy the principle of non-exclusion, by virtue of which an agent who does not want to, or cannot, pay to profit from this good (for example, the case of subscribing to Canal Plus and Foot +). See also Gabszewicz and Sonnac (2006), pp. 14ff.
2. According to Prisma Sports, world sporting broadcasting fees increased by 993 per cent between 1991 and 2001.
3. For a comparative study of the development of broadcasting rights in North America and Europe, see Hoehn and Lancefield (2003); Gratton and Solberg (2004).
4. Four scenarios must be simultaneously confirmed in order to consider that a market is in a situation of perfect competition: the atomicity of supply and demand, free entry to the market, homogeneity of the product, as well as perfect information from different economic agents.
5. Thus, when fixed costs are very high in a market – for example, subscription sports programmes – a monopoly situation makes it possible for TV channels to supply products at a low price and to sell large quantities in order to pay off these costs (the current configuration in the UK, Italy, Spain and Germany).
6. Neale (1964). For an analysis of the TV rights market in the United States, see Fort (2006), pp. 52–91.
7. See Sandy et al. (2004), pp. 127–54.
8. Most jurists agree in recognizing the league as the owner of the rights relating to a competition, insofar as it is the creator of it; participating clubs are only the material organizers. In some countries, the law maintains that broadcasting rights belong to the leagues. Elsewhere, property results from the material right of the sports organizer (the league) over the scene of the event, which makes it possible to grant a right of entry or a broadcasting right, and so on.
9. These cartel practices benefit the clubs to the detriment of the channels and sponsors, who are subject to high fees, and of viewers, who have to pay increasing access costs. See Horowitz (1974); Bourg and Gouguet (1998); Andreff and Bourg (2006).
10. Common law explains the origin of this ownership. Indeed, the IOC has always received broadcasting fees from the Olympic Games, and not the athletes, by virtue of its own statutes.
11. The creation of a channel by the league could also avoid a monopoly situation, which is forbidden by national (a single operator in Italy cannot hold more than 60 per cent of scrambled TV rights) and European regulations.
12. A comparable development could be noted in most developed countries, with, obviously, some particularities linked to the structure of the national audiovisual scene

(especially, the number of payable sports channels). In the United Kingdom, the number of hours of sports broadcasting by BSkyB rose from 9530 in 1995 to 39 835 in 2005.

13. A similar concentration of TV fees and air-time for one or several disciplines can be noticed in most countries. For example, broadcasting fees concerning the five main national football championships (Germany, England, Spain, France and Italy) represent 92 per cent of all fees paid in Europe (€2.8m in 2005–06).

14. From the 2007–08 season onwards, Juventus will receive €109m per season.

15. This media overexposure has increased the advertising receipts of these three clubs, which amount to 57 per cent of the total revenue from sponsorship for the whole of Serie A. In Germany, there is far from being such a concentration: 39 per cent of the Bundesliga sponsorship is collected by Bayern Munich, Borussia Dortmund and Bayer Leverhusen (2005–06).

16. A feature of the European sporting model is the mixture of two levels of competition (national and European), which gives a significant economic advantage to the major clubs involved at these two levels, compared with those that progress solely in the national championships. For 2005–06, for example, €28m for Chelsea, €26m for AC Milan, €20m for Olympique Lyonnais, €18m for Bayern Munich and €16m for Barcelona.

17. Fixing the criteria for distribution by UEFA is guided by two opposing constraints: respecting a principle of solidarity that legitimizes a practice that would be perceived, failing that, as an anti-competitive agreement, contrary to the treaty of the European Union; and favour clubs with a strong sporting and media potential in order to prevent them taking part in a closed and stable Super League, formatted according to commercial logic.

18. In England, the key to distribution is as follows: 50 per cent of fixed premium, 25 per cent premium according to sporting results and 25 per cent premium according to the number of matches shown. Up till 2005–06, 100 per cent of broadcasting fees in Germany were allocated in an equal way. From the 2006–07 season onwards, the sporting performances over the last four seasons are relevant for calculating the share coming to each club.

5. The segmentation of the sports labour market: three examples

In the field of the economics of professional sport, the labour market has a very specific importance, insofar as the sporting spectacle is mainly produced by the human factor. That is why, from the very start of sport economics, many works have been dedicated to the sports labour market, where most of the problems encountered in this branch of activity are concentrated: the mobility of players and the consequences for competitive balance, wage levels, revenue sharing, negotiating collective agreements and so on. The economic analysis of the sports labour market thus exceeds the very restrictive limit of just one chapter and we must try to reduce our field of study.

The first selection concerns the subjects dealt with. The labour economy is generally (Cahuc and Zylberberg, 2003) chock-full of queries relating to very varied issues: the behaviour of agents in the market according to various incentives (salaries and bonuses) and when the information is not balanced; the importance of qualified labour; the analysis of wage formation; determining the causes of unemployment and the impact of working regulations, and so on. With regard to sport economics, it is certainly the analysis of player mobility on the labour market that is at the heart of most contemporary work, and we have used three examples of the problems posed by this mobility and its regulation: player training, player transfers and players' agents.

The second selection concerns the choice of theoretical input. It has, for a long time (Bourg, 1983), appeared to us that one of the essential features of the sports labour market was its segmentation. There are, indeed, deep divisions between star players (primary market) and ordinary players (secondary market), which are manifested by completely different regulatory modalities. Now, this segmentation of the markets does indeed concern the three examples used: training, transfers and intermediation.

In the third case mentioned, we will also think about the problems posed by regulating the market. Indeed, it appears that owing to the deregulation of the sports labour market since the Bosman Case, we are witnessing a deterioration of competitive balance in most team sports. This makes it possible to understand the proposals for reform by national institutions, such as the Ministry of Youth and Sport, or international institutions, such as FIFA or UEFA. These projects for reform aimed to support player training in clubs, to improve regulations for transfers and to clean up the profession of player's agent.

1 PRODUCING SPORTING TALENT: PLAYER TRAINING[1]

The sporting spectacle is defined as an economic activity that uses highly qualified labour. The value of such a spectacle depends on the uncertainty of the result and very high-quality protagonists are needed. However, if player talent is partly innate, it is also the product of training activity. This latter is, therefore, at the very heart of the organization of no matter what sporting system. In the particular case of France, even though the public channels for training are organized in all disciplines (at a national education level, a sport federation level and a state level), professional clubs in team sports have been organizing their own training centres since the mid-1970s. It is from this perspective that one can talk of training "à la française", which represents a model at a time when professional sports are going through difficult times in Europe, resulting from a profound deregulatory movement that has been affecting them since the mid-1990s. And yet, training is perhaps one of the most efficient means of contributing to achieving competitive balance.

The Legitimacy of a Training System

Constitution of the French model

Main historial points of reference The system of training centres for professional football players was progressively put together within the framework of a continual and accelerated process of the professionalism of football between the early 1960s, especially with the start of the Union Nationale des Footballeurs Professionels (UNFP), and the mid-1970s. In a context of crisis, when France had just missed qualifying for the 1970 and 1974 World Cups, and the 1972 European championship, football professionals considered that they were so much behind that this could only be reduced by setting up a rational training system for both players and trainers. Up till then, the only obligation for professional clubs in this area consisted of supporting amateur teams.

The setting up of the National Football Institute on 6 November 1972 in Vichy marked the start of this new policy; its aim was to train tomorrow's elite in a single centre, administered by the Fédération Française de Football (FFF). First devoted to training young players, from 15 to 21 years old, it was repositioned in 1990 on pre-training, in order to satisfy the training supply for clubs. The whole system progressively set itself up around a double obligation: that of developing a training policy for clubs and that of training for professional staff. It was on this basis that the FFF and the state imposed the setting up of training "à la française". The detection of players was ensured through the selection of young players by regional professional staff, who encouraged the young players to join the training centre of the leading club in the area (Faure and Suaud, 1999). At last, local authorities could justify their subsidies to professional clubs by supporting their training policy. The law of 28 December 1999, No. 99-1124, added three new obligations. First, training centres had, from then on, to be authorized by the Minister of Sport. Second, access to a training centre was subjected to the obligation to sign a training agreement between the beneficiary of it, his legal representative and the club. Standard training agreements were subject to a decree, discipline by discipline. Lastly, transactions involving minors were henceforth banned (Article 15-3 of the law).

This text completed state intervention, with a view to protecting young people, in the field of training young sportspeople, by supervising a little more the functioning of training centres. In a general way, this signified that the general organization of the French sports system reserves a prime position for the state in defining legal supervision, directing policies and even participating in managing sport (one thinks here of direct or indirect subsidies by making facilities and professional staff available). In the field of training, this strength of the state is doubtless even greater, for many reasons to do with the characteristics of the French administrative structure. Indeed, not only does the training sector come under public service logic, but also the technicians charged with these issues within the sporting movement are professional government employees; and it must not be forgotten that the professions of trainer and sports educator have been regulated since 1975.

Working of the system   Setting up a training centre is mandatory for all Ligue 1 clubs. The centres are classed into three categories, according to resource criteria (technical and medical supervision, and the like) and efficiency criteria (number of past professional players, number of players having played first-team matches, number of total selections by players in training and qualifications obtained, and so on). The file was submitted to the French Professional Football League (PFL) and the FFF, and is the subject of a report by the Direction Technique Nationale (DTN), the Direction Nationale du Contrôle de Gestion (DNCG) and the Joint Committee on the Charter. Training centres are authorized to welcome a greater or lesser number of players, according to the category in which they are classified.

At the clubs' instigation, this system is today being called into question. Thus, in June 2003, the Joint Committee on the Charter decided to call into question again the obligation of every club in the PFL to have a training centre and to allow the number of players welcomed in each centre to increase. This development is close to an astonishing deregulation, in that the system has proved itself as far as producing French, talented players is concerned. The fact that the Ligue and, above all, the Federation do not to appear to oppose this deregulation is even more astonishing. What can certainly be seen in it, is a development of the power struggle in favour of clubs that denounce the attacks on the free movement of players.

The system was initially set up to promote training by ensuring that the work clubs do in this field is protected. From this perspective, the rules restrict the freedom of movement of players, so that the clubs can collect the fruits of their training. Thus, in the early 1970s, a trainee player who refused to sign a professional contract saw himself banned from every other professional club for ten years, regardless of his most basic rights. If the excesses were progressively erased by reducing the period of restraining the player to five years, the principle remained until the mid-1990s with the advent of the Bosman Case. This, insofar as the sanction could be got round by signing for a foreign club, made the rule, de facto, ineffective. The whole debate concerns the level of constraint imposed on players that is acceptable, with regard to the objective pursued by the training system. Today, a player can join a training centre at the age of 15 as an apprentice, and then he is likely to sign, successively, a contract as a cadet/contender (16–17), as a trainee (19–20) and lastly an engagement as a junior (hopeful) (17–22).

Overall, it could be considered that between 1990 and 1995, the system achieved a certain balance, which ensured:

- very high-quality training in sport (technical, physical and tactical);
- quality schooling up to Baccalaureate level;
- and a fair return on investment for clubs.

In addition, the obligation to sign a first, five-year contract in the professional training club ensured that the latter benefited from the services of a quality player who had become well integrated into the club; compensation for training and/or for transfer, in case the player leaves, to enable it to continue to pursue a real training policy; and the possibility of a strategic management of its workforce in order to ensure good continuity between different seasons.

Lastly, obligations as far as schooling was concerned guaranteed the player the possibility of pursuing head-on his sporting training and his studies. These are all the advances that are likely to be called into question by deregulating the labour market.

Theoretical justification

The lessons of the theory of human capital   According to Gary Becker (1964), training can be likened to an investment from which a return is expected. The first question to be asked is, who must fund this investment? The answer depends on the type of training concerned, with Becker opposing general and specific training. We remain with the second case of specific training, which makes it possible to increase productivity to achieve very specific work that is attached to a given enterprise. Of course, that characterizes training linked to a sports discipline.

The accumulation of specific human capital is based on a rational economic calculation: the amount of the investment is determined by the comparison between its marginal cost and its marginal profit. As long as this difference is positive, investment in training is profitable.

In a situation of pure and perfect competition, it is the employers who must fund this type of training, since it is them who profit from the increased revenue generated by the increased productivity of the trained worker (if one makes the hypothesis that the latter cannot go elsewhere to sell their talent, owing to the specificity of their training). Employers, in the absence of market failure, invest the amount in the training that makes it possible to achieve the social optimum.

Nevertheless, in the presence of externalities, the market can lead to a level of inadequate training, compared with that which is socially desirable. In fact, the worker can use blackmail once trained, because of the power of individual bargaining or the existence of a union. We return to the problem of the hold-up (Cahuc and Zylberberg, 2003): the enterprise loses a share of its profits in salary increases, which encourages it to under-invest in training. We are no longer at the optimum (Phelps, 1990). In this case, state intervention could therefore be hoped for, to fund part of the training.

To sum up, the theory of human capital, as far as specific capital is concerned, leads to two basic conclusions:

● In a situation of perfect competition, this training is payable by the employers and the level that has thus been determined by market conditions corresponds to the social optimum.

- In the presence of various externalities, it could be desirable to have state intervention to make the level of training rise to its optimum from the fact of disinvestment by enterprises.

The problem now is to analyse whether these general conclusions can be applied to the very specific field of professional sport.

The profitability of training professional players   First of all, in the case of restricting the free circulation of players, in order that the investment of the club in training a player is profitable, the number of seasons that are necessary has to be determined, so that the gains brought by the player, who has been trained, allow all the undertaken costs to be covered. Furthermore, within the limits of the rules, one must also ensure that these costs are lower than the cost of recruiting a player of the same level, who has been trained elsewhere. Since the Bosman Case, this scenario no longer exists.

The free movement of players is a real disincentive for clubs to train. It is necessary, in fact, to have compensation for training that would offset all the costs and, particularly, the loss of earnings for clubs, due to the fact that not all trained players become professional. Failing that, the training sector risks showing a deficit and clubs will cease this activity for want of instruments that guarantee them a fair compensation.

Three factors, linked to labour market deregulation, apply in the same way:

- The withdrawal of compensation for transfers at the end of a contract makes a profitable investment possible by clubs that, without having invested in training, succeed in making young players sign their first professional contract.
- The elimination of nationality clauses has prompted the best trained French players to flee abroad. These young players are strongly encouraged to head towards wealthier championships (England and Italy). Exporting young players like this could lead French clubs to wonder about the merits of their investment in training.
- On the other hand, opening the borders has allowed French clubs to extend their field of recruitment for secondary players. Junior players from Eastern and Southern countries are less expensive than French juniors.

For all these reasons, the development of training professional players does indeed follow the lessons of the theory of human capital and is likely to disappear for want of adequate profitability or legal protection. It is on this basis that the proposals for reform from FIFA can be assessed.

The Need for Regulation

The FIFA reform

The new transfer regulations adopted by FIFA in July 2001 are based on respecting 11 fundamental principles. For the problem that interests us here, the main merit of this reform is to make a distinction between transfer fees and compensation for training.

The compensation for transfers corresponds to the compensation for the early breach of a fixed-term work contract connecting a player to his club. The amount depends on many factors (Gouguet and Primault, 2002).

The compensation for training corresponds to the financial compensation granted to the training clubs of the transferred player. In reality, its terms of calculation have given rise to much debate. We would like to emphasize three points:

- The compensation for training will be payable to all clubs that have trained a player between the ages of 12 and 21, once the latter has signed a professional contract with his training club or with another. Later, this compensation will be paid for every professional transfer up to the age of 23.
- To calculate the amount of compensation for training, FIFA divided clubs into four categories according to the level of their investment in training ($2000–$90 000 p.a.).
- Lastly, there is compensation for solidarity, for transfers during the contract, fixed at 5 per cent of the amount of the transaction. This sum is redistributed to clubs that took part in the training and education of the player.

Many questions remain about the real will of international football institutions to pay clubs at the correct value for training. In the specific case of France, it would seem that the real cost of training very largely exceeds the compensation, as calculated by FIFA. This certainly comes from the fact that the multiplier factor is not precisely defined. It should be remembered that this factor aims to take account of the fact that to produce a professional, each club has to train seven to ten players. The real costs of training must not be limited to the cost of a single player, but be multiplied by a factor of seven to ten.

It is still too early to comment definitively about this last rule by FIFA, which was revised in 2004 to be applied on 1 July 2005. It is known that there are many failures, as far as controlling information relating to players is concerned, which does not encourage clubs to apply the directive and to pay compensation for training to those who ask for it. There is a big risk that inadequate remuneration for training threatens this activity, even more so that the supply of labour from countries in the South and East is excessive. It is therefore necessary to analyse the consequences of such a risk on competitive balance.

The impact on competitive behaviour

The talent war   Since the mid-1990s, we have been witnessing a real "talent war" on a global scale. Faced with the growing shortage of qualified labour in the North, enterprises pursued various strategies, depending on the sector, to attract or employ qualified personnel. The problem is to know whether this ferocious competition could be considered a pillaging of a rare resource, in relation to nations that have collectively invested in training their elites, or indeed, whether this "brain-drain" is not, in fact, one of the essential factors of modernization of certain countries. Expatriates actually send most of their salaries to their families; others return to the country with professional experience to set up their own personal projects. It is necessary to talk these days of a brain circulation, rather than a drain (Vaury, 2003).

The problem is, however, not new. As early as 1830, French business-people emigrated to Great Britain to draw inspiration from the British model of industrial organization. As the British bosses were not very cooperative, one could therefore understand the attempts made to lay off the British workers – several thousand then came to France (Girard, 2003). In the 1930s, a whole European elite migrated to the United States. As for the post-war period, it was characterized by a brain-drain. The novelty of the 1990s could be found in the extent of the phenomenon: from localized and unorganized, it became general. One witnessed migrations of skills in all sectors and for various reasons, but on a global scale. One therefore wonders in what way sport and its training are affected by such a global phenomenon?

According to Wladimir Andreff (2004c), one can speak of a real "muscle-drain" from countries in the South and the East. The best players from developing countries are attracted by European clubs and, consequently, these "source" countries suffer from a talent-drain, owing to their ability to train players to an international level. This drain takes place in a context of deregulation of the labour market where, since the Bosman Case in the mid-1990s, the rate of player transfer has significantly increased. Moreover, after a little time, these young talented players can be resold on the European market with a very considerable increase in value, compared with their purchase price.

As with the brain-drain, it is necessary to do a cost/benefit analysis of such a monopolization of young talent from the South and the East. It can be considered that, as in the case of France, players coming from European championships acquire skills that could be used within the framework of national teams. There is, therefore, a positive feed-back effect of these flows; others can be found, especially if one thinks of players who return to their countries as trainers or managers, or of financial flows that can be invested locally.

Nevertheless, beyond these assessments that deserve to be gone into in greater depth, the important thing is to know whether this sporting talent war could harm achieving competitive balance. Paradoxically, the flight of the best players abroad improves the competitive balance of national championships, but at the price of lowering the level of competition of these championships. This situation can be seen very well in the French case, where the championship is much more open since the best players left, but where, in return, French clubs are very little represented in European competitions (Gouguet and Primault, 2006).

The fact that 100 best French players went abroad, which was not compensated by the arrival of equivalent talent, contributed to the levelling down of club potential and to reinforcing the uncertainty of the results. Conversely, at the European level, it seems that the concentration of talent was in favour of the richest clubs, which led to a deterioration of competitive balance that can be verified by considering the list of clubs represented in the last stages of European competitions over the last few years.

It would therefore appear truly discouraging to invest in training players within the framework of a completely deregulated labour market. However, to understand these results, it is necessary to analyse the strategies of the clubs. To do so, we have used the training strategies of three clubs with unusual profiles:

- FC Nantes, a famous club in French football with a long tradition of training and a large budget – a training club by vocation.
- AJ Auxerre, a little town club with an average budget but developing a training policy that fits into a global strategy – a training club by necessity.
- AS Cannes, having developed very high-quality training, sold off for want of a consistent overall project over time – a training club by opportunism.

It is very instructive to analyse the relationship between the sporting results of these clubs and their financial resources. Thus, one observes that out of the four Ligue 1 championships, 1997–2000, Nantes and Auxerre were classified for 75 per cent of the time above the ranking to which their budgets, in theory, destined them. This assessment leaves us to imagine the impact of a training policy on competitive imbalance. As a type, the opportunist training club tends to reinforce competitive balance; its talented players that are sold in advance are going to reinforce the potential of the wealthiest clubs. As for the training club by vocation or by necessity, it tends to strengthen competitive balance by partly compensating for the handicap connected to the relative weakness of its financial resources. Based on these conclusions, one therefore wonders what incentive instruments could be put in place to promote training policy strategies that would improve the competitive balance.

Towards a new training policy   Applying FIFA's regulations as they were initially planned, including calculating a "player factor", has to be a short-term objective, in order to restore consistency to the undertaken reform. The method used, leaving the sporting authorities to define the real cost of training a player, has shown its limitations. An exploratory study on this point must be entrusted to independent experts.

Including a bonus in the calculation of the UEFA coefficient, for countries where the clubs make players trained at the club play in European competitions, would probably promote training. In the same way, and with the same objective, a minimum of players trained at the club could be imposed on the teamsheet for European competitions.

These restrictions could include the terms and specifications provided for as part of setting up the club licence system developed by UEFA. It appears that regulating training on a European level is delicate because of:

- the heterogeneity of the situations;
- the economic power of some clubs;
- the restrictions of European law;
- the difficulty of supervision;
- and the difficulty of implementing sanctions.

However, it is necessary to go further: ensuring the internal consistency and profitability of training cannot be enough; one must still take into consideration the externalities generated by the system. The creation of a retraining fund could offset the deteriorating situation of players excluded prematurely from the market. Moreover, this measure is best accompanied by the obligation made in every country, according to terms that suit them, to put in place a committee to accompany and retrain players who spend at least two years in a training centre without achieving a career as a professional sportsperson.

In addition, young players must not be subject to the financial vagaries of clubs. Every signing of a young player requires the payment of a deposit that guarantees the payment of the remuneration contractually provided for and the payment of accommodation and education for the year.

There are also great differences, from one country to another, in the field of social protection. An effort should be made to ensure the fair treatment of young players. In particular, the likelihood of interrupting a career because of an injury must be subject to an obligatory insurance cover, taken out by the club for the benefit of the player.

These lessons and the thoughts that they generate show the necessity of designing observatory tools for training. If they are not a panacea, they most certainly represent a precondition to any serious evaluation of policies in this field. In order to be effective, it is essential that actors in the system are associated with the measures envisaged. That is why collective bargaining seems to be a relevant legal regulatory tool, if everyone agrees about the objectives. The club licence envisaged by UEFA, understood and negotiated by all the actors, could be the beginning (Arnaut, 2006).

2 SELLING SPORTING TALENT: THE TRANSFER MARKET[2]

The problem of player transfers has been back on the agenda over the last few years, following attacks by the European Commission calling for their abolition, or at least, their reform. This conflict between the Commission and the international football authorities is also in line with the framework of media coverage of the large sums made by the transfer of some football stars between prestigious clubs, whether Real Madrid, Paris Saint-German or Manchester United, and the like.

In order to throw light on the debate relating to the legitimacy or otherwise of such amounts, let alone their influence on the competitive balance, it seems necessary to go back to economic theory to describe the problem correctly and, especially, pose two unavoidable questions. First of all, how can one objectively determine the value of the transfer of a player between two clubs? And then: why is there a discrepancy between the price of the players and the previously determined economic value?

As far as the functioning of the transfer market is concerned, it is a question, on the one hand, of understanding why it is necessary to regulate and analyse the proposed agreement made at the European level. On the other hand, the consequences of such a regulatory failure on competitive balance must be shown, as must the possible remedies for them.

The Economic Legitimacy of the Transfer System

The two theoretical approaches

The transfer fee is the financial amount that accompanies a player transferring from one club to another. The basic problem is to know how, and for what reason, to determine such amounts. Thus, we would like to go against the idea currently spread by the media, that the transfer fee is arbitrarily based. It would seem that some form of parallelism could be established between the economics of culture and the arts, and the economics of sport. Since the pioneering work by William Baumol (Baumol and Bowen, 1966), economic theory has set out to answer the question: how to determine the value, the quoted value, of such and such a painter or such and such a picture? In order to do this, two approaches have been developed: a cost-based approach and a talent-based approach. After having recalled the basis of these methods, we analyse how they can be applied to sport and thus clarify the value of transfer fees.

The cost-based approach   In order to determine the value of an artist or a footballer, we rely on traditional economic theories that propose, it will be remembered, two different bases of value (labour and utility) and are based on two different levels of analysis (macroeconomic and microeconomic). Therefore, a good has a value: either because it incorporates a large amount of labour or it brings a great utility to the individual who uses it. It is necessary, therefore, to consider the notions of "production cost", then the "training cost".

In the first instance (production cost), we can go back to the traditional wage theory of Adam Smith and David Ricardo, which would explain the price of labour, the monetary expression of its value. Labour, according to Ricardo, has a natural price (corresponding to a kind of social minimum) and a current price (which depends on the supply and demand of labour in the market). Based on that, Ricardo showed that the current wage fluctuates around the natural wage without being able to diverge from it permanently.

It was necessary to wait for Marx to go beyond this vision of a natural order, where wages no longer appeared exclusively as the equivalent of labour being socially necessary for the support and reproduction of the worker and his or her family (exchange value of the labour force). This labour force is also allocated a use value, depending on the work capacity of the worker. For Marx, the worker hires his or her use value to the capitalist, but only receives in compensation his or her exchange value, which is, of course, greatly inferior to his or her use value – the difference being the increase in value, which the capitalist pockets, hence exploitation.

This theoretical basis could possibly be used for transfer fees, seen from the clubs' point of view (paradoxically!). Indeed, it is possible to liken the transfer fee to the use value of the player for the club. It is the employer who invested in football, who took the risks; he or she could therefore consider his or herself to have every right to recover the total of his or her contribution and to ask, in compensation for the loss of a player, for a sum of money equivalent to the use value of the latter. In this hypothesis, it is assumed, of course, that the club is owner of the player. We will subsequently see that it is the market that will allocate this use value to the highest bidder, hence a discrepancy between the transfer fee (price) and value. In the opposite hypothesis, where it is postulated that the player is completely free to use their abilities, one could look for the theoretical basis of transfer demand in G.S. Becker (1964) with his theory of human capital.

In the second instance (training cost), the rational individual invests in human capital in order to optimize the overall return of his or her asset portfolio (monetary, financial, real and human). In order to do this, he or she carries out a standard calculation of opportunity cost: the actualized cost of the capital acquisition must be inferior to the actualized sum of the anticipated income.

Training is very often considered as the main means of increasing the stock of human capital. The individual follows their training until the actualized cost of this investment (the income of which is relinquished while not working during training, the time spent studying, and school fees, and so on) is equal to the actualized income due to the training being completed.

Can this theory of human capital be used as an explanation of transfer fees? It could, in fact, be thought that every player has invested in human capital, the actualized value of which could constitute the basis for calculating their wages or their transfer fee.

Finally, whatever the theory called on – labour value or utility value – the economic basis of transfer fees can always be found in the use value of the player. Of course, the problem is to know, speaking in concrete terms, how to measure such a value. It is at this level that economic analysis has more difficulty. It has to be recognized that there is a severe lack of study applied to sport. We will subsequently present the market answer, which will allow us to return again to basic analysis. Indeed, in perfect market conditions, the price will reflect the value of the exchanged good. But in the case of malfunctioning (asymmetrical information, lack of competition, speculation and various externalities, and so forth) the price can diverge from the value. It is this that must be analysed in the particular case of transfer fees.

The talent-based approach   The value of the transfer fee lies here in the quoted value of the player, just as the value of a painting lies in the quoted value of the painter. The problem is, therefore, to determine such a quoted value relatively objectively. In the field of art, econometric studies carried out by analysing multiple regressions have given convincing results (Pommerehne and Frey, 1993). Four determining factors in the value of an artist and his or her work have become apparent:

- the number of exhibitions already shown and the number of prizes received;
- the time passed since the first exhibition;
- the flexibility of the artist;
- the price of previous sales.

As far as we know, this type of exercise has not been carried out in the sporting field, but could be the subject of econometric tests that would certainly confirm the results obtained in the field of art; all the more so, as the main variables to be used are known:

- the number of years spent at the top level;
- the list of sporting honours;
- the position occupied;
- the flexibility of the player;
- age;
- nationality.

On this basis, it should be possible to establish a quoted value for the players that could be used to calculate the transfer fee. Nevertheless, although the principle is simple, we are going to come up against a formidable question, as in the field of art: who has to set the quoted value? A basic question that leads to others: can this task be entrusted to an independent external operator? Can it be left to the market?

Up till now, it is the second procedure that has prevailed, which would not necessarily be a bad solution, if the labour market in professional sport and transfers were functioning correctly, which is not the case. This is something to which we will return. Talent intervenes in a decisive way in determining the relative value of players, along with other elements that disturb the transactions. That is why, before coming back to the discrepancies that are produced on the transfer market, we would like to assess in the light of theoretical contributions that have been presented, the content of the agreement on the reform of transfers between the European Commission and interested parties, signed in 2001.

The real working of the transfer system

Determining the price of transfers   The level of the transfer fee is the result of the confrontation between the willingness to pay of the club that is buying (purchasing) and the willingness to receive of the club that is selling. The purchasing club here forecasts discounted future receipts due to the acquisition of the player: strengthening the team that manifests itself in better sporting results, financial receipts directly linked to the player himself (merchandising, increasing spectator receipts, increasing TV rights and sponsoring contracts, and so on). From this perspective, the examples of the transfers of Zinedine Zidane (July 2001) and David Beckham (June 2003) to Real Madrid, or Hidetoshi Nakata to AS Roma (January 2000), are interesting to detail in order to show the profitability of the investment, mainly as a result of merchandising receipts.

For the selling club, three factors have to be taken into account: first, the assessment of this willingness is based on the actualized sum of the investments made by the selling club in the training, care and improvement of the player; second, the club estimates the amount of net losses that the departure of the player is likely to cost it, both from the sporting point of view and financial one; and third, the club estimates the cost of replacing the player from which it has separated.

Moreover, the extent of this willingness to pay and to receive depends on which category the player transferred belongs to. It is known that the labour market for professional footballers can be broken down into two radically different segments. For France, for example, it is possible to identify a primary market (made up of 40 star players, who are the talk of the town) and a secondary market (made up of 350 anonymous players, with a relatively precarious status). It is, of course, at the level of the primary market in all countries that the consequences of the Bosman Ruling have made themselves felt the most on the European scale, as far as transfer fee inflation and wage bills of the major clubs are concerned. Studies are therefore needed to clarify a little more the nature of transfer fees, about which only the overall trends are generally known. Three variables are decisive here:

- The position occupied. For example, defenders are never the subject of the highest transfer fees.
- Nationality, which is in fact linked to player achievement. It is worth mentioning the case of French footballers, who were absent from international rankings a dozen years ago and who were then subject to strong demand since their victories in the World Cup and European Championship.
- Age, insofar as speculation appears strongest about young players.

If these variables, in theory, enable the level of transfer fees to be understood, as well as the "segmentation" of the market, what remains to be explained is why, in the highest segment, a difference between the value and the price is noticed. It is this that fuels all debate concerning the highest transfer fees, which are claimed to be too high.

The difference between value and price   Can it be said that the player's market price reflects his true value? If the market functions in perfect conditions (information and power, and so on) one could certainly answer in the affirmative. The levelling out of willingness of the clubs concerned to pay and to receive would allow a "fair" price to be fixed, if it were determined on an objective basis (by cost and talent). However, the market is often imperfect, owing to the presence of externalities (asymmetry of information and power information and power, and so forth). Three factors have to be taken into account.

The disconnection between sporting value and economic value is the first. The revenue structure of the best-paid sportspeople on the planet clearly highlights the fact that they live as much on their image, as on their work. Clubs have also absorbed this aspect. Nowadays, they recruit talented sportspeople, but they are as much vehicles for communicating their brand name. The examples of Zinedine Zidane and Hidetoshi Nakata, quoted previously, perfectly illustrate this. One cannot, therefore, reduce the value of a player to just his sporting value: this represents only a part of his total economic value and the non-sporting value of the player could then be subject to many speculative offers from the purchasing club or the selling club, which has an effect on the final price of the transaction.

The second factor for analysis is information asymmetry. The best players and their intermediaries (agents) have great power in the market, which can lead to an abuse of dominant power (see later, the point about intermediaries).

Lastly, it is necessary to consider the speculative aspect of transfers. This speculates mainly on young unrecognized players, on whom the clubs bet for the future concerning their transition from hopeful to star. So it is that many young players from French training centres leave to go abroad to highly paid championships – in Italy and England, mainly. Speculation can also play a part in including very high termination clauses, aimed at making financial gain. Here, too, more study would be needed to pinpoint these differences between player value and price, so as to suggest later some instruments for market regulation. From these simple criteria, it seems to us that we should be able to pinpoint the extent of doubtful transactions. This is all the more important because, in the presence of such malfunctioning, all the competitive balance of championships is threatened. Ultimately, one naturally arrives at the question of the *necessity* of regulating the transfer market.

The Necessity of Regulating the Transfer Market

The agreement on transfer fees

Presentation   According to Viviane Reding, the European Commissioner for Education, Culture, Youth, Media and Sport, 1999–2004, this agreement can be summed up in the following way: how to guarantee, at the same time, the free movement of players, team stability and the integrity of competitions (competitive balance)? The Commission worked out this difficult compromise, which took more than two years (December 1998– March 2001) of negotiation with the concerned parties for it to be signed. Five major themes structured the 11 principles of the agreement, which took place at the end of the discussion between the football authorities, the European Commission and the players' representatives:

- the protection of minors;
- better payment for training;
- the stability of contracts;
- a solidarity mechanism;
- a specific authority for managing disputes.

Compared with the theoretical analysis that we previously developed, it would seem that all possible approaches to founding the value of transfers are more or less present but without any real explanation:

- The value based on training costs is fully recognized and a series of compensation systems is even planned to highlight the role of small clubs, which are at the start of professional players' training. It remains to perfect the technical details of calculating such compensation that rests both on validated theoretical bases (human capital theory, status theory and efficient wage theory) and on recognized methods of economic calculation (present value, productivity and total economic value). Further study is necessary.
- In case of negotiated breach of contract and with the agreement of the club, there will be transfer compensation, the amount of which refers to, mainly, wage theory. The compensation should be based, according to FIFA, on objective criteria: total salary, remaining length of contract and total compensation of previous transfer. Here

again, all that deserves developing, both theoretically on the use value of the player and empirically on the details of calculation and the criteria to be used.

● Whether it is for calculating the training compensation or the negotiated transfer fee, a half-hearted reference to the talent-based approach is made. But it must be recognized that this method is not really clarified, either as far as its content (criteria to be used in order to define talent) or its organization is concerned, which could establish the quoted value and thus the players' ranking, unless, it should be remembered, it is left to the care of the market.

Critical analysis   We have organized our analysis around two issues: the legitimacy of the transfer system in contemporary football and the need to find a compromise between the different partners. Of course, the first question to be asked is: what is the legitimacy of the transfer?

The answer certainly comes from the idea one has of sport and, in particular, the thorny question of the sporting exception. Is the footballer an employee like any other, with total freedom to change employer? For some (the Fédération Internationale des Footballeurs Professionnels – FIFPro), the player must regain freedom of movement; it would be enough for the new club to pay an amount equivalent to the wages owed to the club that has been left. For others (FIFA, UEFA), the player must not unilaterally breach his contract, for fear of harming the competitive balance. This is the point of view that the Commission accepted, while suggesting sanctions in the case of unilateral breach and offering to control the transfer compensation, in the case of negotiated breach. Whatever the actors' clear-cut opinions, the transfer has never been called into question because it well expresses, despite everything, the attempt at reconciliation between an increasingly invasive industrial economic logic and also the need to respect a sporting logic, without which the spectacle and the profit will be destroyed.

This signifies that it is only possible with difficulty to abolish the transfer system, which, contrary to what had been traditionally written, has a genuine usefulness and that is based on an unquestionable economic logic.

On the one hand, the transfer indemnities constitute a way of internal funding that has the merit of enabling the sporting sector to keep a certain autonomy. This system is not perfect, but nobody at the present time knows what to replace it with, at the risk of generating new, pernicious effects (black market and wage inflation, and so forth).

On the other hand, it is difficult to accept the comparison made by the Commission between mutually agreed transactions between clubs for fixing the amount of the transfer fee and an arrangement. It is in the name of this argument for the non-respect of competition rules, that the Commission for a while proposed the abolition of transfer fees. However, nothing is more competitive, at an international level, than negotiations for transferring a star.

We come to a second debate, touching on the necessity of finding a compromise between the different partners, a point that is no longer disputed. The Commission itself has greatly appreciated the importance of that condition. Viviane Reding herself, in the period after signing the agreement, correctly declared it was better to have a negotiated solution than an imposed solution. This has, above all, allowed the most difficult-to-reconcile points of divergence to emerge.

The example of the reaction to the reform by the professional players' union, which was removed from the final negotiation because its position was judged too radical (the clubs emerged strengthened), is very significant. The players' position was basically structured around an opposition to the training compensation, which was judged too high and to the system of sporting sanctions in case of unilateral breach of contract. Conversely, the union declared itself in favour of total freedom for players and a transfer system based on the payment of the salary owing.

Transfer reform is only in its first stages. Agreement about several major principles has, with difficulty, started and the concrete details of methods have advanced a little (calculation of compensation, dispute and staged solidarity, and so on), but there is still much to do. It is the responsibility of the actors in football themselves to continue the dialogue. It seems to us that it is on this point that progress has to be made. From this perspective, one could resort to the instruments of industrial economics, insofar as it has now been recognized that football is comparable to an industrial or commercial branch, in which groups of actors interact in a complex and confrontational way. It is necessary to promote a collective bargaining process, in order to settle the problem of disputes relating to revenue sharing from the sporting spectacle. Transfer fees are affected by divergent positions:

- between clubs and unions;
- between agents and clubs;
- between leagues and clubs;
- between players and agents.

Behind this bargaining, we find again the attempt to reconcile two demands: an equitable economic competition and a balanced sporting competition.

The issue of competitive balance

Inter-club dualization   The point of departure for analysis is the recognition here that football clubs are now subject to a logic arising from the financial globalization of the world economy (Andreff, 2000). The investment necessary to stay in such a competition is increasingly heavy, which calls for looking for new sources of funding for the major clubs. To obtain them, these clubs have consequently to achieve good sporting results; hence the connection with transfers.

In an exaggeratedly competitive environment, the richest clubs find and buy the best players. So it is that the poorest championships are used as reserves for the richest (as in the minor leagues in the United States). This helps us to understand the very large inter-club dualization that has become established in Europe over the last few years, particularly with the G14, which was pushing for the creation of a sort of European Super League.

The question is, of course, to know if such an investment in talent is manifested in improved sporting results. The English championship shows that the answer is positive: "Sporting performance is tied at 94 per cent of player salaries", reported *Les Echos*[3] in 2001. The fact remains that, here again, further statistical analyses have to be envisaged. In particular, and if it is possible, it is necessary to test the relationship between sporting results at time t and transfers at time $t - 2$ or $t - 3$. Indeed, it is very likely that a transferred player will only be efficient at the end of one or two seasons. Such a study would perhaps make it possible to check the speculative behaviour by certain clubs.

The elements and analyses that are currently available seem to be partly contradictory. Stefan Szymanski and Tim Kuipers (1999) consider that there is no correlation between sporting results and transfer expenditure. The position of the experts at Deloitte & Touche,[4] is more qualified, but they do not conclude that there is a correlation.

Whatever the uncertainties about the effective causality between transfers and sporting results, it has indeed to be recognized that since the Bosman Case, the differences in wealth between clubs have deepened and efforts to buy sporting talent are very uneven, which has put competitive balance at risk in many countries. Solutions must be found.

Possible solutions   The debate about transfers cannot be separated from a much more general debate about the organization of the professional sporting system, which we will come back to later. In this chapter, we will limit ourselves to some information relating to the labour market. The essential point, of course, concerns mainly the problem of the free movement of players. The consequences of the Bosman Ruling on the increase in club wage bills are now well known. In the same way, transfer reform risks making players' salaries rise once again. Different proposals need to be discussed:

- the general setting up in all of Europe of financial control committees, on the French model;
- establishing a US-style salary-cap system (but difficult to transpose, as it is);
- improvement of the quality of information about the labour market;
- better distribution of talent between clubs.

Overall, efforts must be made to carry on in this attempt to regulate all of the system, because of the growing power of some clubs and star players who risk either distorting the competitive balance or sending us towards the US-style closed leagues.[5]

3   SPOTTING SPORTING TALENT: THE AGENTS' MARKET[6]

The labour market in professional sports does not put the supply of players in direct contact with the demand of clubs. Agents, serving as intermediaries between players and clubs, appeared at the very beginning of professionalism in sport. Working first for clubs and then for players, their position seems much more ambiguous nowadays. But whatever their effective employer, their justification that is officially advanced is always the same: they are there to compensate for market failures caused by asymmetrical information between players and clubs.

Nevertheless, beyond this theoretical legitimacy of agents, the problem is to know whether their growing weight in player transactions gives them excessive market power. In this case, they could possibly have an impact on competitive balance. Therefore, the question arises of whether this state of the market, which is linked to the presence of these intermediaries, is preferable to a direct encounter with the supply and demand of work with asymmetrical information.

The position of agents today is such that one does not hesitate to ask the question: "Have agents taken over power?"[7] And this is without talking of the pernicious effects that they could be responsible for (for example, dirty-money laundering, fiscal fraud, and the like). That is the reason why voices have been heard for some time, demanding reforms of the labour market for professional players (Bennahmias, 2002; Denis, 2003; Collin, 2004; Arnaut, 2006).

The Legitimacy of Players' Agents

Historical reminder
Three periods in the history of intermediaries in France can be distinguished. In the first (1890–1961), the intermediary was given a mandate by all-powerful clubs. During the second (1961–95), the intermediary took over power to help players. Lastly, during the most recent period (1995 to the present day), more balanced bargaining between clubs and players led to specialization by intermediaries.

Thus, at first, there was the time of the all-powerful managers (1890–1961). With a small delay compared with Great Britain, it was mainly after the First World War that French football saw significant development with the democratization of the practice, a change in the social origins of players (the arrival of workers) and the generalization of false amateurism. Moreover, with the growing success of the sporting spectacle and the increase in gate receipts, the rules of the market economy started to reach football with the refunding of expenses, match bonuses and the start of blackmail by players.

It should be remembered that players then had the right to change club without limitation in the name of individual freedom. Thus started the touting for players that made it possible to fix the beginning of intermediaries, or agents, in football. Clubs, therefore, acquired "touts", who tempted players away from other clubs. These were the intermediaries working for clubs who managed the careers of players, as opportunities dictated.

To fight against touting, which was a source of instability for teams, the FFF established the Licence A system; this had to be obligatorily issued to a transferred player, so that he could play in the first team. Therefore, on 18 April 1925, a new rule stated that Licence A would be automatically given to a transferred player, if the club that he left gives its agreement. The transfer system had just been created. Indeed, a club that wished to acquire a new player made a double offer: one to the coveted player and the other to the club that had been left, which could have increased the bidding.

Alfred Wahl and Pierre Lanfranchi (1995) emphasized that the transfer period thus opened a vast "footballers fair". They report, for example, a complaint by the director of a club that had been left, for whom, "the horse-traders of sport are too experienced to leave any trace of their transactions".[8]

Beyond false amateurism, professionalism arose in France in 1932 on the initiative of the directors of the most powerful clubs, who wanted to impose their power on players. This was also the start of a huge wave of recruitment of foreign players. During the period 1932–39, there were about 30 per cent of foreign players playing in France. French clubs thus had intermediaries abroad to spot players who were in disagreement with their clubs and who were ready to emigrate. These intermediaries acted for the demand of clubs that were sometimes only looking for profits by selling players as expensively as possible to other clubs. Moreover, these intermediaries could turn out to be "dealers in men, who would not hesitate to supply ill or injured players and who deceive French clubs".[9]

This forced mobility of players who could not refuse their transfer thus gave rise to the start of a players' organization, in the form of a mutual benefit society (in 1934) and then as a union (in 1936). But the aim of reforming transfer rules did not see the light of day, because of the war.

Progressively, footballers came increasingly from the working class, and mining areas became reservoirs of players, with a strong contingent of Italians and Polish. All the amateur clubs in these areas, therefore, were subjected to special surveillance by recruiters on behalf of the major clubs. Many players also came from Latin America (Argentina and Brazil) with resounding setbacks, owing to the fact that the agents had inflated their reputations to deceive credulous directors.

In short, as early as the 1920s, the player became merchandise. He was bought and sold by clubs who speculated on his value and it was in his interest to be bought and sold as often as possible. From this period on, the footballer was compared not to an employee, who was free to work with the employer of his choice, but to a real slave, whose owner could sell him to another owner. Alfred Wahl and Pierre Lanfranchi even quote remarks that evoke "brokers dealing in human flesh"[10] who organize the market for players. Numerous examples have also been given by these two authors, showing how directors, or managers, made their interests prevail against those of players unable to defend themselves.

This makes it possible to understand that from the mid-1950s on, disputes between players and club managers became the rule about the double problem of wages and transfers. As a general rule, players lost, which made their dependence with regard to clubs increasingly explosive. A reaction ensued, comparable to a "players' revenge", which ushered in the second period: 1961–95.

In late 1961, the UNFP (the French players' union) was formed in France, marking a delay compared with England and Italy, where players' unions already existed. This creation led to the signing of a collective agreement for football, in November 1962. But the most important negotiations started later, concerning the basic reform of the life contract.

In June 1969, the freely negotiated fixed-term contract came into force. At the end of his contract, the player could negotiate with a new employer without the club he was leaving being able to interfere or receive any compensation. This new market regulation was subjected to much criticism concerning:

- the likelihood of unemployment for average players, who no longer benefited from a life contract;
- the impossibility of poor clubs to bail themselves out, because of the sale of a good player;
- the lack of interest by clubs in training, which could easily find good players;
- the transformation of players into true mercenaries;
- and the risk of a massive exodus of French players abroad.

In the 1960s, French football thus saw an inversion of the balance of power in favour of players; this was the cause of many abuses. Managers sought to call into question the limited time-based contract, which triggered a reaction by the UNFP who decided on the first players' strike in France in 1972. An arbitration meeting, on the initiative of the new president of the FFF (Fernand Sastre) and in the presence of a member of the Council of State (Philippe Séguin), initiated negotiations that led, in June 1973, to the signing of the Football Charter, that is, a real collective agreement on football professions.

Within this framework, the footballer's situation improved considerably, to the point that it weighed heavily on club budgets from the 1980s onward. This could partly explain the massive arrival of intermediaries. In reality, since the middle of the decade, agents imposed themselves on clubs and players, who entrusted them with the management of their careers. Clubs could no longer dictate their conditions to disarmed players, as in the previous period.

This long period, when players could do what they want, was succeeded by a new time for owners. Indeed, with the Bosman Case in 1995, there was an increase in player salaries and an increase in the frequency and the amount of transfer fees. This made it possible to understand the growth in pay of agents involved in such transactions. Nevertheless, despite this development that seemed to result in a favourable balance of power for players, clubs started to regain a certain power: beyond the primary market for star players, the secondary market was made up of anonymous players with a new, relatively precarious status; and the biggest European clubs had an increasing influence on the transfer market.

In such a remodelled context, agents have had to adapt; we are witnessing both a specialization and a dualization of the profession: for those working for the stars from major clubs, more and more agent agencies from outside football can be found; for those players in the secondary market or from small clubs, it is rather a question of agents having been involved in football.

But the most important thing in this period was the return of clubs as the representative of agents. As in the time of the touts, the clubs gave a mandate to agents to manage the transfer. It would seem that there was more and more mixing of the roles of manager and agent, which apparently disturbed nobody at the European level, but that presented more and more ambiguity. One even saw agents take a stake in, or take control of, clubs. It is necessary to have better information about these new elements, in order to assess the power of the effective market of agents.

Theoretical analysis

The sports agent can be justified insofar as transaction costs are such that they can put someone who offers a service (a player) in contact with a club where there is a demand, at a lower price than what it would cost them directly, whilst still making a profit. The transaction costs come essentially from the asymmetrical information about the labour market:

- Clubs cannot collect all the necessary information for a player to make a good choice. There are various qualities looked for in a player (human, sporting, mental, and so on) and clubs cannot allow themselves to be mistaken, taking into account the financial sums at stake and the exaggerated competition for winning sporting talent.
- Players should also support the costs of access to information in order to really know the clubs likely to employ them. Beyond the fame and sporting project, the player could want to know better the internal workings of the club and its financial health.

The search for this type of unavailable precise information easily justifies resorting to the services of an agent, who thus acquires market power. Analysing agent power could concern different factors: quantities, prices and competitive balance.

Quantity exchanged It could be first thought that the market power of the agents would manifest itself in an increase in the number of players employed, from a perspective of profit motives. In reality, it appears that this number is the result of regulations, the increase in club budgets or the effectiveness of a training policy.

Although agents have a relatively marginal role in increasing the number of players employed, they do, on the other hand, have an influence on player mobility. Agents lack the power to act effectively on the number of posts, and in order to maximize the number of contracts signed, and thus their income in a growing economy, they are the origin of the accelerating number of transfers between clubs. Their actions have been helped since 1995 by the deregulation movement produced by the Bosman Case.

As a result, we are therefore seeing a reduction in the effective average length of contracts. The agents' interest in player mobility thus leads to many excesses: door-to-door selling at competing clubs, encouragement of controversial situations within clubs, media pressure and player manipulation, and so on.

The interest of agents in this mobility is even greater, as their way of being paid is an extra incentive. Indeed, agents receive a percentage of the total amount of the transfer fee and of the bonus once the player has signed.

Lastly, encouraging a player to leave his club for a more lucrative contract is also a favoured tool of competition between agents. It is often by this means that agents try to take away a player from a competitor. Nonetheless, this market power depends largely on the type of player and agent concerned, in accordance with the analysis of the segmentation of the labour market already mentioned.

Wage levels   The power of agents necessarily results in a general wage increase or a wage increase for certain players. Although wage inflation in undeniable in Europe, it would seem to be difficult to attribute a direct role in this inflation to the actions of agents. Even though no restrictive regulation of agents' power has been implemented, the stagnation in the increase of transfer fees would tend to prove that. Analyses attribute the reasons for this inflation rather to the structure of the market, and the segmentation and disappearance of nationality quotas within Europe (Gouguet and Primault, 2005).

Finally, agents play a minor role as vehicles for information that has increased competition between the best clubs for the best players. The impact of agents on wages would seem to result rather from certain abuses, of which they are either the instigators or the simple instruments. They are instigators when they use the market power they have in being mandated by a major player to tie in the success of the negotiation to the prior signing, at a prohibitive price, of one or more other players from his "stable". Such behaviour, in a small market dominated by one or two agents behaving in such a way, can be a significant factor of inflation. This was the case seen in France in basketball, before the Bosman Case.

Agents are the instruments of other abuses using, in particular, the support of transfer fees. More or less sophisticated systems of overbilling, as revealed particularly in the "Olympique de Marseille accounts affair", have been used to further corrupt practices and/or fiscal fraud.

Competitive balance   One of the common criticisms made about players' agents is that they can promote one category of club to the detriment of another, in such a way that the uncertainty of the championship finds itself diminished. Developing such a claim, it would be helpful to test the relationship more scientifically between a club's wealth, the share of the budget made in payments to agents, the type of agent concerned and sporting results. Do the richest clubs spend more to use the best agents? Do the best players systematically pass through the hands of the best-known agents? In the end, does this have an influence on competitive balance? Are top-class agents only strengthening the strongest teams? Work is needed to answer such questions. Given the importance of the stakes, it is relatively surprising to note an almost total lack of interest by sports economists in this problem.

Towards New Regulation

Reforming the status of agents

The US precedent   According to Robert C. Berry (Berry et al., 1986), even if the professional player has existed since the Civil War, it is only from the mid-1960s onwards that players used agents. In fact, player bargaining power up till this date was very weak, but the 1970s saw the reserve clause called into question and the rise in power of player unions. In this context, the balance of power in negotiations was reversed in favour of players who obtained better conditions, wages and other things overall. This change of conditions therefore created a demand for professional services, as far as tax and financial consultants, and so on, are concerned. This demand, of course, accelerated with the considerable growth in turnover linked to professional sport (outside broadcasts, sponsorship, merchandising and gate receipts, amongst others). We witnessed the birth of the job of sports agent, on the same model as that of an artistic agent.

Although the development of this profession brought many benefits to players, the practices of certain agents concerning the following problems have been denounced:

- breach of ethics;
- excessive commissions;
- conflict of interests;
- generalized incompetence;

- poor income management;
- and fraud.

Faced with such dysfunction, it was decided, along with applying the general law, to strongly regulate the profession of agent. According to Rodney Fort (2003a), the access of agents to collective bargaining, which is characteristic of the US professional leagues, was limited; they did not have a place at the negotiating table. Rodney Fort pointed out that, insofar as players gave the exclusivity of their power to the unions, it was the unions themselves that did not want to totally exclude agents, and they preferred to regulate their quality. Team owners thus accepted only negotiating with agents who had obtained the agreement of the players' unions. Amongst the conditions laid down in the agreement are:

- mentioning a criminal past;
- proof of experience in a sporting background;
- mentioning conflicts of interest;
- and revealing their fees.

History teaches us no lessons. It is curious that after a 30-year interval, Europe is seeing the same problems with players' agents and is preparing to put in place the same remedies.

FIFA regulations   In 1994, FIFA adopted regulations concerning players' agents and they were applied on 1 January 1995. These imposed a licence that allowed someone to work as an agent; it was granted for the payment of a €136 000 deposit and an interview! In 1999, the European Commission sent FIFA a statement of grievances concerning football players' agents, on the grounds that the established regulations were a barrier to entering the profession.

Consequently, FIFA modified its regulations on 10 December 2000 (applicable on 1 March 2001). The deposit was replaced by a compulsory insurance, covering professional civil liability (Art. 6 of the regulations). The examination was henceforth a written one (Appendix A of the regulations – examination modalities) and came within the competence of national federations (Art. 5). The then licensed agent had, in addition, to sign a code of practice (Appendix B) and use the proposed standard contract of agency (Appendix C). They were authorized to practice their activity for an indefinite period, but they could not sign mandates for longer than two years; only their named principal was authorized to pay them (Art. 12). Possible sanctions (Art. 15) could be taken by the associations and could go as far as withdrawing the licence. Players and clubs resorting to unlicensed agents also could incur sanctions, which could go as far as a 12-month suspension for players (Art. 16) and a suspension from all football activities for clubs (Art. 19).

It is up to the national associations to control the activity and this is a source of legal insecurity and iniquity. This is the weakness of the system in place.

The French example   For the first time, French law interceded to regulate the profession of an agent with a text on 13 July 1992 that modified that of 16 July 1984. Article 15-2 of that law thus legalized a profession that up till then had been forbidden, because of the state monopoly concerning employment of labour in France.

The text provides for a duty of disclosure and certain operational rules, including (Karaquillo, 2000):

- the imperative to intervene "only for one of the parties, who alone can pay him";
- a ban on remuneration of more than 10 per cent of the agreed contract;
- and the incompatibility of the profession with certain functions or professions, the list of which was drawn up by decree (No. 93-393 of 18 March 1993): for example, management or sporting supervision in a club.

In addition, a national commission was created, chaired by a representative of the Sports Minister. It never worked properly. The proposed sanctions were never applied.

A modification of the 1984 law was made on 6 July 2000. It aimed to introduce possession of an obligatory licence to work as an agent instead and in place of the simple declaration established by the previous text – which rapidly reached its limits. This licence was issued for three years by a competent federation, at the end of an examination. The state, acknowledging its own shortcomings during the previous period, off-loaded control of the activity to the federations. The clauses concerning remuneration, incompatibility and obligation to act for only one of the parties remained. It introduced a ban on transactions involving minors, as well as the idea of a sports agent's associate.

Since early 2005, another modification of the law has been envisaged by the Sports Minister[11] in order to compensate for the drawbacks of the legal framework in force up till now. It aims, on the one hand, to clarify its function and its environment and, on the other, to strengthen the sense of responsibility of the actors, and their control:

- the licence to be only issued to individuals (physical person);
- the sports agent's licence to be issued to foreign nationals from outside the European Community;
- the improvement of measures relating to conflicts of interest;
- the establishment of a numerus clausus to limit the number of people entering the profession;
- the modification of the terms of remuneration with a desire for transparency;
- and the definition of the idea of a sports agent's associate with a restriction to only administrative tasks.

Towards more ambitious instruments

It is essential that specific policies are implemented to supervise the job of agent. But they are not enough. Agents are often pointers to deficiencies in the system for finding appropriate regulation, thus it is essential to follow up the specific measures with a more overall regulation of the activity, in order to fight against the listed abuses. We deal with this last point in the next chapter, while considering models of organizing professional sport.

In a limited way, and without exhausting the subject that is being examined on the legislative level in France, here are several recommendations:

- to better ensure the transparency of information;
- to require the financial control and licence commissions of UEFA to publish annual accounts and, within this framework, the amounts paid in commission to agents;
- to require agents to give their audited accounts to the financial control commissions of the disciplines in which they are involved;
- to require the publication of the list of all mandates of every agent, every year;
- to require clubs to publish their commissions paid, corresponding to every transfer, just like Manchester United, for example, does at the moment;
- to make publication of players' pay compulsory;
- to guarantee the protection of training;
- and to favour competitive balance and ethics.

All these recommendations aim to reduce the risk of intermediaries turning the sports labour market to their own advantage with, as a consequence, a deterioration of competitive balance. To conclude this chapter, it is necessary to evaluate the real weight of players' agents.

The Effective Role of Agents

The typology of agents

There are many criteria that make it possible to draw up a typology of players' agents: the profile of the individual, their positioning in their market, the nature of their mandate, their mode of remuneration, their legal status and the extent of the services offered. After interviews with various experts, it appeared that only the first two variables are really relevant in irrefutably determining the various categories of players' agents.

The agent is, first, a person with a network, previously integrated into the professional sports environment. It is their social capital in this sector, therefore, that allows them to start up as an agent. Above all, these sporting networks made it possible for current agents to establish themselves in the market. The agent is frequently a former sportsperson or comes from the world of professional sport. This integration allows them to get to players, who entrust them with a mandate and then makes it easier to put them in contact with clubs, the first stage of their mission. In addition, they must be a negotiator since, as well as putting them in contact, they have to prove their efficiency by getting the player and club to sign a work contract. The other variables (for example, legal competence) appear more incidental to be used in this analysis.

The strong segmentation of the labour market has led to a strong dualization of agents. The more the agent works in the star market, the greater their power, the more substantial is their share of the market and the more they will work internationally. On these bases, it is possible to describe three classes of agent with very unequal market power.

The upper class   Relying on a breeding-ground of national talents (Brazil and France in football, the Balkans and the United States in basketball) or a strong economic championship (England and Italy in football), the "upper class" agent comes from a professional sports background or is introduced from other power networks connected to sport. They are good negotiators, knowing the discipline well. They are surrounded by highly specialized financially and legally skilled people. The activity developed thereafter as part of commercial companies, but despite everything remains very personalized. The difference here is significant compared with the United States, where major law firms have invested in the market. The agent in this category is positioned semi-exclusively on the stars (the leading segment of the European/world market), which represent their entire "portfolio" of players. In the leading segment, they have a significant share of the European market and a major part of the national market. Because of that, they appear to be the essential agent for a player wanting to achieve a certain level of fame.

The middle class   Relying on a breeding-ground of national talents or a strong economic championship, on favoured relationships with one or more clubs or a particular segment (young players, goalkeepers or a certain nationality, or such like), the national agent benefits from their historical presence in the sector. They are good negotiators, technically and tactically precise in the field of sport, but not competent in legal and financial areas, not having the critical size to manage complex dossiers on an international scale. Their players are, for the most part, positioned in the secondary sector and they are present only marginally in the leading segment of players.

The lower class   This category brings together two types of agent, developing, for different reasons, economic activities on a nearly equivalent level. The dilettante is the parent of the player or a jurist who intercedes only in drawing up the contract, possibly in favour of the clubs. The category is rather heterogeneous. The underqualified one is a tradesperson who works alone and in a not very professional way. They have taken up the profession owing to their inclusion on the margins of the system, linked to an opportunity (for example, an acquaintance in the sector). Their legal skills are very limited and their network limited. They struggle to develop and master their activity.

Risk of abuse
Although the function of the intermediary is to ease the meeting between the labour demand of the club and the labour supply of the player, in reality it is the players who predominantly approach the intermediary, so that they can better manage their interests. However, for tax reasons and although French law forbids it, very often agents are paid by clubs, which also give them a mandate. In addition, the intermediary is likely to intercede jointly as part of two distinct operations: negotiating the transfer between two clubs and negotiating the transfer fee between player and club.

It appears that the lack of clarity in the relationships between different actors, and the overlapping of several simultaneous transactions, leads to conflicts of interest that have contributed to certain pernicious effects of the market power acquired by agents.

First of all, the agents of star players can acquire an exaggerated market power from the moment that certain stars in key positions have no substitute. The agent can thus take advantage of their dominant position by linking the lot of one player to that of another; and/or by imposing very high financial conditions on the value of the player on the market.

In addition, agents can use information that they have available improperly, either by spreading false information about their player's qualities and overestimating them to buyers; or by holding back information from their player, in order to direct him in their own interests; or, lastly, by manipulating information in order to increase bidding during the transfer period.

It should not be forgotten that agents can make use of their dominant position to establish illegal practices. Here, the list is long, but justifies listing in short:

- As soon as the player has signed the contract (for several years), agents cash their commissions in their entirety. In case of breach of contract, they again receive a commission for the same period, tied to the new contract.
- Agents bill the clubs for commissions for services rendered to the player, which is an abuse of a social good. Clubs are complicit in such activities, because they therefore escape social security costs.
- Agents resident in tax havens could be used as screens for tax or social fraud.
- Agents could issue false invoices and sell part of these commissions back to other actors.
- Agents could practice in an illegal capacity when finding themselves in an obvious conflict of interest situation, either because they have already been the subject of a criminal conviction or they themselves or a relative have a position of director in a club.
- Agents could contribute, either voluntarily or by culpable negligence to the development of illegal work.
- Agents could take part in or organize illegal nationality violations (the false passports affair in France in 2000).
- Agents could behave with players as real labour smugglers (cf. affairs in Belgium).
- Agents could even sometimes demand a payment for business they have not dealt with.

Endless examples could be given.[12] Be that as it may, the conclusion is clear: in a growing market, the position of intermediaries is all the more favourable when the market is opaque. Without improving the transparency of information, it is therefore justifiable to believe – to fear – that market failures, linked to the position of agents, will be perpetuated.

It is the clubs who pay the cost of this operation, as they pay transfer fees that are more expensive than they should be. We have arrived at a situation in which intermediaries, who are supposed to improve the functioning of the market, are the origin of pernicious effects with the complicity of most of the actors: the amount of the transfer fee does not necessarily reflect the value of the players, but rather what the protagonists are ready to share among themselves; and the commissions of agents do not correspond to the value of the services rendered, but are divided up between players, managers and agents. We are now in a classic situation in the sports world (doping is another example of it), where all the actors seem to be aware of the real functioning of the system, but appear to get what they want from the situation. This also concerns the supervisory authorities, which have closed their eyes for a long time – until the law gets involved. To counteract such failure, regulating the profession has to be planned. Indeed, a lack of competence can be observed with regard to the financial stakes, and a lack of control of a profession that is at the heart of the crisis in the football industry. The agent represents the weak link in the system that does not avoid the risks of corruption and even money-laundering. That is why the agent symbolizes and crystallizes what is wrong in the sector. Although it is therefore necessary to supervise the profession, the solution to the problems that have arisen requires a much better overall regulation of the system. That is what we will examine in the following chapter.

NOTES

1. This section partly uses and brings up to date Gouguet and Primault (2003).
2. This section reworks and updates Gouguet and Primault (2004).
3. 10 April 2001.
4. Cf. diagrams pp. 34–5 of the 2000 Deloitte Report.
5. For a theoretical analysis, see Cavagnac and Gouguet (2006).
6. This section partly reuses and updates Gouguet and Primault (2005).
7. *La Lettre du sport*, 9 April 2004.
8. Wahl and Lanfranchi (1995), p. 50.
9. Ibid., p. 80.
10. Ibid., p. 147.
11. A bill relating to the status of sports agents, proposed by François Rochebloine and Edouard Landrain. National Assembly, 9 February 2005.
12. *Libération*, 1 October 2004; Robert, *Le Milieu du terrain* (2006).

6. Models of organization of professional sport and competitive balance

The competitive balance of professional sports competitions has always been at the heart of sports economists' thinking (Zimbalist, 2002a; Fort, 2003b; Fort and Maxcy, 2003; Kahane, 2003; Sanderson and Siegfried, 2003). Indeed, in professional championships of team sports, the spectacle is produced by two teams in competition and its quality depends on the balance of forces present. That means that the more the competition is balanced, the higher the supporters' interest and the greater the championship receipts. That is why improving competitive balance appears a legitimate objective for most analysts.

Nevertheless, this objective is not easy to achieve within the framework of an unregulated market. Competitive balance can actually be considered as a public good that benefits all the actors; this means that clubs can obtain a maximum of wins and a better classification, whilst not unbalancing the championship too much. That means, as for all public goods, that there is a great risk of free riders, that is, clubs that do want to profit from the financial advantages procured by improving the competitive balance, but without paying the price for it. That is why a regulatory system for some markets was envisaged, so that the excesses induced by this desire of clubs to maximize their wins could be avoided.

As well as the theoretical responses that have been given to this question through Rottenberg's (1956) invariance proposition, we take the concrete example of the European football championships. We would like to show that competitive balance is a very difficult notion to understand owing to the numerous explanatory variables that interact with each other. The results are very uneven, concerning the role played by variables that are considered to be the most representative: wage bills, club budgets, market size, institutional variables, and so on.

In order to throw light on the discussion, we consider that the competitive balance of a championship depends on two distinct sets of explanatory variables:

- Territorial economic variables that make it possible for the club's ability to acquire sporting talent to be assessed (wage bill and total budget, and so on). The value of these variables depends on the size of the local economic base.
- Institutional sporting variables (regulating the labour market, income sharing, player training, administrative control and so on), which make it possible to understand the discrepancy between "natural" competitive balance and the balance achieved.

We want to show that if one wants to fight against natural competitive imbalance that comes from the unequal wealth of areas that support clubs, comprehensive policies for regulating national championships have to be established. There are two competing models: the US closed-league model and the European open-league model. After having presented the general characteristic of these two models, we analyse the capacity of the European model to compensate for the territorial inequalities that are partly responsible for the competitive imbalance.

1 THE MAIN FEATURES OF THE TWO MODELS OF ORGANIZATION

Since the mid-1950s, US economists have indeed shown that achieving competitive balance within professional leagues necessarily had to happen by regulating economic competition, if one did not want to see the richest systematically dominate the championships – which would make it impossible to maximize the overall profit of the league. Economic analyses carried out in Europe are noticeably different, insofar as the promotion and relegation mechanism for teams push those responsible in clubs to look to maximize their sporting wins.

Paradoxically, and unlike what happened in the United States, Europe has seen a huge deregulatory movement of its markets, the best known of which was after the Bosman Case in 1995. One should, therefore, wonder not only what the future of these two models could be, by analysing the problem of their relative effectiveness, but also that of a possible transposition of the US model, which world mean ending the European open leagues.

General Presentation

The US model

Birth and development In order to understand the major place professional sport has in US society, it is necessary to return to the history of the
main professional leagues (Scully, 1995; Staudohar, 1996), which shows
the influence of three factors:

- Sport became a professional activity in the United States more
  quickly than in most other industrialized countries. In baseball, for
  example, a generalization of false amateurism in most clubs was
  initially seen; this led to the creation of the National Association of
  Professional Basketball Players in 1871.
- Club owners transformed sport into a full commercial activity facing
  the profit opportunities offered by competitions.
- Values linked to sports culture have been considered useful to the
  liberal economic model, hence the very important position that
  sport has in the US educational system, including universities, which
  practically serve as a reservoir of sporting talent for the professional
  sector. Moreover, the champion personifies liberal values, those of
  pursuit of performance, of the worship of the elite and the hero, and
  of rise in social status (Bourg, 2004b).

It was in this market economy context that, paradoxically, a true col-
lectivist system of organizing professional sport appeared. According to
Gerald Scully (1995), club owners have always considered that restricting free competition was necessary to achieve competitive balance on the
ground. Clubs are actually franchised businesses that have paid an entry
fee and this commercial licence is tantamount to granting a monopoly
in a given geographical area. The leagues determine the reception conditions for new franchises, in such a way that causes no concern for
already established teams, and so that all the big cities are represented.
In that way, no local market is left vacant. Every league operates according to a closed system, which excludes progression to another level of
competition. Such stability allows each club to pursue, in preference,
an objective of profit maximization and to conceive strategies over
the long term, without being constrained by the short-term vagaries
of sporting results. The specificity of team sports, therefore, lies in the
paradox that sees clubs being opponents on the ground, yet partners in
producing the sporting spectacle. Now, the market value of the event
depends on the uncertainty of the result, which can only be guaranteed

by establishing mechanisms to regulate markets, in order to equalize the forces present and to avoid the richest teams systematically winning all the time. Therefore, the US model was structured around several major leagues that are cartels, organizing their own championship. The best known concern team sports: MLB (baseball), NFL (football), NBA (basketball), NHL (hockey) and MLS (soccer). All these leagues were created in the late nineteenth century, after the Civil War, when the industrialization and urbanization of the United States was taking place. In addition, although the British roots of some sports should be noted (baseball, hockey and football), the US model of organizing leagues quickly had its own specificities. The most significant example is certainly baseball, the oldest and most popular sport in the United States, but certainly anti-British and anti-cricket. At first, baseball was organized around a national association of players, which authorized what today is called free movement. Every player had the freedom to go from one club to another that had offered them better remuneration. But when the National League was founded in 1876, power passed into the hands of club owners who succeeded in imposing the famous "reserve clause" (1880), which enabled no matter what club owner to decide unilaterally whether to keep a player or not for the following season. This rule spelt an end to the system of free movement. According to Paul Staudohar (1996), this reserve clause was the origin of many disputes in professional sport and certainly led to the creation after 1885 of the first players' union in order to defend their interests during negotiations with club owners. US professional sport had just entered the era of collective bargaining.

Collective bargaining The US system of professional team sports can be analysed like any other industrial or commercial sector. Many actors interact, as shown by Figure 6.1.

The many disputes between these actors are regulated by collective bargaining. Over the last 30 years, all the main disputes involved the revenue sharing from the sporting spectacle:

- between club owners and players' unions for the breakdown of the total value-added between wages (for the players) and profits (for the owners);
- between the players' agents and clubs for determining the wages of each player;
- between the league and the clubs for sharing broadcasting fees and relocating teams, and so on;
- and between clubs for income sharing.

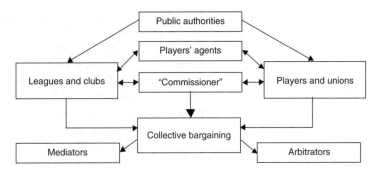

Source: Staudohar (1996, p. 72).

Figure 6.1   Collective bargaining in US closed leagues

Behind these negotiations, the fundamental issue is to try to reconcile two objectives. On the one hand, competitive balance: in order to maximize the overall profit of the league, it is necessary to ensure the uncertainty of the result by having a balance between the teams. On the other hand, economic competition: every team must receive fair remuneration for its contribution to the overall income of the league.

Without market regulation, these two objectives cannot be achieved simultaneously and can, on the contrary, show that total freedom leads to segmentation between teams, players and towns, and so on. The rich therefore become richer, calling competitive balance into question again. That is the reason why the professional sports system in the United States acquired regulatory instruments for the sporting spectacle market, to try to reconcile competitive balance and economic competition.

In reality, in this closed league system, clubs look to maximize their profit. The income for each of them depends on three factors: sporting results, which needs investment in talent; the power of the club to attract, which depends on the area where they are located; and the power of the league to attract, which depends largely on the media. In such a context, the free operation of the market is likely to result in a competitive imbalance, hence the justification for the regulatory instruments put in place within the framework of extensive collective bargaining between all the actors involved. It is this model, the effectiveness of which has to be assessed, that some authors would like to transpose to Europe, in order to rethink the organization of professional team sports and replace a model considered as obsolete.

The European model

In the European model, clubs are win maximizers. This is unlike US leagues, as access to competition is not made on financial criteria but on sporting results, with the risk of relegation to a lower division at the end of the season. This does not mean, however, that all financial logic is absent from the European model. Indeed, to reach its sporting objectives, every club calls on suitable financial resources. In the absence of market regulatory instruments, there is a risk of competitive imbalance between rich clubs in the major markets and the others.

We do not describe here all the complexity of detail of the institutions that govern the organization of sport, at each of these territorial levels. For our argument, let us just recall that two types of actor can be distinguished.

On the one hand, there are governmental institutions whose powers and functions vary according to the administrative culture of each country: for example, centralization in France, federalism in Germany. In addition, there are non-governmental organizations: the Olympic hierarchy, at the local to international level (IOC), as well as amateur and professional clubs. The former are grouped together within federations (national and international); the latter within national leagues.

Beyond the general principles of organization, the European model is based mainly on voluntary work, which is thus the main foundation of the organization of amateur sport. The problem, therefore, is to know if the hegemony of economic logic in sport threatens such an organization.

The basic contradiction   The sporting spectacle has become an industry. Therefore, it has to obey European legislation concerning economic competition (cf. Articles 85 and 86 of the Treaty of Rome). Nonetheless, faced with the consequences of a blinkered application of these competition rules, it was recognized that the specificities of the sports sector needed to be taken into account (without going as far as recognizing an exception!). The contradiction, which Peter Sloane (1976) has analysed, can be summed up in two proposals:

- If the logic of maximizing private profit is dominant, there is a risk of a breakdown of competitive balance. Inequality between clubs will deepen: on the one hand, those that are part of small markets will make do with national championships; on the other, those that are part of large markets will choose the much more lucrative European competitions.
- If strictly regulated sporting activity is adopted to have competitive balance, it is virtually inevitable that leagues will have to become closed, as in the US model, so that regulatory instruments are efficient.

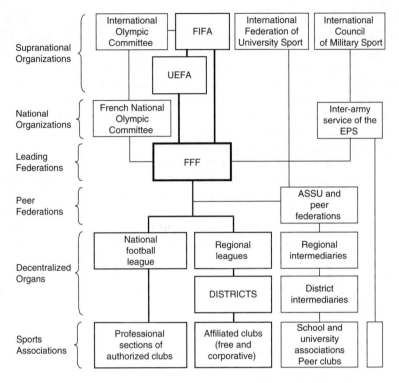

Notes: ASSU = Association du Sport Scolaire et Universitaire; EPS = Education
Physique et Sportive.

Source: CDES (Centre de Droit et d' Economie du Sport), Limoges, France.

Figure 6.2   Organigram of French football

In both cases, it is the whole structure and originality of the European
model that is threatened, either by market liberalization in the name of
economic competition or by strong market regulation in the name of
achieving competitive balance. We discuss later whether a third way is
possible.

Instruments of Regulation

Strong US regulation

The labour market   In this market, competitive balance is sought by the
action of two instruments: first, by allocating talent to avoid one team

monopolizing all the best players (the draft system); and second, by controlling the wage bill for the same reason (the salary cap system).

The draft system is a rule favoured by clubs for rookies from universities, high schools or abroad. Players are ranked according to their sporting value and each club chooses a player in inverse proportion to their ranking in the championship. It is, therefore, possible for the last-placed in the championship to choose the best young player, which is supposed to improve competitive balance (reverse order draft). The player cannot refuse the choice of their new club. This readjustment of club potential concerns about a quarter of the workforce and limits wage escalation. This system was considered too rigid and was made more flexible with the possibility of inter-club negotiation.

The salary cap system determines the ceiling on the league's wage bill. Collective bargaining between players and owners establishes the percentage of league revenue that has to go to the players. By dividing this amount by the number of teams, the maximum wage bill a club can have is obtained; individual work contracts negotiated between players' agents and owners are drawn up on this basis.

In this way, the salary cap stops a rich club buying all the best rookies on the market. However, its impact on competitive balance must be assessed according to the kind of system really in use in the leagues. A distinction must be made between the "soft salary cap" (NBA) from the "hard salary cap" (NHL). In the first case, the ceiling on salaries only concerns new young players; in the second case, all players are concerned (old and new). Lastly, it should be said that the NHL and the NBA have not set up such a system.

Revenue sharing   In theory, the best way to achieve competitive balance would be to redistribute the total revenue of the league in equal shares between all the clubs. That would avoid the risk of the richest clubs dominating the market. Obviously, this solution deeply shocks orthodox (neoclassical) economists: they are afraid of "free riders" and the unfounded remuneration of clubs that do not participate in the collective effort.

Nevertheless, it has been recognized that some form of revenue sharing is necessary, and thus rules were drawn up leading, on the one hand, not only to the antitrust laws being reconsidered, but also a redefinition of a new process of collective bargaining, on the other.

The largest receipts for all the major leagues (excepting, perhaps, ice-hockey) are broadcasting fees. It is the leagues that collectively negotiate these fees with the national networks, for all the clubs. This collective sale of rights was removed from the application of the antitrust laws (Sports Broadcasting Act, 1962), in the name of the social utility that was created by the equal sharing of the fees, which improved competitive balance and therefore the well-being of television viewers. It should be remembered, in fact, that US courts do not consider it illegal if a cartel increases the level of social utility.

Through this collective sale of broadcasting rights, collective bargaining was organized in each league, so that revenue sharing between clubs could be defined. This sharing is the origin of many disputes and two types of revenue must be distinguished: shared revenue and unshared revenue.

In the case of shared revenue, national broadcasting fees are distributed equally between all the clubs and represent a relatively large share, depending on the league (from about a third for the MBA or NBA to two-thirds for the NFL). As for "ticket" sales, they are roughly shared according to the league (60 per cent for the home team and 40 per cent for the visiting team in the NFL, but 100 per cent for the home team in the NHL).

As for unshared revenue, the receipts from merchandising, and above all the local broadcasting fees, could lead to a breakdown of competitive balance between the teams in small markets. This risk is particularly high in ice-hockey, which combines an absence of sharing of "ticket" receipts with that; but Paul Staudohar (1996) has also noticed a difference of 1–30 between a baseball team in New York and one in Seattle.

The main conclusion of this reminder of US regulatory tools concerns their effectiveness in achieving competitive balance – which is the principal justification given for their exemption from antitrust laws. It would appear that achieving competitive balance is positively connected to the scale of revenue sharing. The NFL set up the biggest system of sharing and is also the most balanced, unlike the NBA, which has not adopted such a system.

European deregulation

The labour market   Before the Bosman Case (1995), rules issued by sports institutions could be considered as attacks on player mobility: setting a ceiling on the number of foreign players in a club, compensation for transfers, life contracts and the like. These terms of employment that, before 1995, impeded the freedom of movement of sportspeople, reflected the archaism of working relationships in professional sport very well, with a total absence of collective bargaining. However, these special conditions did enable the concentration of talent in just a few clubs to be limited and to maintain competitive balance (Bourg and Gouguet, 1998). These were the constraints that the Bosman Case made disappear, by abandoning the authorized maximum number of foreign players, as well as by banning transfer compensation for players at the end of their contracts.

The Bosman Case has sparked off much controversy between economists, amongst those who are concerned with assessing its impact on competitive balance. For some (Késenne, 1997), Rottenberg's invariance theorem remains valid: the big clubs attract talent. For other analysts (Primault and Rouger, 1999; Lavoie, 2000), the turning point of 1995 has led to a deterioration in competitive balance by increasing player market segmentation, increasing the number of transfers and, lastly, challenging once again national training systems. That is why, faced with this deficiency in regulating the labour market, many authors have demanded revenue sharing.

Revenue sharing   The US experience of revenue sharing suggests that this tool could be usefully transposed in Europe. To illustrate this idea, we take the example of professional football in England (Moorhouse, 1999). There, the regulatory system has three main characteristics:

● Disputes have always arisen between clubs on the subject of redistributing revenue.
● Club managers have never felt the need to establish a mechanism for revenue sharing.
● Sports bodies have preferred to favour rules that limit player mobility.

Since 1980, and especially since 1992 (the date when the Premier League was created), all instruments for revenue sharing have been abolished. The consequence was inevitable: increased segmentation between clubs, with the rich club becoming even richer.

In conclusion, and unlike what happens in the United States, it appears that there is a serious risk of market deregulation in the professional sports market in Europe. New modalities of revenue sharing will probably have to be invented, if one does not want to see all the small countries (especially, Ireland, Scotland, Wales, Denmark, the Netherlands, Switzerland and Portugal) excluded from major European competitions.

The Future of the Two Models

These two models have seen great operating difficulties over several years. A lively debate has raged on their respective futures. On the one hand, it appears that the US model is not as profitable as is generally supposed (Lavoie, 2004). It is necessary, perhaps, to review the hypothesis of profit maximization by club owners and take the strategies of new public and private actors who influence the organization of professional sports into account. On the other hand, if the European model is in danger, it does not, after all, appear possible to transpose the instruments of the US model into closed European leagues. If we want to keep the European model, we should therefore invent new regulatory tools for open leagues.

The real effectiveness of the US model

The profitability of the major leagues   According to Marc Lavoie (2004), a drop in profits and an increase in the wage bill of players can be seen over the period 1989–2000. The relative proportion of wages in the turnover never stopped increasing over the decade, reaching 50–60 per cent, accord-ing to the leagues – which is comparable to what happens in French or English football. The consequence of this situation was a cut in profits, which varied according to the sport: baseball and hockey saw net losses; basketball just achieved a balance and only owners of football teams made a profit.

Another result established by Marc Lavoie is fundamental: he shows that despite the negative returns from the usual overheads (except for football), owners could make gains in capital by selling their team. And, indeed, ownership of clubs changes often: during the 1990s, 25 out of 30 teams in the NHL and MLB changed owners.

The problem with such an analysis lies in the reliability of the statistics used to reconstitute club accounts. These come from specialized financial reviews, which, as Marc Lavoie indicates, produce reliable statistics. On this basis, it is possible to maintain that the financial situation of profes-sional team owners deteriorated during the 1990s (with the exception of the NFL). When these owners do not have the capital resources to get into debt, they can become bankrupt (Pittsburgh Penguins in 1998 and the Ottawa Senators in 2003 for the NHL).

Faced with such results, a central question cannot be avoided: why do capitalists continue to invest in an activity that is unprofitable? That means that it is perhaps necessary to revise the hypothesis currently posed by US sports economists: profit maximization by club owners.

Which maximization hypothesis?   The controversy between European and US sports economists revolves around a key question: which is the correct maximization hypothesis: profit or win? It is traditionally sup-posed that US owners are profit maximizers, while European owners are win maximizers. An intermediary hypothesis, put forward especially by Stefan Késenne (2001), suggests that European owners are win maximiz-ers, but constrained by a minimum profit.

This last hypothesis is certainly the most credible, unlike that put forward by economists like Rodney Fort (2006) on the universality of the hypothesis of profit maximisation. As Marc Lavoie (2004) has shown, US owners make losses, just like Europeans. It could be provisionally concluded that they are looking to maximize wins under the constraint of a non-negative profit. That means that many US owners behave like Europeans.

Do the European leagues have to become closed?

Is the transposition possible? According to Thomas Hoehn and Stefan Szymanski (1999), the organization of the system of professional sports in Europe is not viable because it mixes two levels of competition: national and European – the first being the condition of access to the second. Thus, clubs wanting to take part in European competitions invest more in talent than others, upsetting the competitive balance of national championships. The solution proposed by Hoehn and Szymanski to avoid such a market failure is that the strongest European clubs leave their national championships to make up a closed league. In this new context, the relationship between the clubs belonging to the Super League and the national clubs would likely to be the same as that between major leagues and minor leagues in the United States.

Moreover, with a closed league, it would be possible to use US regulatory instruments like the draft, the salary cap or revenue sharing. It is recognized that these instruments are difficult to imagine in an open league. As Jean-François Bourg (2003a) reminds us, applying the salary cap in a single country would handicap those clubs taking part in European cups who would be facing foreign teams not subject to the system.

Is the transposition desirable? The answer can be given insofar as the main consequences of making the European leagues closed are now known. Let us list them:

- National championships would lose a lot of their prestige and therefore their financial resources.
- International matches would turn to the advantage of clubs, while national teams could encounter problems. In particular, major clubs could be reluctant to loan their stars to national teams for fear of injury of tiredness, and so on.
- The connection between club and the local area could disappear. As in the United States, a great geographical mobility of clubs could be seen, whose owners would look for the best profit opportunities.
- The balance of power between professional leagues and federations could turn to the advantage of the former. What is more, if these

leagues became totally closed, this connection could disappear. We then wonder what would become of sporting ethics.
● Overall, it is the total relationship – which is a founding principle in France – between amateur and professional sport that will be changed.

All these questions mean that we must ask ourselves whether, in fact, the US model is well-adapted to European culture. It may, in fact, be that the tools used in the first model could improve the level of competitive balance; but to do that, it is necessary to have closed leagues. Conversely, the real problem in Europe is to know if the principle of entering into the sporting spectacle market based on sporting criteria and not financial ones, as in the United States, must be kept. Moreover, beyond being a simple spectacle that is organized on a fair and efficient basis, sport is also a vehicle for a code of ethics that must be preserved. In our opinion, the European model seems more capable of reaching that objective, thanks to its connection with the amateur sector.

Four tracks for further study could be envisaged:

● If importing the US-style closed-league system into Europe is not wanted, it must be possible to create original regulatory instruments that are effective in open leagues. Such regulation should be thought of on a European scale (cf. the previous chapter).
● If talent is intended to be distributed between clubs in order to strive for competitive balance, reliable methods must therefore be developed to evaluate this talent and to pay for its training at its true value.
● If European culture is to be respected, it is necessary to defend the European idea of sport, so that it is not reduced to a simple economic activity. This makes it essential to take sporting externalities into account.
● If the opportunity to restore the competitive balance of national and international championships is wanted, it is necessary to take account of the very large regional inequalities that persist in Europe.

With regard to the last point, no matter which option is taken, comparing the two models of professional sport shows the importance of the regional aspect in achieving competitive balance. In the United States, particularly, the problem of blackmailing local authorities to build new facilities, by owners threatening to relocate the leagues, has been a recurrent issue for many years (Baade, 2005b). We would like to show that this regional problem is also at the heart of achieving competitive balance in Europe.

2 ACHIEVING COMPETITIVE BALANCE

It appears to us that achieving competitive balance is at the crossroads of two forms of logic: a vertical, sectoral logic and a horizontal, spatial logic. Thus, if one does not want to see competitive imbalance deepen in Europe, it is necessary to take these two forms of logic into account simultaneously: territorial and sectoral.

From a territorial point of view, it is a question of assessing the impact of the local economic potential of acquiring sporting talent by each club. The problem is to know whether it is always the most powerful that win.

From a sectoral point of view, it is necessary to evaluate the regulatory instruments that have been put in place to compensate for previous inequalities and strengthen competitive balance. That comes back to our wondering if it is possible to neutralize the territory and make the present forces equal, independent of the importance of local markets.

The Territory: A Source of Competitive Imbalance

General presentation

The territory–competitive balance relationship Many works, both in the United States and in Europe, have shown that a club's wealth was a major explicatory variable in sporting wins. Thus, for the French football championship, Eric Barget and Arnaud Rouger (2000) have found a correlation coefficient of 0.781 between the percentage of wins and the wage bill; and of 0.766 between the percentage of wins and the budget, with a positive relation between these variables. For a club, therefore, the higher the budget, the more competitive it is, on average.

Wladimir Andreff and Jean-François Bourg (2006) came to the same conclusion on a European level with calculating a coefficient of Spearman's rank correlation between sporting ranking and club turnover ranking. The wealthier a club, the higher its probability in reaching the top of the ranking.

In view of these results, it could be thought that since a club's wealth often depends largely on the wealth of the supporting territory, a club's sports results will depend, in the end, on the economic health of the host communities. However, according to Marc Lavoie (1997), there is no clear connection between the size of a market and its team's performance. This is certainly a reflection of the fact that this connection is the fruit of the interaction of many variables, as Trudo Dejonghe (2004) has clearly shown in Figure 6.3.

It appears that the local economic potential largely determines the

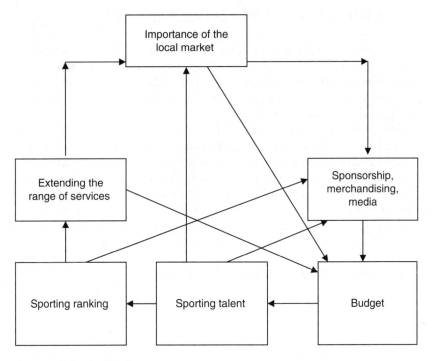

Source: Dejonghe (2004).

Figure 6.3   The model of endogenous growth

amount of a club's resources in terms of sponsorship, merchandising and the media. With a substantial budget, the club can buy the best available players and maximize its wins. Beyond this simple linear relation, other loops, with multiplier effects, could be put in place, for example: more wins generate more gate receipts, which makes it possible to buy more sporting talent, and so on. Such amplification effects differ according to the club. In the end, the general relation between local economic potential and sporting results is not easy to test, owing not only to the complexity of the interactions as a whole, but also to the fact that all these causalities are not automatic.

Territorial imbalances in Europe   It is essential to determine the economic weight of cities in order to assess the support they can bring to their pro-fessional football teams. There is much debate between economists to determine what variables should be used to measure such a weight. Very often, for want of more precise data, only a demographic indicator is used.

Table 6.1   European urban framework: city size

Class	Size	Number of Cities	Cities
1	+ 7 million	2	Paris, London
2	3–5 million	6	Essen Madrid, Barcelona Milan, Berlin, Athens
3	1.5–3 million	13	Cologne, Düsseldorf, Hamburg, Munich Manchester, Birmingham, Leeds Rome, Naples Brussels, Lisbon, Vienna, Stockholm
4	1–1.5 million	23	Rotterdam, Amsterdam Copenhagen, Dublin, Helsinki Lyon, Marseille, Lille
5	500 000–1 million	36	Zurich, Oslo, Bordeaux, Toulouse. . .
6	200 000–500 000	100	

Source: Rozenblat and Cicille (2003).

However, some studies show that, in order to go beyond this simplistic vision, the demographic approach must be supplemented by an analysis of the functions performed by the cities.

Demographic criteria   Based on city size, it is possible to show an urban framework on six levels, as displayed in Table 6.1.

In France's case, it can therefore be noticed that there are no French cities in Class 2 and that there are only three of them in Class 4 (Lyon, Lille and Marseille). This constitutes what one could call the French territorial exception – which could still be measured by the ratio between the size of the capital and that of the second biggest city, or even the sum of the three biggest cities (Table 6.2).

The extent of the French territorial imbalance is measured here. If France and the United Kingdom are compared, for example, it will be easier later to understand the very differing situation of football clubs. The five largest British cities, excluding London (Birmingham, Glasgow, Leeds, Manchester and Liverpool) total 11 million inhabitants, that is, the equivalent size to Greater London. In France, it would be necessary to add together the nine largest cities to get the same result compared with Paris. Excluding London, cities with more than 500 000 inhabitants total nearly 20 million inhabitants, that is, twice as many as in France.

Table 6.2   The French territorial exception

	France	Germany	UK	Italy	Spain
Difference between the biggest city and the sum of the three next biggest	2.6	0.6	1.3	0.5	0.7
Difference between the biggest city and the second biggest	7.1	1.3	3.4	1.3	1.2

Source: INSEE.

Further than these first results that make it possible to highlight the very great difference between the demographic weights of European towns, it is necessary to take other variables into account to describe their economic weight and, in particular, the functions they perform.

Urban functions   It is possible to arrange European cities into seven classes, based on 15 indicators (see Table 6.3). The indicators used are: the population of conurbations in 2000; the change in population 1950–90; the trade in goods by ports; airport passengers; the accessibility of cities, on a European level; the head offices of major European groups; the financial markets; international fairs; international conferences; museums; tourists; cultural sites; students; scientific reviews; and European research networks.

For the purposes of this argument, it is interesting to comment on the differences that exist between this classification, drawn up on the basis of urban functions, and that obtained from the demographic weight of the city (see Table 6.4). The example of Amsterdam is certainly the most significant: this city is in 34th European place for its population, but in 4th for its urban functions, that is, a difference of 3 between the two rankings. Conversely, Essen is the most under-classified with a difference of −3.

From this perspective, we can return to the comparison between France and the UK. As a general rule, the largest British cities are ranked below where they should be because of the hegemony of London on many international functions. Thus, there is a difference of 2 between the two rankings for the cities of Liverpool, Manchester, Nottingham, Sheffield and Newcastle. Conversely, the largest French cities are rather ranked above where they should be (except Lille), which means that they compensate for the weakness resulting from their relatively small size. The importance of this result will be shown in understanding the results of French football clubs.

Table 6.3   Ranking of European cities according to 15 criteria

	Points	Rank
Class 1		
Paris	81	1
London	76	2
Class 2		
Madrid	62	3
Amsterdam	59	4
Milan	57	5
Class 3		
Barcelona, Berlin, Rome	55	6
Brussels, Vienna	53	9
Munich, Stockholm	52	11
Lisbon	51	13
Class 4		
Athens, Cologne	50	14
Copenhagen	49	16
Dublin, Lyon	47	17
Frankfurt	46	19
Düsseldorf, Helsinki, Zurich	45	20
Florence, Hamburg, Marseille	44	23
Geneva, Oslo	43	26
Toulouse	42	28
Class 5		
Naples, Rotterdam, Stuttgart	40	29
Bologna	39	32
Edinburgh, Turin	38	33
Birmingham, Manchester, Strasbourg, Valence	37	35
Anvers, Bilbao, Bordeaux, Essen, Lille, Nice, Seville	36	39
Basel, Glasgow, Gothenburg, Montpellier, Nuremberg	35	46
Hanover, Luxembourg, Venice	34	51
Leeds, Nantes, Porto, Salonica	33	54
Granada, Palma de Majorca, Utrecht	32	58
Grenoble, Malaga	31	61
Class 6		
Cannes, Rennes, Salzburg, Verona	30	63
Alicante, Bari, Genoa, Trieste	29	67
Dresden, The Hague, Munster, Nancy, Saragossa	28	71

Table 6.3   (continued)

	Points	Rank
Bremen, Bristol, Dijon, Ghent, Leipzig, Padua, Pamplona, Rouen	27	76
Aix-la-chapelle, Angers, Cadiz, Clermont-Ferrand, Eindhoven, Lausanne, Mulhouse, Palermo Southampton, Tarragona, Wiesbaden	26	85
Berne, Brest, Cagliari, Freiberg, Graz, Liverpool	25	96
Class 7		
Belfast, Cardiff, Cordoba, Karlsruhe, Leiden, Luton, Malmö, Mannheim, Rostock, Saint-Sebastian, Santander, Tampere, Tours, Valladolid, Vigo	24	102
Brunswick, Coventry, Darmstadt, Liège, Metz, Newcastle-upon-Tyne, Nottingham, Rheims, Toulon, Turku, Vitoria-Gasteis	23	118
Brescia, Corunna, Murcia	22	129
Augsburg, Bergamo, Bielefeld, Bournemouth, Brighton, Halle, Le Havre, Leicester, Lübeck, Messina, Orleans, Portsmouth, Salerno, Taranto	21	132
Aldershot, Arnhem, Carrara, Charleroi, Enschede, Kassel, Kiel, Linz, Nijmegen, Osnabrück	20	146
Blackpool, Breda, Koblenz, Haarlem, Heerlen, Saint-Etienne, Sarrebruck, Sheffield, Swansea	19	156
Caserta, Kingston, Middlesbrough, Preston, Southend-on-Sea	18	165
Chatham, Chemnitz, Derby, Erfurt, Magdeburg, Plymouth, Stoke-on-Trent, Valenciennes	17	170
Bethune, Lens, Mons	16	178

Source: Rozenblat and Cecille (2003).

Testing the territory–sporting results relation

Method   Faced with the difficulty of obtaining information, we content ourselves with the two existing series: ranking cities according to their economic potential that we have just shown; sporting ranking of clubs at the end of each season. The problem lies in the fact that the second ranking is relatively unstable in the promotion/relegation system that is characteristic of European championships. It is therefore difficult to use temporal series made up of different clubs every year. Two solutions are possible.

Table 6.4 Difference between demographic and economic weight

Ranking of European Cities	
Difference between 32 British conurbations	
−2	Belfast Liverpool Manchester Nottingham Sheffield Newcastle Birmingham Brighton Coventry Leeds Middlesbrough Portsmouth Southend-on-Sea
−1	Aldershot Blackpool Bournemouth Bristol Cardiff Derby Glasgow Kingston Leicester London Luton Chatham Plymouth Preston Stoke-on-Trent
0	Southampton Swansea
1	Edinburgh Dublin
Difference between 30 French conurbations	
−1	Lille Toulon Valenciennes Bethune Bordeaux Le Havre Lens Metz Orléans
0	Paris Reims Rouen Saint Etienne Tours Angers Brest Cannes Clermont-Ferrand Dijon Grenoble Lyon Marseille Mulhouse Nancy
1	Nantes Nice Rennes Strasbourg Toulouse
2	Montpellier
Difference between 17 Benelux conurbations	
−1	Charleroi Liège Haarlem The Hague Rotterdam Antwerp Mons Arnhem Breda Enschede Heerlem
0	Leiden Nijmegen
1	Brussels Ghent Eindhoven Utrecht
2	Luxembourg
3	Amsterdam

For the first, time $= t$, the sporting ranking of clubs is drawn up on the basis of qualitative data enabling the value of a club to be determined from results obtained over a period of a dozen years, for example. This ranking can be obtained from consulting experts about the significant criteria, such as: the history of the club, its training policy, the current dynamics, the financial power and the level of popularity (Bullion, 2002). Of course, as with any classification, we come up against well-known methodological problems relating to: selecting the variables; their quantification; their weighting; and their aggregation. That is why we have not used this option.

The second solution consists of testing the ratio year after year, based on the sporting ranking of the season. The volatility of clubs is mainly, in fact, most important at the end of the season. There is, therefore, a hard core in all European championships with which one can try to test the ratio.

It is interesting to test before and after the Bosman Case, in order to see the influence of free movement of players on sporting results. Lastly, we make the hypothesis, which seems reasonable, that between these two dates, at a ten-year interval, the European urban framework was not modified. Over such a period, the structural modifications of cities are, on average, not very perceptible.

Under these hypotheses, we tested the correlation between sporting and economic ranking with the help of the Spearman rank correlation. In principle, calculating this coefficient is very simple, but in reality, the nature of information available obliges us to look at a certain number of options. Indeed, the Spearman coefficient is obtained in the following way:

$$R = 1 - \frac{6\sum_{1}^{n} d_i^2}{n(n^2 - 1)}$$

with: d, the difference between two places in the rankings (economic and sporting); n, the size of the sample.

This coefficient lies between -1 and $+1$, according to whether there is a discordance or concordance between the two rankings. For example, if $d_i = 0$ for all i, the concordance between the two rankings, is perfect $R = 1$.

The difficulty in calculation comes from certain specific points relating to the two rankings:

- The European city classification only uses those that have a minimum of 200 000 inhabitants. That means that, especially in France, some cities that have a club in the first division do not appear. In order to do that, we have taken the classification of these urban entities with regard to their demographic weight in their respective countries, even if we have denounced the shortcomings of this criterion.
- The largest European cities often have several clubs. This could distort the correlation, insofar as an average club in a very large city will considerably decrease the value of the Spearman coefficient. We have chosen to retain only a maximum of two clubs for the very big cities (London, Madrid, Barcelona and Milan, and so on).
- The European ranking of cities has been "nationalized", that is, that every city has been classed nationally according to its European place: if Madrid and Barcelona were respectively 3rd and 6th in the European ranking, they would be placed 1st and 2nd nationally.

Table 6.5   Comparison of Spearman coefficients

	France	England	Spain	Italy	Germany
1990	0.287719298	0.582142857	0.392105263	0.67079463	0.545923633
1995	0.297744361	0.12745098	0.587969925	0.62641899	−0.22910217
1996	0.266165414	0.283823529	0.462450593	0.5624355	0.271413829
2001	0.014447884	0.194014448	0.272932331	0.45510836	0.143446852
2004	0.418796992	0.140350877	0.47593985	0.67801858	−0.14654283

Source: Lepetit (2005).

Results

On a European level   The main conclusion to draw from Table 6.5 is that the results are not as clear as one would have thought a priori, owing to the great instability of the Spearman coefficients that were obtained. Italy seems to set itself apart by relative coefficient stability, which is an expression of compatibility between the two rankings. In this country, local economic potential and sporting results have a strong correlation. It is similar in Spain, but with a weaker degree of correlation. This could be explained by the fact that the clubs of San Sebastian (102nd in Datar Ranking), Vigo (120th) and Corunna (129th) are regularly ranked in the first five of the championship. In other championships, the Spearman coefficients are unstable over time. But, above all: it seems that after the 2000s, they have relatively weak values; the result of a less defined correlation between economic ranking and the sporting ranking of cities.

Perhaps, in view of these last results, it is necessary to wonder about the capacity of the Spearman coefficients to reflect accurately the reality of sporting championships. For the coefficient to fall, it is enough that a small town or city comes top of the sporting ranking, or that a club from a very big city finishes badly, even if the four or five biggest teams in the championship always occupy the top of the ranking, over time.

These two scenarios are particularly present in England: beyond some London clubs, the modest performances of the second Manchester club (Manchester City) or Birmingham (Wolverhampton) lower the value of the coefficient. Conversely, clubs from towns or cities with a weak economic potential fitted into the top of the table: Blackburn (1995), Newcastle (1996 and 2004) and Ipswich (2001). Yet the English championship is always dominated by the same teams: Manchester United, Arsenal, Chelsea and Liverpool.

These last results mean that a more qualitative analysis of each national championship needs to be carried out, in order to understand the distortions between sporting and economic ranking. This is what we will do with France, in order to return later to the explicatory factors of such a difference.

The specific case of France   Two types of city can be distinguished, based on sporting ranking:

- Those that belong to the higher level of the French urban framework and that obtain uneven sporting results:
    - There are cities that are regularly at the top of the ranking, despite occasional accidents: Marseille, Paris, Bordeaux, Monaco, Nantes and Lyon have been the best teams over the last 20 years. However, to a lesser degree, one could add: Lens, Lille and Rennes.
    - There are cities that are clearly ranked below their level: Montpellier, Nice, Strasbourg and Le Havre. Some years, large clubs in the previous category fall into this class, such as Paris or Lille.
- Those that belong to the average or lower level of the French urban framework and that obtain uneven sporting results:
    - There are communities that are clearly ranked above their level: Auxerre is the typical example of this. Guingamp can be added, for certain seasons.
    - There are communities that are regularly in the lower half of the ranking, such as Bastia or Ajaccio in Corsica.

Therefore, it appears that there is no linear relationship between the economic weight of cities and towns and their sporting ranking, except for two obvious cases: on the one hand, the wealthiest cities that regularly achieve good sports results; on the other, the smallest communities that succeed, with more or less difficulty, to stay in the bottom part of the ranking. Between these two extreme cases, the non-linear quality of the relationship is confirmed, with the situation of the wealthy clubs, which are clearly ranked below their level. That means that if economic wealth is a necessary condition for being very well placed in sporting terms, it is not reason enough. The example of Paris is sufficiently explicit. Conversely, cases like Auxerre, small communities that are regularly over-ranked confirm the complexity of the relationship or the necessity of taking other explanatory factors into account for sporting performance.

In order to understand these French paradoxes, it seems necessary to present the regulatory instruments that had been established to try to maintain competitive balance. This balance would certainly have been upset to the benefit of the most powerful cities, if the market had been allowed to function freely. That means that regulatory instruments can lessen the consequences of the differences in wealth on sporting ranking and improve the competitive balance of the championships.

Regulatory and Compensatory Instruments of Territorial Imbalance

Competitive balance in Europe

Measuring competitive balance   Such a measurement raises much debate amongst economists, as no instrument is perfect.[1] The most common criterion used to characterize competitive balance is the ratio of the standard deviation of the effective percentage of teams wins to the theoretical standard deviation.

This measurement has been subject to much criticism. For example, Marc Lavoie (1997) considers that, as well as a measure of dispersion of effective performances around an ideal theoretical situation, it is also necessary to have a measurement of correlation. This means that it is necessary to verify whether, from one year to the next, it is the same teams or not found at the top of the championship. In fact, a very balanced and very close championship with a weak dispersion index could be perfectly achieved, but one in which the top places would still be monopolized by the same teams.

Marc Lavoie has thus revealed a real cycle of wins in the NHL:

- Winning teams see their probability of remaining winners decrease over time.
- Nevertheless, after seven to eight years, those teams that tend to be winners become winners again (and vice-versa).
- Certain periods are more favourable than others for maintaining the same teams at the top of the championship.

This ties in with analyses carried out by Jean-François Bourg (Bourg and Gouguet, 1998) for the French football championship over the long term. Just six clubs, between 1946 and 1997, won 41 of the 51 titles of Champion of France. In total, 12 teams won the 51 titles.

To sum up: besides all the theoretical squabbling over measuring competitive balance, we must not focus too much on the measurement itself. It is preferable to bring out the sluggish development trends of a championship and to analyse the institutional factors at work alongside traditional factors connected to the local economic potential, tackled in the first section.

Main results   Several levels of analysis are possible in order to comment on Table 6.6. On average, over the whole period, it appears that the French championship is the most balanced, followed by Germany. In a general way, major fluctuations in all the championships can be observed over time; to such a point that it is difficult to extract reliable general information from them. Nevertheless, some interesting trends can be pointed out: on average, England and Italy seem, more than other countries, to stay at a high level of competitive imbalance: Since 1999–2000, all countries appear to have experienced a deterioration in the competitive balance of their respective championships.

These general results were confirmed by an analysis of clubs taking part in European competitions (Ineum Consulting, 2004). According to the UEFA index, compared with clubs from other major European championships, French clubs are behind since the Bosman Case. There are fewer French clubs regularly present at the highest level of European championships. That means that the internal balance of the French championship is, for this country, a handicap at the European level, where the clubs are no longer competitive.

All these results were confirmed by a study coordinated by the CDES (Centre de Droit et d'Economie du Sport) for UEFA, relating to the consequences of the Champions League on national competitive balance. In order to understand the very great differences that exist in European football, as well as the great instability of measuring competitive balance, it is necessary to analyse the market regulatory tools set up not only on the national level, but also on the international one. They mainly concern the labour market and income redistribution.

Explanations and recommendations

The current debate about the competitive balance of the football championship is focused on three questions:

- Is there a permanent competitive imbalance in all national championships?
- What could be done about it on a national level?
- What could be envisaged at a European level?

A structural imbalance   Throughout Europe, championships are dominated by certain major clubs that stay systematically at the top of the ranking, year after year. As a result, the Champions League could be considered as tantamount to a true closed league. Virtually all the clubs are the same from one year to the next and most were members of the G14.

The first factor in explaining such an imbalance is to look into the size

Table 6.6   Measure of the competitive balance level in European football

Season	France	England	Italy	Spain	Germany	
1989/90	1.04377856	1.27010153	1.52109352	1.71525662	1.06181495	Before Bosman Case: 1989/90–1995/95
1990/91	1.05755428	1.54834377	1.53073095	1.16866996	1.34917065	
1991/92	1.28554719	1.29684933	1.74614421	1.36593904	1.23224229	
1992/93	1.41793029	1.03509834	1.33333333	1.62545540	1.27571587	Bosman Case: 1995/96
1993/94	1.50350468	1.51971175	1.54454554	1.29269201	1.13471657	
1994/95	1.42717977	1.62901186	1.71403282	1.46449201	1.68033610	
1995/96	1.26345391	1.59934197	1.58423607	1.48877474	1.09961372	
1996/97	1.46808145	1.22903471	1.33210728	1.61164593	1.42686640	After Bosman Case 1996/97–2003/04
1997/98	1.31357915	1.28452326	1.75777658	1.39359437	1.13902837	
1998/99	1.41652248	1.52177182	1.34553243	1.40768567	1.51514384	
1999/2000	0.88191710	1.68741472	1.64793394	1.02726002	1.43372088	
2000/01	1.15470054	1.43178211	1.59758805	1.28759261	1.13759292	
2001/02	1.17989697	1.71602356	1.70925967	1.13670808	1.53783944	
2002/03	1.27630222	1.62221421	1.56242647	1.32088487	1.23006987	
2003/04	1.45909128	1.57363140	1.86119647	1.28452326	1.60676674	
Average	1.27660266	1.46432362	1.58586249	1.37274497	1.32404257	

Note: The figures correspond to the measurement of the level of competitive balance (the ratio between two standard deviations: effective and theoretical). The higher the ratio, the higher the competive imbalance.

Source: Filloux (2005).

of the national market, since there appears to be a negative relationship between these two factors. The competitive imbalance in small countries (Portugal and Belgium) is more pronounced than in the five major European championships (Germany, England, France, Italy and Spain). Nevertheless, among the latter countries, the relationship is more ambiguous, since the championship seems to be more open in two countries (France and Germany), than in the other three.

A second factor seems to confirm this analysis. In nearly all countries, the coefficients of the Spearman rank correlation showed the same factors are connected to sporting results: TV rights, wage bills and level of player transfer fees, and so on. That means that there is a positive correlation between the economic weight of towns and sporting results. However, as we have previously shown, exceptions exist in some countries with badly ranked large markets (Paris) or small markets with good sporting results (Auxerre). In such conditions of economic inequality, the European Champions League reinforces this trend of increasing national competitive balance. In fact, the income redistributed by UEFA is concentrated in only a few clubs and can represent up to 50 per cent of their budget. In France, for example, just the European revenue received by Monaco in 2004 represented the equivalent of the total budget of the French clubs belonging to the bottom half of the championship.

The conclusion is that although the Champions League is not responsible for European competitive imbalance (which is due to the specific characteristics of each national championship), it increases such an imbalance by redistributing considerable sums to the richest clubs year after year, which can therefore buy more sporting talent than the others. Double regulation is to be envisaged, both on the national and European level, to try to fight against the lasting effect of this imbalance, which turns the Champions League into a virtually closed league.

National regulation   A first analysis places itself in the relationship between the degree of regulation of national championships and its impact on achieving competitive balance. We have, in fact, shown that although the French championship is the most open in Europe, it is also the most regulated and is built on three pillars: solidarity, training and control. Conversely, the Portuguese championship is one of the most unbalanced (with the systematic domination of three clubs), as well as one of the least regulated (weak governance with little training, no control and no income redistribution).

Between these two extremes, a more in-depth analysis is needed in order to understand the effectiveness of the regulatory terms implemented in other countries. Even in the absence of such data, one clear conclusion appears: all clubs are not treated in the same way, as it depends on the country to which they belong. In these conditions, how can it therefore be said that competition is not distorted?

This is certainly the reason why one sees, today, the most powerful clubs lobbying to fight against the national market regulatory systems that sports bodies are looking to set up. For example, the best French clubs look with envy at the situation of their Italian counterparts, for negotiating their own terms for broadcasting rights – which benefit the richest. It is this heterogeneity of national rules that distort European competitions and it must be modified.

European regulation As part of the general framework of European construction, two avenues can be explored: that of inter-governability and that of supranationality. In the first case, we are satisfied with coordinating and harmonizing national rules; in the second case, a European regulatory body imposes new common rules.

Whatever solution is adopted, the basic problem to be resolved is the same, but is not unanimous among researchers. It is the question of the connection between competition and equity; the free exchange between countries where social and tax systems are different and therefore cannot be fair. According to Jacques Sapir (Sapir, 2006), competition is either free or non-distorted, but cannot be both simultaneously. It is therefore necessary to wage war on "free riders" who do social or fiscal dumping.

This is particularly true in the case of the European football championships. For example, in the European market, where wages are negotiated net of expenses and taxes, the competitive disadvantage of French clubs is undeniable, especially at the level of the market for star players. The overall cost in this segment in Germany, Italy, Spain or England is, on average, 40 per cent lower than it is in France.

France is currently looking for solutions (including image rights), but that involves the whole problem of European tax harmonization . . . or even the whole problem of setting up a real social Europe, which could not be done tomorrow. But is it always necessary to pull everyone down, owing to the social, fiscal or ecological dumping of some countries in the name of triumphant liberalism? There are some possible solutions, which we have already mentioned.

As far as the redistribution of income is concerned, it is perhaps necessary for UEFA to review its terms for redistribution, in order to avoid even more unbalancing those championships that are already profoundly so. Specialized studies would be necessary at this level to analyse the incentive character of the income distributed to clubs, as well as their perversity from the moment when clubs are tempted to adopt adventurous behaviour – if the sums at stake are large.

As for player training, UEFA plans a reform aiming to impose a quota of locally trained players on clubs, which could eventually be raised to eight out of 25 professional contracts. For the 2006–07 season, it was proposed that every team having a maximum of 25 professionals must include at least two players trained in the club and two other players trained in other national clubs. For the 2007–08 season, these two quotas rose to four players. This measure could slow down the deepening differences between the major European clubs and the others, with the former systematically "pillaging" the best talented players of the latter.

As far as management control is concerned, we can only be pleased with the Europeanization plans for this type of control by means of, for example, putting in place the UEFA licence. In fact it has been very much understood that a European standardization of the governance of football clubs as businesses is increasingly needed. Without a generalized control system for club spending (in particular, the wage bill), the whole sector is in danger as a result of the irresponsible behaviour of just a few, as well as preventing competitive balance from being achieved. We hope that UEFA succeeds in setting up effective national systems where there are none.

In conclusion, it appears that local economic potential, regulatory instruments for the sporting sector and competitive balance are all closely connected, without one being able to establish general indisputable laws. There is a positive relationship between local economic potential and sporting results, even more pronounced when the market works freely. In this case, clubs from the richest areas largely dominate the others. Regulatory instruments for the markets, along with specific terms for the redistribution of income, can help improve competitive balance. The French market shows that such instruments can be effective at a national level, but can, at the same time, put in danger the international competitiveness of clubs.

It has become increasingly clear that a solution to the financial crisis that is affecting many European countries will come from the political ability to set up European authorities to coordinate and regulate national championships. As far as competitive balance on the European level is concerned, there are still too many free riders who would like to benefit from the advantages of this state, without paying for it.

We have already suggested that the French regulatory model could be used as a basis. It is a question of thinking globally about the future of the European system of football, which is built on three pillars that are inseparable and that cannot, in isolation, constitute an answer: solidarity, training and control:

- Solidarity consists of distributing a share of income to balance the distribution of sporting talent.
- Training consists of encouraging a minimum production of sporting talent at club level, which presents many advantages compared with a highly speculative transfer market.
- Control consists of avoiding the many unfortunate financial consequences, which are customary in the world of professional football.

In these conditions, as the French example shows, national championships could balance themselves; but, above all, it would be possible to avoid setting up a European closed Super League. However, this poses the problem of knowing whether such a segmentation of the competitions between the European and national levels is tenable in the long term. Several questions, therefore, should be asked: is it necessary to consider a semi-closed league for the wealthiest clubs? Is it necessary to reconstitute balanced national championships with the remaining clubs? Can one imagine regional leagues, as in the United States?

Undoubtedly, the coming years are likely to be charged with major decisions, relating to the organization of professional sports in Europe. Nevertheless, one should not reason under the assumption of "all things being equal", as most economists very often do. For many reasons, fundamental transformations in the world governance of tomorrow, amongst which figure the important position of global environmental problems, are likely to have even greater consequences than just organizational reforms aimed at improving the level of achieving competitive balance. It is this that we must examine to conclude this work.

NOTE

1. See Zimbalist, 2002a; Fort, 2003b; Fort and Maxcy, 2003; Kahane, 2003; Sanderson and Siegfried, 2003.

7. The false justification of sport as a global public good

In the decades from 1896 to 1980, the current market dimension of competitive sport did not emerge because of the domination of a Courbertinian and Anglo-Saxon concept of sport, based on amateurism and voluntary work. In fact, according to the modernizer of the Olympic Games, sport should remain outside the market and follow a disinterested logic. In 1896, Pierre de Coubertin drew his inspiration from an aristocratic morality and a virtuous aestheticism: "I will make weak and restricted youth healthy again, his body and his character, through sport, its risks and its excesses. I will widen his vision and his understanding by contact with grand, sidereal, global and historical horizons".[1] A century later, in 1998, Juan Antonio Samaranch, the then President of the IOC, again defined the Olympic spirit as "a lifestyle founded on the joy of effort, the educative value of good example and the respect of universal, fundamental, ethical principles".[2]

At the same time, the Olympic sponsors explained in the media the reasons for their financial participation, in the following way: "The Olympic Games have a history, that of men and women who have worked to offer the world the occasion to find itself, around sporting feats which equal many strong sensations and unforgettable emotions. Today, international companies are united for a single plan: make the legend live".[3]

Therefore, and following this the model of development of the Olympic spirit, the recent conversion of top-level sport as a spectacle to the globalized market economy (Andreff, 1989) has generated significant financial flows – the origin, management and distribution of which raises basic theoretical questions concerning the status of sport:

- Are we facing a private good or a public good?
- Does it come under the status of a global public good (GPG), insofar as its universal placatory and humanist message still constitutes the corpus of reference for directors of the sports movement (Bourg and Gouguet, 2006)?
- Or even: are we in the presence of a private good obeying a classical logic for achieving turnover, new markets and profits?

● Is it necessary to improve the world governance of sport or find an alternative to the current organization?

Admittedly, by constituting a multinational sporting spectacle, the IOC and the international federations (IFs) have been exposed to the temptations of the business world. However, and contrary to the international sports movement, no company has built its business on the Olympic spirit and its moral demands. The Olympic ideal has been profoundly changed by its relationship with money. Consequently, can the Games still bring such values as disinterestedness, loyalty and education? Is the founding speech of Pierre de Coubertin anything more than a simple commercial excuse? After undertaking an analysis of opening sport to the market place and drawing up a list of the weaknesses in regulating world sport, we discuss reorganizing sport and about new governance.

1 SPORT: WHAT ECONOMIC STATUS?

The example of the Olympic Games illustrates this discussion with the swing, during the 1980s, of sport into the market era.[4]

From an Original Public Good to a Private Good

The present-day Olympic Games have existed for little more than a century (1896–2008), whilst the Games in ancient Greece took place every four years at Olympia for nearly 12 centuries (776 BC–AD 392). Could it be said that the modern Olympics have revived those of antiquity? Historians have shown that there was a radical break between, on the one hand, the ancient, medieval and classical eras and, on the other, the contemporary era as they belong to profoundly different societies. The recognized decline in religions, especially Christian ones that are hostile to money, along with the development of a capitalist economy within the framework of a political parliamentary system, have moulded a new type of sporting event. For sport has not always existed. Admittedly, physical exercise made its appearance at the same time as humankind and responded to a practical function (security and survival). The sports instinct appeared suddenly with the first leisure activities around 3500 BC, in the form of running and jumping. Surpassing oneself and records are two notions that were absent from the first ancient Games in Greece, the cradle of the Games (Queval, 2004). Unlike their modern counterpart, they had a specific spiritual connotation that motivated the participants much more than seeking material gains. However, the Emperor Theodosius I, a Christian convert,

Table 7.1   Statistical development of the Summer Olympics (1896–2004)

Date and Organising City		Number of Countries	Number of Athletes	Number of Events	Number of Sports
1896	Athens	13	280	43	9
1924	Paris	44	3070	136	18
1952	Helsinki	69	4879	149	17
1980	Moscow	80	5217	203	21
1984	Los Angeles	140	6797	221	21
1988	Seoul	159	8465	237	23
1992	Barcelona	169	9368	257	25
1996	Atlanta	197	10310	271	26
2000	Sydney	199	10321	300	28
2004	Athens	202	10500	301	28

Source: IOC.

abolished the games in AD 392, which were then considered as pagan ceremonies that had too close a connection with Greek pantheism; they also transgressed certain principles of the Christian religion, which condemned worshipping the body and showing nudity.

Military training, the development of physical strength and recreation prevailed for 15 centuries. It was only in the nineteenth century that the Olympic spirit was reborn in a context marked by the rise of capitalism after the Industrial Revolution. Inspired by the Hellenic tradition of the ancient Games, Baron de Coubertin drew on the Anglo-Saxon culture of competition and rivalry to make in 1896, at the first modern Olympics in Athens, a humanist event aimed at reconciling body and spirit, muscle and thought.

Until 1980, the influence of the Olympics was directly affected by all the geopolitical unrest of the twentieth century: world wars (for example, 1916 Games planned for Berlin were cancelled), Palestinian terrorism (11 members of the Israeli team shot in Munich in 1972), the struggle against apartheid (37 countries boycotted the 1976 Olympics) and the invasion of Afghanistan by the USSR in 1979 (65 Western countries protested by refusing to take part in the Moscow Olympics in 1980) (see Table 7.1). But this susceptibility of the Olympic spirit to ideological confrontation has never called its existence into question.

In order to develop, the Olympic system (the IOC, the National Olympic Committees [NOCS] and IFs) has set itself three objectives: to universalize the practice of sport, to internationalize competitions and to make sporting events profitable. In 1896, at the time of the first Olympic Games in

Athens, 280 athletes from 13 countries took part in 43 events. In 2004 in Athens for the second time, more than 10000 sportspeople representing 202 countries competed in 301 events. In a century, sporting culture has therefore become international, but in an asymmetrical way.[5]

From an economic point of view, the financial disaster of the Montreal Games in 1976 (with a deficit of $990m), then Moscow, four years later ($169m), for which the taxpayers were still paying the bill until recently, nearly spelt death for the organization of the Olympics, for lack of cities wanting to host them. In fact, there were only two in 1980 (Moscow and Los Angeles), one in 1984 (Los Angeles), and two in 1988 (Seoul and Nagoya). Since then, the movement has reversed the trend with six candidates in 1992 and 1996, five in 2000 and, lastly, 11 in 2004.

The process of internationalizing sport is old, at least since the first modern Olympics. It is true that the globalization of competitions corresponds to a natural historical construction of the sports movement (IOC and the IFs), whose ultimate objective has always been the universality and confrontation of the best athletes.[6] From the 1980s on, the conjunction and intensity of various societal elements have put into movement the globalization of sporting issues (Table 7.2). New information and communication technologies (television, cable, satellite and digital) wipe out distances and borders from a spatial, temporal, linguistic and ideological point of view. The market has also established itself in sport as a common scale of measurement.

After nearly a century of immobility, the Olympic order was completely reorganized around those two new dynamics, in order to draw a profit from it. The opening of the Olympics to all amateur and professional athletes, as long as they are accepted by their federation (1981), the possibility of using the Olympic symbols commercially (1986), the decision to alternate the Summer and Winter Olympics every two years (1986, applied since 1994), and the creation of a global marketing programme (1986) illustrate the IOC's will to promote the spectacle by a double reinforcement: of the competition between sportspeople, and the competition between sponsors and television to obtain exclusive rights.

The privatization of the Los Angeles Olympic Games in 1984, linked to the refusal of the city to commit public funds, along with the profit from them ($225 million), were two totally new decisive events for the future of the Games. A real alternative to their public financing is therefore growing, thanks to television, which gives these events a global dimension, and which interests major companies wanting to increase their reputations and their turnover: Coca-Cola, McDonald's, Kodak, Visa, Panasonic, and the like (see Tables 7.3 and 7.4). In addition, the progression from a local sale (negotiations with every NOC) to a global sale (overall sponsorship

Table 7.2　　Stages in the conversion of the Olympic spirit to globalization (prevailing trend of the period)

Period	1850–1914	1918–1980	Since1980
Object	Moral, education	Spectacle	Commerce, communication, finance
Institutional and legal framework		National and international federations	Commercial companies
Type of technique used	Muscular strength	Instrumentation of practices	Technological and scientific support
Area of competition	National	International	Global
Number of countries present at Summer Olympics	13 (1896)	83 (1960)	202 (2004)
Media coverage	Written press	Radio	Television
Number of countries receiving televised images of Olympics	0	21 (1960)	220 (2004)
TV broadcasting rights (world)	None	$1.2m (OG 1960)	$1603m (OG 2004)
Number of TV viewers worldwide	–	200 000 (OG 1936)	$3.9bn (OG 2004)[a]
Number of international sports competitions	20 (1912)	315 (1977)	1 000 (2006)
Funding	Contestants	State, spectators	State, TV channels, sponsors, shareholders

Note:　a.　Number of different people who followed the Olympics at least once during the fortnight; each viewer being taken into account just once. As a combined audience, the IOC announced a total of 40 billion viewers for the 2004 Games (OG).

Source:　Bourg (2004d, p. 65).

agreement with the IOC) immediately opened all markets to sponsors, by simplifying the negotiations.

This opening-up strongly contributed to the emergence of a sporting system of mass production/consumption (Harvey and Saint Germain, 1995), which thereafter included a virtually unified competition space, sports bodies and companies (sports equipment manufacturers, sponsors,

Table 7.3   Olympic sponsors (The Olympic Partners [TOP], Winter and Summer Olympics)

Programme	Period	Number of Sponsors	Receipts (in $m)
TOP I (Calgary – Seoul)	1985–88	9	95
TOP II (Albertville – Barcelona)	1989–92	12	175
TOP III (Lillehammer – Atlanta)	1993–96	10	350
TOP IV (Nagano – Sydney)	1997–2000	11	500
TOP V (Salt Lake City – Athens)	2001–04	11	650

Sources: IOC; press.

Table 7.4   Broadcasting fees for the Summer Olympics (in $m)

Year	Summer Olympics	Total
1960	Rome[a]	1.2
1964	Tokyo	1.5
1968	Mexico	9.8
1972	Munich	11.8
1976	Montreal	34.8
1980	Moscow	101.0
1984	Los Angeles	287.0
1988	Seoul	403.0
1992	Barcelona	636.0
1996	Atlanta	895.0
2000	Sydney	1331.0
2004	Athens	1603.0
2008	Beijing[b]	1800.0

Notes:
a.   First Olympic Games to have been the subject of payment for broadcasting rights by TV channels. Those years marked in italic correspond to the years of upheaval (1960 and 1984) or to economic dominance of the Olympics by broadcasting rights (1996, 2000, 2004 and 2008).
b.   Estimate.

Source: IOC.

broadcasters and operators), who manage their activities on a worldwide basis with global mechanisms that belong to the market economy and liberal logic (access to financial markets, winning new markets, developing marketing programmes, international search for creating value for shareholders and the free movement of labour and capital, and so on).

The most dynamic vector of the commercial globalization of sport was television. The increase in private and public channels, whether subscription or "free", increased the supply of programmes, while the competition they generated in obtaining broadcasting rights increased the revenues for sport. The organization of a market monopoly by the Olympic movement allows it to control and offer prices, without any competition. By eliminating all competition on the supply side, this collective bargaining puts higher-bid mechanisms into operation, which are all the more effective, as the demand by channels extends and becomes more diverse.

Since the IOC, which is the owner of the Olympic Games – an event that has neither rival nor substitute – holds a monopoly of the supply, the money from the rights is rising considerably. For $500000 in today's terms, CBS obtained the exclusive US rights for the Rome Olympics in 1960. In 1984, ABC had to pay $225 million (Los Angeles), whilst NBC had to pay $793 million for the 2004 games (Athens) and $894 million for the 2008 games (Beijing).

The exchange value of the Olympic Games has prevailed over its use value; and the educational and health values of the Olympic Games and their intrinsic aesthetics have been replaced by instrumental market values. It is, therefore, not globalization that is the problem in itself – insofar as that constitutes its original spirit – but its privatization. It is the latter that, henceforth, will give sport its resources and its direction. Increasingly, the issue is the ownership of the financial resources generated by top-level sport. From the beginning, a non-profit-making organization, the IOC, has been the owner of the Olympic Games. Holding the monopoly for running this event has created a shortage, which has made it possible to increase their turnover and to make a growing profit from it. But linked to an increase in established or claimed property rights (radio-TV broadcasting rights, Internet, marketing and by-products, and so on), is a corresponding increase in economic actors and jobs in the sports industry, in the widest sense of the term: agencies specializing in marketing, communications, financial investments and career management, amongst others.[7]

This chain of values is both segmented and privatized. However, in many respects, the Olympic Games are a mixed good because of the public funding of the training of athletes and of facilities, tax exemption, granting commercial companies the right to run public sports facilities, direct subsidies and the securement of the positive externalities created by amateur sport.[8] However, although taxpayers are frequently called upon, only shareholders of the commercial partners (sponsors, private television and equipment manufacturers) receive the dividends. The legitimacy of this double concomitant movement of the socialization of the costs and of the privatization of the profits appears questionable – even if this process

Table 7.5   Ways of funding the Summer Olympics[a] *(in percentages)*

Summer Olympics	Montreal, 1976	Los Angeles, 1984	Seoul, 1988	Sydney, 1992	Athens, 2004
Public funding	95	2	46	39	74
Private funding	5	98	54	61	26

Note: a.   All investment expenditure (sports facilities, transport facilities, and so on) and operating expenditure (budget of the local organizing committee) needed for the organization of the Olympics.

Sources: Preuss (2000); *La Lettre de l'économie du sport*, 18 October 2000, 19 December 2003.

intervenes in order to strengthen the financial autonomy of the Olympic Games, along with the return on investments by private operators.

With €3.59bn, the total bill for the 2004 Athens Olympics, ex ante, represented the GDP of many least developed countries LDCs. Such a budget covers investment expenditure (€2.14bn) and that connected to the proceeding of the events (€1.45bn). Going from the premise that all these expenses were necessary to respond to the IOC's specifications and to meet the organizational constraints (for example, spreading the competitions over 33 sites), a cost of €3.59bn should indeed be considered, even if a part comes from creative sustainable investments of positive externalities (airports and motorways, and so forth).

Even if it is difficult to compare privately financed Olympic Games, with objectives of maximizing short-term profits (1984 Olympics), and publicly financed Olympic Games, which emphasize the structural changes for the city, region and state (1976 and 2004 Olympics), it is interesting to identify the three major models of funding the Olympic Games: public (95 per cent for Montreal), mixed (45 per cent for Seoul) and private (2 per cent for Los Angeles) (see Table 7.5). Obviously, comments must be put in perspective because of the methodological uncertainties due to different levels of territory and, especially, to the lack of homogeneous instruments of analysis. Despite everything, the collectivized cost remains important, even more so since it must include a long-term cost for the upkeep of facilities. These costs, assured by the state, are the basis of forming private profits and media and commercial advantages that benefit firms that only cover short-term costs (funding the spectacle). In the short term, the induced effects on economic and touristic activity of the Olympics appear weak and short-lived. Therefore, access to facilities and promotional advantages of the Olympic Games often appear expensive. However, it should be mentioned that for Athens 2004, the Greek state received substantial aid from the European Union and that the prospect of the Olympics had the effect of concentrating such a work programme in a short period of time (several years instead of ten or 15) that allowed Greece to reduce its delay, as far as transport infrastructure is concerned.

Sport: A Global Public Good (GPG)?

The idea of GPGs appeared in international negotiations at the end of the 1990s, mainly concerned with the issue of sustainable development. Faced with the extent of global environmental problems (the greenhouse effect, biodiversity loss and the increase in North–South inequality, and so on), reference was increasingly made to the demand for global governance (Kaul et al., 2003). For example, the United Nations Development Programme (UNDP) recommends carrying out human development through an extensive strategy of coordination between all the groups of concerned actors: individuals, NGOs, businesses, public authorities and international organizations (PNUD [UNDP], 2005).

Since the founding world conferences in Stockholm (1972) and Rio (1992), followed by that in Johannesburg (2002), some positive signs of attempts to create synergy amongst these actors have appeared (Sacquet, 2002):

- The emergence of global citizenship in the form of citizens' forces of opposition (anti-globalists), information and expertise networks, NGOs and the like. As far as human rights or the improvement of human "abilities" are concerned, unquestionable results have already been noted in certain countries of the South (Sen, 2003).
- The strengthening of the role of local authorities, particularly in applying local Agenda 21s and the values that they bring (transparency, solidarity, responsibility and so on).
- The promotion of corporate social responsibility in many forms: the appearance of rating agencies, the development of ethical and interdependent investment funds and the involvement of multinationals with annual reports on sustainable development.
- The appearance of a new type of consumer, concerned about fair trade.

It is in this new international context that the debate about GPGs arose. The conceptual origin of GPGs should be looked for in economic theory, with the traditionally established distinction between public goods and private goods, with regard to two principles. In particular, pure public goods are goods to which the principles of rivalry and excludability do not apply: non-rivalry means that consumption of a good by an individual does not prevent another individual consuming the same unit; non-excludability means that an individual cannot prevent another individual profiting from the good in question (for example, national defence policy).

Nevertheless, pure public goods are relatively rare in reality. It is more common to come across public goods characterized by rivalry (in the form of congestion or saturation) or by excludability (owing to paying access). It is a question, therefore, of near-public goods. Lastly, there is the existence of public goods, the use of which the state makes mandatory: merit goods (health, education and sport, and so on).

Finally, this distinction between public goods and private goods is based on recognizing market failures that involve state intervention – and that is in contradiction with liberal logic. However, this approach to public goods is in keeping with the idea of regulating the economy, as it is traditionally understood within the framework of the nation-state (Keynesian policy). Now, the logic of economic globalization has called this approach into question over the last 20 years (Michalet, 2003). On the one hand, market failures that justify state intervention no longer concern the national market, but rather the global market; on the other hand, this intervention should be under the authority of a global institution – which poses the problem of global governance.

Faced with the collapse of the traditional framework for analysing public goods (national), different options were adopted for approaching global public goods. Some economists consider the second are simply an extension of the first (from national to global). On the other hand, others think that GPGs are of a different nature from traditional public goods. In particular, they include an ethical dimension that cannot be ignored; especially, as far the survival of humanity is concerned.

These then, are the fundamental rights and needs of a human being, as well as the environmental constraints on which the recognition of a global public good must be based (Lille and Verschave, 2002).

Therefore, can sport be categorized as a GPG? We make the following proposition: by definition, a GPG is a good that the market cannot produce, so sporting events elude this category; on the other hand, an idea that is completely outside the sports market could be categorized as a GPG alongside culture, education or health – to which it is closely connected.

Basically, this means that it is necessary to distinguish carefully between these two categories of goods and, moreover, to describe completely different realities as "sport". In one respect, "merchandising" sport, which has become an industry like any other and that obeys market logic. In another respect, "true" sport; sport as a leisure activity and that, for those who do it, is more concerned with pleasure, aesthetics and culture, and so on, than performance. It is also necessary to stop the hypocrisy that consists of claiming to be representative of the second, in order to put forward the regulatory principles of the first.

It is as part of this general debate about sport that questions must be asked about the status of the Olympic Games. If they are considered to be private goods, an economic analysis can be carried out using the traditional economic tools. In particular, the subject of the economic impact of the Games can be understood in a broader sense, by taking externalities into account. One comes back to the debate over Olympic values, which could be considered as positive externalities, increasing the level of well-being in society.

On the other hand, by considering the Olympic Games as public goods, belonging to the shared heritage of humankind, one could wonder what real social loss the disappearance of the Olympic Games would represent, as they are understood at the present time. This means that we are presently very far from defining the Olympics as pure GPGs: goods that benefit all countries, all population groups and all generations.

In other words, if one wants sport in general, and the Olympics in particular, to become a GPG, a new model of organizing our society must be envisaged.

2 TOWARDS A NEW GOVERNANCE OF SPORT

The phenomenon of globalization nowadays means the idea of complete integration of the economy into a vast market dominated by worldwide multinational companies (Andreff, 2003). In particular, this development of world capitalism means a loss of autonomy of nation-states, as far as monetary and financial policy is concerned – which also tends to call into question the very idea of territory or border (Adda, 2006). The world economy has, therefore, become an area for the mobility of capital, knowledge, labour, culture and so on, subject to a growing logic of privatization that states are finding increasingly hard to resist.

The IOC and the IFs could only achieve their goals of permanence and development (universalizing the practice of sport, internationalizing the Games and making sporting events profitable) at the price of sacrificing the founding principles of the modern sport. The ills of the Olympic ideal are now characterized by things on a giant scale: wheeling and dealing, nepotism, doping, opacity and corruption. Indeed, this strategy gives priority to exploiting these reserves of financial rights, rather than perpetuating the original Courbertinian ideals. It is therefore necessary, first of all, to analyse better in theory the malfunctioning; and consequently study the necessity of profoundly reforming the Olympic institutions.

The Main Weaknesses of World Regulation of Sport

The international sports system currently in force was set up from the end of the nineteenth century onwards, at the instigation of the IOC and the IFs – but only from a symbolic and moral point of view. Admittedly, the IOC these days includes as many NOCs as the planet has sovereign states. True, the IOC has at its disposal a restraint power, which raises questions of an ethical nature. But the IOC, which is the supreme authority of the Olympic movement, is a non-profit-making NGO, endowed with few legal instruments concerning worldwide sports organizations and athletes. Moreover, its governance of sport is not very effective, because it is affected by a crisis in its aims, which are uncertain and not very clear (sporting objectives/commercial objectives).[9] Indeed, even though the sporting movement has for decades defended the heritage of the values of the Olympic spirit defined by Coubertin, this official position has now become unconvincing.

The structure of the sporting system is incomplete and unsuitable: weak direct power, limited role and functions, opaque decision rules, insufficient democratic legitimacy and loss of sovereignty, and so on. Attempts to favour a new form of governance based on a greater transparency (for example, the procedure for designating the organizing cities for the Olympic Games) appear insufficient for the challenges presented by the liberal globalization of sport. This globalization itself creates a demand for a global public good, for which there is no supply at any level. Sporting institutions are trying to be intermediaries for a demand for sustainable and ethical sport, but national regulations – against doping, for example – are ineffective since control of the legal, sporting and scientific aspects require a response on the world level. It is, therefore, the logic of the market itself (merchandisation) which is increasingly denounced as a cause of the appearance or increase in these public "ills".

The deregulation and privatization of the economy of the Olympic spirit also involves the disappearance of the instruments of sovereignty for the sporting power. Although the IOC and the IFs from 1890 to 1980 were the police for the sports world, vehicles for its development and guarantors of its ethics at the same time, it would appear that from now on the sporting movement must very often be content to interpret the new rationality, which some 20 outside companies in the sports markets are pushing (sponsors, broadcasters, manufacturers of sports goods and marketing

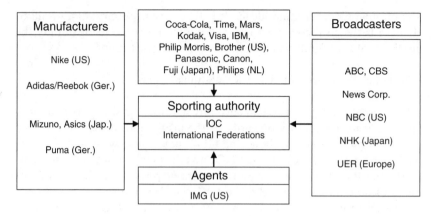

Source: Bourg (1996).

Figure 7.1   The economic centres of world sport

agencies). It forms a community of interests that acts as a network and that occupies a central place in the new system of producing the sporting spectacle (see Figure 7.1). Sports institutions are, therefore, placed under the supervision of private companies, which are responsible only to their shareholders. Admittedly, they retain the symbolic legitimization of sporting feats and official validation of competition results; but for the rest, the global market will, from now on, supplant sports regulations. Many examples of this submission of sports institutions to the market could be given (Andreff, 1999).

The Need for Profound Reforms

"Good governance" too often comes down to improving working conditions of international organizations (Chavagneux, 2004). It concerns the problem of optimizing, under constraint, the distribution of tasks between organizations (IOC and the IFs). This is a largely inadequate approach. Therefore, we will look at things from a critical perspective critical of the established order, founded on the primacy of market relationships imposed on all interactions between sport and the environment.

The return of sports culture: towards an Agenda 21 for sport
From this perspective, several series of difficulties of a conceptual nature emerge. Traditionally, sport has been defined according to four cumulative criteria: a dynamic situation (muscular effort), a competition (winner and losers), rules and an institution (Loret, 1995; Defrance, 2000; Queval,

2004). Since sport has pervaded our social representations in its competitive and media-focused version, it has been granted a semantic monopoly
that aims to convince that all physical activity is sport. Now, this notion
covers a wide range of activities having often contradictory properties.
The purposes of physical education (training, health, building up self-
knowledge, learning moderation and limits) or "Californian" sports (especially, boardsports) appeared in the 1970s (maintaining physical potential,
participation, user value, emotions and cooperation) differ from those
of the current competitive sports model (exploiting physical potential,
surpassing oneself, performance, exchange value and domination). It is
therefore more necessary than ever to no longer provide "a" definition of
sport, but "definitions" of various forms of activity, since, de facto, not all
physical activity is sport.

The anthropological characteristics of the person currently competing
in sport are very close to those of someone in the past (Vigarello, 2002).
The pleasure of physical play, the regular comparing of performance
to see who is the best, the objectification of movement by independent
measurement, the increasing of individuality, the worship of excellence
and the pleasure of transgression are not traits that are specific to the
modern athlete. On the other hand, contemporary sociological and economic developments encourage a hegemonic uniformity, although they do
impoverish the meaning of sport. With several hundred thousand professionals in the world and several billion TV viewers, top-level sport can no
longer be presented as a simple game or physical activity.

In addition, the originality of sport – but also its complexity – is that
it is based on two opposing systems of representation and values: in one
respect, the Olympic spirit draws on exulting nature, equilibrium and
health; in another, it comes close to the ideal of surpassing oneself that
leaves it open to excess and to all sorts of tricks, which become the very
negation of sporting ethics and public health. Consequently, what are the
values that are likely to promote sustainable sport? What compromise
can be found between the many paradoxes that the sporting institutions
have to manage: the status of sport as a strictly codified educational
human activity and commercial issues, the globalization of sport and its
local raison d'être, the demands made by performance and that of human
dignity, and financial means and sporting purposes?

The key question relates to the difficulty of creating a common representation of sporting values and the model of top-level competitive sport:
exchange value only and/or a factor for health, education and integration?
The non-existence of an a priori sporting social contract, prior to the production of a global public good, probably partly explains the weakness
of the governance of world sport – as does the non-existence of a global

sporting citizen (sportsperson, spectator, viewer or taxpayer) who has yet to appear.[10]

These reservations show the difficulty of radically opposing, or even separating, two ideas about sport: on the one hand, top-level sport that is, globally commercialized (a private good); on the other, sport as the heritage of humanity (a public good). The catalyst of such a challenge could only be the "meaning" given to collective action, that is, a set of shared values on essential data concerning the future of sport and a common assessment of the means to implement them. The building of this global sporting general interest or this common universal good must necessarily involve public opinion. From this perspective, the production of a sporting global public good (SGPG) supposes strong regulation from the public actors and/or independent private authorities (cf. Box 7.1).

New regulatory instruments

Governance will be defined as a business management technique (businesses, states and international organizations) and implemented when a multiplicity of actors with differing interests have to find an area of agreement. In other words, it is a question of a continuous process where conflicts of interests can be overcome and a cooperative approach established. "Good" governance depends on the ability of the system to control deviant behaviour, the "global public evils" (doping, corruption and cheating, and so on), by economic and moral incentives. The globalization of sport, therefore, poses the question of its world governance.

To do this, it would therefore be appropriate that collective rules be developed, decided, legitimized, applied and controlled by a set of transactions (Conseil d'Analyse Economique, 2002). This governance depends on the effect of specialized institutions in sport (IOC, and the IFs and so on), equipped with their own instruments, as well as on the standardizing effect of private operators (sponsors, television, manufacturers of sports goods and shareholders, and so forth). It works both at a world level and through the channel of continental and national organizations. It holds, in part, its legitimacy from the delegation of the states and from the consensus of the sporting community; but it comes under no central political authority and is subject to no democratic sanction. This system of governance, which is in a state of constant transformation, responds to a threefold movement of the intensification of interdependencies, to the extension of these to new disciplines and to the enlargement of the geographical field to new countries (the number of nations represented and the NOCs and so on).

The natural tendency of the market is to produce public goods with positive externalities in an insufficient way; and to overproduce public goods with negative externalities – that is, those whose production includes an

BOX 7.1   THE AGENDA 21 OF WORLD SPORT: CAN THE OLYMPIC IDEAL BECOME A GLOBAL PUBLIC GOOD?

List of 21 priority recommendations for the twenty-first century

- Carry out epidemiological studies to undertake a health appraisal of top-level sport.
- Study the short-, medium- and long-term effects of the use of doping substances and techniques on the health of sportspeople.
- Unify detection procedures, as well as the list of banned ways of doping and their sanctions, with the full application of the World Anti-doping Code.
- Research and develop activities aimed at strengthening the efficiency of anti-doping monitoring.
- Create an individual medical passport for sportspeople (the validation of which is essential for taking part in competitions).
- Promote information initiatives for sportspeople concerning the risks incurred to their health in case of doping.
- A monitoring, control and suppression system for the whole of the doping ring (dealers, buyers and consumer motivators, and so on).
- Help promote sport in least developed countries.
- Initiative against money-laundering in sport.
- Fight against corruption and cheating in sport.
- Research the consequences of high-level competitive sport on the health and life expectation of sportspeople's lives.
- Promote a precautionary and preventative principle in relation to all sporting excesses (intensive sport for children, and overloaded training and competition schedules, and so on).
- Protect the environment during the carrying out of any sports infrastructure.
- Fight against all forms of violence in stadia.
- Clarify the values and purposes of diverse activities that are currently grouped together under the term "sport" and distinctly designating these views and practices.
- Promote sport as a public utility and as sustainable.

- Create global sporting institutions of governance (United Nations Sports Programmes and agencies, and so on).
- Implement regulatory instruments for world sport (taxes and fines, and so on).
- Institute initiatives against the giant scale of major global sporting events.
- Fight against the waste of public funds in commercialized sport.
- Promote a sporting world order (world sporting citizenship, a common sporting social contract and a legal framework, and so on).

Source: Bourg and Gouguet (2006).

inconvenience (Conseil d'Analyse Economique, 2002). That is why the external effects should correctly be taken into account by the appropriate management systems from the legal and economic points of view: it is the challenge for global sporting governance to devise.

The bases of new governance must be defined. From this point of view, the idea of the World Anti-doping Agency (WADA) is a first. The WADA was set up in 1999 with the intention of promoting and coordinating the international fight against doping in all its forms. Made up of representatives of the IOC, the NOCs, IFs, sportspeople and governments from the five continents, this agency is independent only theoretically – insofar as its composition, its funding and its leanings are closely linked to the sporting movement and to the states who have direct interests in breaking records and winning medals.[11] Despite everything, the World Anti-doping Code, which was adopted in 2003, is the first international instrument to harmonize the rules concerning doping in every sport and in every country.

However, the slow gestation of the WADA – with delicate negotiations concerning its mandate, its financing and its working – show the limits and deadlocks in leading to a global agreement about a subject of common interest, in a context where national and individual preferences diverge; whether it is the attitude in relation to the risk of doping, to its cost, to its definition, to its damaging nature, to its regulation or to its sanctions.[12]

In spite of significant advances, the fight against doping is unfortunately not currently a priority, since the health risk for sportspeople is judged to be acceptable. The result of that is a statute of doping comparable to that of "rare diseases" in the field of health: those whose impact and extent are so weak in developed countries that there are not enough commercial incentives to warrant any research and development being devoted to them.

World governance, as far as the fight against doping is concerned, has to make it possible to reduce these divergences of appreciation, as well as the transaction costs (reducing procedure costs, shortening the time taken to scrutinize the cases and improving the legal readability and predictability) by rationalizing the then unified procedure.[13] Thanks to economies of scale that could be produced, world governance could thus make this fight effective (decline of current immunity and disputes) and less costly (cooperating in producing useful scientific knowledge). Indeed, the example of the difficulties of the fight against doping shows the harm done to the development of a global public good by three gaps (Kaul et al., 2003): the "jurisdiction gap" (the lack of an institutional framework which could manage a global public good); the "participation gap" (the lack of legitimacy of international authorities and of citizens' sovereignty); and the "incentive gap" (the lack of incentives and sanctions).

New institutions
International sporting authorities are too numerous, not active enough and often questionable concerning their role and their aims. Consequently, it would be advisable to look again at the instruments and fields of governance in order to clarify their functions, legitimize their mandates and strengthen their powers. It is not only and mainly a question of compensating for the failures of the market – and to make it more efficient – but, beyond that, to protect global public sporting domain and to find an alternative model by changing the paradigm.

Three different, non-conflicting ways could be explored as a way of contributing to (re)founding true global governance (Michalet, 2003):

- The creation of a democratic and recognized coordination authority integrated into revitalized United Nations and Bretton Woods institutions. This could take the form of a World Humanity Organization constitutionally based on the Universal Declaration of Human Rights and successive declarations as far as economic, social and cultural rights are concerned (Petrella, 2004). An extensive study has been going on for several years on the necessity of completely changing international institutions. In particular, it has been henceforth recognized that a true "democracy of world governance" (Lille and Verschave, 2002) must come about and that the emergence of a global right at the service of justice for all is possible (Latouche, 2003).
- The increase in independent and specialized regulatory agencies. Producing standards and incentives on a world scale would favour

the development of a sporting global public good to compensate for failures of the market (mechanisms, instruments and taxes, and so on). Each of these agencies would be in charge of a particular field of activity: the fight against doping, assistance to the least advanced countries for access to sport, the fight against corruption, sporting ethics and the links between top-level sport and health and so on. Their intervention would extend to the whole planet and to all sports, taking account of the globalization of competitions and what is at stake.

• The drafting of charters and codes of good conduct by major international companies. Companies tend to behave as free riders in the field of commercialized sport, as elsewhere, leaving it to the care of others to finance and produce global public goods, whilst benefiting at the same time from their positive externalities (ethics and the fight against doping increase the market value of sport) since, by definition, the public good is freely available once produced. Why, consequently, accept to share the cost and the obligations? However, one manufacturer (Nike) and one sponsor (La Française des Jeux) did rally after pressure for a boycott of their products and with a view to business ethics, when it concerned the disrespect of children's rights (working conditions in the sports goods industry), of the expectations of sporting ethics and of public health (the confirmed doping of racing cyclists). Along with about 50 multinationals, Nike joined the Global Compact initiative launched by the United Nations in 2000, committing itself, in particular, to give up using child labour; and La Française des Jeux by means of a foundation to finance the fight against doping.

This means that to be effective, voluntary commitments must respond to at least two conditions: third parties must exert credible threats (spectator boycott and removing sponsor support), and implement initiatives that must be monitored by independent inspectors. Sanction mechanisms, in case of breaches, must be instituted. We note that more and more NGOs, such as WWF or Greenpeace, take part in monitoring operations. So it was that during the Sydney Olympics, Greenpeace was given the responsibility of checking the application of the Charter on the environment of the organizing committee. In case of non-compliance, the organizer runs the risk of a media campaign that could damage its reputation. Nike was subjected to such a campaign during the 1998 Football World Cup and has, since then, reoriented its external quality strategy for its products, particularly its working and employment conditions in its Third World factories.

A new organization for the Olympic Games
The previous proposals tackle the subject of the efficiency of the markets for sport (Bourguinat, 1998; Sen, 2003). It is the same as far as the Olympic Games are concerned.

In order to do this, discussions should begin on solutions likely to radically reform the Olympic ideal: to restore the primacy of sporting values, by returning money and the market to the role of means and not ends; to change the Olympic motto, "Faster, Higher, Stronger", which is synonymous with all the ills of the Olympic Games; to give real credibility to the performances, by an effective and worldwide fight against doping; to reform fundamentally the operating rules of the IOC (eliminate co-opting, limit the age and length of members' mandates, modify the way of designating the host cities, and to ensure the financial transparency of the Olympic Games); to create the United Nations Programme for Sport in order to exercise a legal and deontological supervision over the IOC; to put mechanisms in place that guarantee the unity of sport, by, in particular, a cross-subsidization of receipts between the professional and amateur sectors.

Based on the model of a British English club of over 100 years ago, the IOC is a democratic heresy because of its admission by co-opting members. Between 1894 and 1974, out of the 300 personalities appointed, one king, four dukes, seven lords, 12 barons, 22 princes, 24 counts and 25 generals could be counted – that is, a 30 per cent aristocratic and military membership. Thirty years later, the composition has only slightly progressed. Amongst the 123 members, about 50 come from a royal family or are soldiers, ambassadors, ministers or former ministers. Sportspeople, trainers and managers are very badly represented.

More than this necessary reform, the Olympic programme must be revised to stop the giant scale of the event: fewer athletes, accompanying personnel and journalists (12 000 accredited in 1992 and 21 500 accredited in 2004); fewer heats (257 in 1992 and 301 in 2004) and fewer sports.

To that end, it should refocus on the basic Olympic disciplines – a dozen, such as athletics, gymnastics, cycling, rowing, fencing, horse-riding or sailing – and to organize a rotation, every four years, of five or six new sports needing promotion. Those sports with the most media coverage could be withdrawn from the Olympic Games (basketball, football and tennis) because they have absolutely no need for this exposure to expand. The programme would also be reduced by removing obsolete disciplines (the pentathlon, dressage, synchronized swimming and throwing the hammer) or overlapping events (certain swimming relays, several weight categories in judo, the apparatus finals in gymnastics, racing for points in cycling and some Greco-Roman wrestling tournaments). In the same way, limiting the number of the selected sportspeople to two per discipline, instead of three per country, would reduce the number of athletes.

In order to contribute to a real financial "downscaling", the Olympic Games could take place in the same area – Olympia, for example – which would avoid the waste of the candidate cities (communication and promotion expenses) and the successful ones (building oversize facilities in relation to usual needs and that are difficult to adapt). These budgetary restrictions would make it possible to carry out another fundamental reform, consisting of the IOC being made to give the broadcasting rights to a single television team, whose images would be offered to every country – which would restore the universal and free character of the Olympic spirit. This less wheeler-dealing environment would be favourable to a less "chauvinistic" treatment by national broadcasting media, which are increasingly showing only the feats of their own athletes (see the example of NBC during the Atlanta Olympics in 1996) in order to increase audience numbers and advertising receipts intended to cover the rights that they have paid for. With the same aim in view, eliminating national anthems and flags, organizing the opening procession of the Games according to sport rather than country, as well as getting rid of ranking countries according to the number of medals won, would all restore a sporting spirit, which has been corrupted by nationalist and ideological discrepancies.

These proposals will seem to be utopian. But does not utopia lie in maintaining the current operating method? Could it be said, by adapting the phrase of Amartya Sen, that modern sport is "unethical", insofar as it is more interested in the means rather than the ends, because of the productivist path that it has taken? However, from another point of view, is it not possible to defend the theory, according to which nothing is less ethical, a priori, than competitive sport, in that it exploits biological inequalities for domination purposes and that it represents a reactionary myth? Are we witnessing an internal crisis in sport or a general crisis in society? How can sport be transformed without calling into question its instrumentalization by productivist logic? Do not the current unfortunate consequences of competitive sport as a spectacle really come, beyond the spirit of the capitalist market economy, from the ideology of progress, the central foundation of modernity?

In conclusion, it seems that the notion of a sporting global public good helps to renew the traditional approaches of GPGs. From this point of view, clarifying the word "sport" is an absolute precondition for defining the conditions that must be fulfilled for sport to become a global public good.

NOTES

1. de Coubertin [1920] (1967).
2. *Revue olympique* (1998), Lausanne, August–September.
3. In 1992, during the months preceding the Winter Olympics in Albertville, the 12 official sponsors thus explained to the world media the reasons for their partnership with the IOC.
4. For an economic history and these macroeconomic aspects of the Olympic Games, see Bourg and Gouguet (2004); Preuss (2003).
5. Indeed, this globalization process must be put in perspective by the assessment of a spatial concentration of practice, spectacle and performance within the EU–North America–Southeast Asian triangle (cf. Chapter 3).
6. See Bourg and Gouguet (2005); Houlihan (2003b).
7. For example, as far as the wish to create new property rights is concerned, the NBA considers itself as the exclusive holder of the points scored, minute by minute, in the matches organized under its aegis. Indeed, the running of a live sports information service by a company (Motorola) should depend on its agreement and the payment of a fee. The New York Court of Appeal revoked the decision by the District Court and dismissed the NBA, judging that it was a question in this instance of "factual information" and not of "an author's original work" (cf. United States Court of Appeals for the Second Circuit, *The NBA* v. *Motorola Inc.*, 1997).
8. Generally, to describe the intervention of public authorities in a sector, economists resort to the concept of merit goods. In the field of sport, the state entrusts the public service missions to duly authorized federations. It is true that sport has a considerable influence on forming communal values and, therefore, plays a social and political role. These are important reasons that justify the regulatory supervision of sport by the public domain, as well as its funding.
9. For a documented illustration of the unfortunate consequences of the international sporting movement, see Jennings (2000); *Carton rouge! Les dessous troublants de la FIFA* (2006), Paris, Presses de la Cité.
10. But the supporter has become a consumer, the athlete a worker, the club a brand and sport merchandise.
11. For the sporting movement, as for the United Nations, rational productivist rationality moved from the field of means to that of aims. It is around a liberal, commercial and technological vision that top-level sport is organized. That is why the specialization of WADA in itself would not enable it to eradicate doping.
12. For many doctors, it is top-level sport itself that is harmful to health in the short, medium, and long term, rather than the doping, which is intended to lessen traumatic consequences. Would it not be also advisable to clear up this controversy by financing an extensive programme of international scientific research into the general problems posed by the precautionary principle?
13. Until now, the multiplicity of actions and recourses at stake before national, international sporting federations and state jurisdictions and legal institutions would engender controversies and contradictions linked to national specificities, and to regulatory differences according to the discipline; which would be equivalent, in the final analysis, to a virtual impunity for sportspeople.

8. Doping as a by-product of professional sport

From 1998 onwards, the extent of doping was revealed by many scandals that successively touched the Tour de France and the Tour of Italy in cycling, rugby in the Southern Hemisphere, Italian football and international athletics. Effectively, this practice appeared no longer as an isolated act, but very much as an organized and well-established massive practice. Doctors (de Mondenard, 1987, 2000, 2004; Laure, 1995, 2000, 2004; Carrier, 2002), sociologists (Yonnet, 1998, 2004; Waddington, 2000; Mignon, 2002; Houlihan, 2003a), historians (Vigarello, 2002), philosophers (Siri, 2000, 2002; Queval, 2004) and jurists (Caballero and Bisiou, 2000; Breillat et al., 2004) have all understood, with their own concepts and methodologies, the problem of doping.

As for this study, we intend to examine the possibility of applying economic reasoning to the behaviour of the champion who takes drugs. Can doping avoid economic analysis? Are its foundations to be found in economics? Can resorting to this practice simply be seen as the reasoning of *Homo oeconomicus*? Economic research has recently become interested in doping in order to confront some of its theories about the real behaviour of the drugged sportsperson (Bourg, 2000, 2003b, 2004a, 2005) and the anti-doping policies of sports bodies (Eber, 2002; Maennig, 2002).

In order to understand why sportspeople resort to drugs, one should straightaway distinguish between the two traditional levels of economic analysis. On the microeconomic level, according to the classical approach to the rationality of the consumer who is looking to maximize an objective function (utility) within a budgetary constraint (scarcity), the sportsperson is led to choose the optimal allocation of his or her resources based on a cost/benefit calculation: the costs of doping and the sanction, the amount of earnings linked to wins, and the amount of earnings without drug-taking.

On a microeconomic level, the commercial and institutional environment of the sportsperson makes it possible to explain the previous individual calculation. This latter relates back, first of all, to the high financial stakes of the sporting spectacle, which concern a lot of economic agents (clubs, federations, leagues, sponsors, industrialists and media, and so forth), as well as to the characteristics of the control system and of the suppression of drugs.

In such a context, the individual act of doping seems to result in complex sequences linked to the collective organization of the sporting spectacle. Indeed, the abstract *Homo oeconomicus* has to give way to the sportsperson anchored in a specific universe, whose decisions depend on pre-established rules and traditions. Other non-material variables also have an influence on the act of drug-taking, such as those linked to the very principle of sport, to his or her connection to performance and his or self-image (Vigarello, 2002; Yonnet, 1998, 2004). In the end, it is possible to consider doping as a by-product of professional sport. From now on, the value of top-level sport is only assessed by the yardstick of its records. In the same way as the functional drugs whose status has changed over the last three decades, drug-taking is in fact a tool and not an end in itself: drugs are taken "to be better, to be oneself, to be better than oneself" (Mignon, 2002, p. 6).

Faced with doping, what new questions have cropped up that threaten the traditional definition of sport? In other words, where is the incompatibility between drugged behaviour and sporting ethics? Are we heading towards two sporting worlds: one guaranteed "pure", following ethical principles and the second helped by pharmacology and biotechnology, instrumentalized by the logic of the spectacle?

Where theoretical analysis and a holistic approach converge, bringing in experimental economics[1] can help to shed light on the cognitive processes that underlie the decision to take drugs or not.[2]

1   DETERMINING THE FRAMEWORK FOR ANALYSIS

Drug-taking behaviour is conduct where products are taken to improve performance.[3] The fact of using medicine to surpass oneself intellectually or physically is widespread in many sectors and in very different situations: to overcome an obstacle (examination, job interview or public speaking) and to improve one's professional or private performances. Doping is a particular form of drug-taking behaviour, in that there is no legal meaning and is only sanctioned in sport, which, it is true, is built on several myths that explain this specificity: purity of effort, equality of opportunity, uncertainty of result and a healthy and natural activity. Doping is in line both with a societal transformation (a spirit of rivalry and competition and the obligation to get a result), which demands that the individual surpasses him or herself (Ehrenberg, 1991) and in a general movement of the medicalization of society that is accompanied by the instrumentalization of the body.

Using these first comments as a starting point, the scope of our study is defined by the following factors:

1. The sportsperson, whose determining drug-taking factors will be identified, is a professional, that is, an athlete living off very high-level sport and spectacle, to the exclusion of any other activity.[4]
2. The career of a sportsperson is short (four to eight years on average, depending on the discipline), precarious and insecure because of both the increasing demands of competition and spectacle and their risks (injuries, lack of form and not feeling accepted by the team, and so on). It is also subject to strong existing competition in the labour market, where the supply is plentiful with young players from training centres and who have been able to move freely within the European Union since the Bosman Case at the Court of Justice of the European Communities (1995).
3. Insofar as highly competitive sport has adopted the market economy, the free play of the spectacle, the media and advertising has segmented distribution of income. The consumer chooses his or her programmes, products and stars in sport, in the same way as in cinema and music (Bourg and Gouguet, 2005). Consequently, champions who benefit from worldwide media exposure acquire an exceptional market value: in 2005, the three highest incomes in sport in the world were those of Tiger Woods the golfer (€69.5m), Michael Schumacher, the Formula 1 driver (€65m) and André Agassi, the tennis player (€37m). Such levels of pay can influence doping in two ways: in one respect, by increasing the temptation to resort to cheating; and in another, by giving sports-people the resources to finance this behaviour while minimizing the risks.
4. Doping is the act of consuming illicit substances by a sportsperson or resorting to specifically forbidden practices named in the Anti-doping Code of the Olympic movement and that are subject to regulation (Laure, 2004). The aim of this practice is to push the organism to levels of performance that it could not achieve without drugs, because of the physiological limits, tiredness, anxiety and pain of the subject. Unlike the definition of drug-taking behaviour, that of doping is based on the ideas of banning, transgression and potential sanction.
5. Sportspeople know that they are in competition with three categories of athlete: those who do not, or no longer, take drugs (a minority); those who take drugs in an artisan way, which is careless and not very effective because of their modest budget; and those who take drugs

Table 8.1   Progression of world records in four men's sports (1896–2006)

Disciplines	1896	2006
Athletics		
100 m	10″ 8	9″ 78
Shot-putting	14.32 m	23.12 m
Pole-vaulting	3.61 m	6.14 m
Long jump	7.21 m	8.95 m
High jump	1.97 m	2.45 m
Cycling		
Speed	38.220 km/h	56.375 km/h
Tour de France (average speed)	25.451 km/h[a]	40.940 km/h
Weight-lifting		
Super-heavyweight	111.5 kg	213 kg
Swimming		
100 m freestyle	1′ 22″ 2	47″ 84

Note: a.   Average speed of the winner of the first Tour in 1903.

scientifically with undetectable and effective molecule synthesis (most of the elite).

6. Therapeutic advances, coming from endocrinology and molecular biology and brought into the sports sphere, have considerably widened the possibilities of doping over the last few years. Certainly, the use of new methods of preparation and the development of material and equipment have made performances improve in a spectacular way (Table 8.1). All the same, resorting to doping has strongly contributed to improving records.

7. The sportsperson has to make a choice: use certain banned substances and methods included on the list drawn up by the World Anti-doping Agency (WADA), with the risk of being caught during an unexpected check or in competition and then sanctioned; or not to use them, which comes back again to the athlete imposing a handicap on him or herself, in that winning and records are determined with a very small difference (less than 0.5 per cent in most disciplines), whilst resorting to certain products allows his or her ability to increase by 10 per cent or more.

8. The risk of being subjected to a positive anti-doping control is very low: 0.14 per cent during the football World Cups (1966–2006), 0.39 per cent during the Summer and Winter Olympics (1968–2006), and

Table 8.2   The official statistics of anti-doping tests

	Number of Tests	Number of Positive Tests	% of Positive Tests
France 2005 (all sports)	8 805	338	3.84
Tour de France (1966–2003)[a]	3 811	80	2.1
WADA 2005 (all sports)	3 114	63	2.02
Australia 2002 (all sports)	6 263	34	0.54
Summer and Winter Olympics (1968–2006)	25 388	99	0.39
World Athletics Championships (2005)	708	2	0.28
Football World Cup (1966–2002)	2 112	3	0.14
World Swimming Championships (2005)	437	0	0

Note: a.   These statistics do not apply to the years 1992, 1995, 1996 and 2000 (data unavailable). The number of sanctioned positive tests (80) does not take into account illicit, or subject to identified restriction, substances and that are covered by a therapeutic justification – for example, 37 "doubtful" cases during the 2003 Tour de France, with only one confirmed positive test.

2.1 per cent during the cycling Tour de France 1996–2006) (Table 8.2). These levels do not necessarily mean that there are only irreproachable athletes. It simply means that of the products analysed or analysable, there was no confirmed doping, or only in very small numbers. The shortage of the number of tests and the impossibility of detecting the most used substances explain the unreliability of the controls. According to the testimony of athletes, trainers, doctors and managers, the percentage of drug-takers exceeds 75 per cent in certain disciplines.

9.   The risk of being sanctioned, in sporting terms, is still lower or even zero, for several reasons. There are many ways to cancel the disciplinary procedures: legislating for a medicalized management of doping (the use of illicit products could be subject to a therapeutic justification, if it is registered beforehand on the athlete's health card), and resorting to a legal logic that exploits any technicality, any scientific uncertainty, any mismatch or incompatibility between sporting or state regulations.[5] Thus it was that 38 out of 152 samples taken during the 2004 Tour de France included banned products. All the riders concerned had a medical cover in their file. During the Summer Olympics, increasing numbers of athletes resort to medical prescriptions: 383 in 1996, 618 in 2000 and 600 in 2004 (96 per cent of them came from the

main countries winning medals). The number of positive tests was two in 1996 (0.1 per cent) and 24 in 2004 (0.85 per cent).

10. In most countries, the risk of being criminally sanctioned for using doping products does not exist – with the notable exception of Italy. In France, from 1965 (the Herzog law) to 1989 (before the Bambuck law), the user was likened to a delinquent and could be taken to court. Henceforth, the drugged sportsperson has been considered as a victim of this scourge, encouraged by the unfortunate consequences, and doping is not supposed to disturb public order.

11. Asymmetric information represents a permanent element in drugged behaviour in sport. This term designates a situation where an individual has more information than another about a good or a service. For example, the person insured knows his or her own characteristics better than the insurer. A comparable observation could be highlighted as far as the relationship between the sportsperson and the doping regulator is concerned. In fact, a frequent and long interval of often 20–30 years appears between the start of athletes using unlawful medicines and the date of its banning by the sports authority and, above all, the possibilities of screening.[6] Parties taking part in the market for sporting spectacle (federations, clubs, sponsors, television, agents and athletes, and so on), carry out their transactions without having the same information. This information is both imperfect and asymmetric, since it is distributed unequally between the actors of the exchange. Now, from a theoretical point of view as from an empirical point of view, we know that the more a market is opaque, the greater the number of failures. The effectiveness of anti-doping control therefore depends directly on the reduction, or even the elimination, of asymmetric information, which is an indispensable condition for transparency, and a return to founding sporting ethics[7] (Table 8.3).

12. In a context of the strong growth in turnover in the "sports" sector (€580bn in 2005) and rapid advancement in pharmacology (the "official" world market for medicine was €520bn in 2004), a veritable international market in doping substances has developed since the 1980s. On the whole, and taking into account the number of top-level athletes defined as such from their professional status (about 200 000 potential consumers), the sums devoted to such "preparations" in several disciplines (1–3 per cent of the total budgets of teams), from the turnover of the most-used substances, the financial flows generated every year by an effective demand and a plentiful supply for all activities in this international market for drugged sportsmen,[8] are probably €6–10bn in 2006. The comparison of these figures with the budgets for the fight against doping (€17m for WADA) can only be worrying (see Table 8.4).

Table 8.3   Asymmetric information: the example of the difficulties of anti-doping control

Substances	Year of Discovery	First Use in Sport	Date of Banning by the IOC	Year of Identification
Amphetamines	1930	1936	1968	1968
Anabolic steroids	1940	1954	1974	1976
Beta blockers	1958	1978	1985	1985
Corticoids	1936	1960	1987	Undetectable
Erythropoietin (EPO)	1959	1987	1990	2000[b]
Ephedrine	1934[a]	1964	1968	1968
Growth hormone	1944	1980	1989	Undetectable
Probenecid (masking agent)	1954[a]	1976	1987	1987
Testosterone	1935	1952	1982	1982

Notes:
a.   Date of French medicine being put on the market.
b.   Exogenous EPO has certainly been detectable since 2000, but its use can be masked by other substances.

Source: de Mondenard (2004).

Table 8.4   The doping industry (2006)

Data	Estimated Costs in €
Annual drug-taking of a basic amateur	500
"Pot belge" (2 millilitres of a cocktail composed of cocaine, amphetamines, morphine, caffeine and analgesics)	500
Anti-doping tests (France)	600
Annual drug-taking of a top-level champion	100 000
Value of a kilo of anabolic steroids	150 000
Annual salary scale for sports medicine doctors	1–2m
Image fees paid by Cofidis to its riders in a tax haven (2001, 2002, 2003)	5m
Budget of anti-doping control of the World Anti-doping Agency (WADA)	5m
Budget of the World Anti-doping Agency (WADA)	17m
Global sales of creatine	250m
Worldwide turnover of doping	6–10bn

Source: Press.

2 THE HYPOTHESIS OF *HOMO OECONOMICUS* APPLIED TO THE ATHLETES WHO TAKE DRUGS

The neoclassical approach is that which, amongst all the economic theories, holds that rationality is the most important (Becker, 1964, 1968). In a society made up of rational individuals, who know what they want and are consistent in their choices, agents look to maximize their utility when they take decisions, such as to marry or divorce, to commit offences or crimes or not, to drive a car carefully or not, and so on. Can the act of doping be likened to the fiction of *Homo oeconomicus?* In this case, the athlete's behaviour consists of reasoning in terms of opportunity cost: he or she would be left to compare the costs and benefits of consuming doping substances with those of an alternative and lawful allocation of his or her resources.

The basic hypothesis, therefore, is that potential drug-taking sportspeople are free and independent individuals who base their decision to take drugs on a comparison of the costs and benefits of this act, practised within the certain institutional framework specified earlier. Such a cost/benefit method emphasizes the existence of a choice to be made between the return on this "investment in human capital" and that which would be obtained by using these resources for other activities, between personal interest and morality, the short and the long term, and between actual or immediate goods and future goods.[9] The athlete is constantly making an economic calculation that will enable them to arbitrate between contradictory choices. So they will only cheat if the net advantage to be gained is big enough. According to a market calculation, the net profit for the drug-taker will depend on the following elements:

1. The amount of earnings connected to wins.
2. The cost of doping.
3. The amount of earnings obtained without doping.
4. The cost linked to the sanction, in case of a positive test. It is necessary here to take into account both the amount of the conviction and the probability of being punished.

The net advantage drawn by the drug-taker will be equal to (1) – (2) – (3) – (4). If this amount is positive, it could be considered that it is rational to take drugs.

If the economic calculation is widened to take externalities into account, the decision could be swayed by two variants, reflecting the case of a sportsperson who has certain "moral values" and who measures the real risk for their future health engendered by doping. For this category of athlete, the clear advantage to be drawn from doping must exceed a certain threshold in order for them to cheat. This threshold is determined according to the personal ethics of the sportsperson concerned, as well as by their estimate of the "value" of the quality and length of their future life that they have to give up, by resorting to dangerous substances.[10]

This model shows variations linked to the sportsperson's behaviour and, consequently, illustrates the choice of policies for fighting doping. According to this analysis, inspired by work on "crime economics" of Gary S. Becker (1968), the fact that a sportsperson gives him or herself up to an illegal activity by taking drugs is the result of a rational calculation. Therefore, the level of doping depends on the balance that exists between positive (earnings) and negative (sanctions) incentives to commit this act or not. This trend of neoclassical thought is founded on a predictive approach to the economic consequences of the law. In order to dissuade the sportsperson from taking drugs, three rules have to be respected: the strong possibility that the guilty will be caught, the punishment must be dissuasive and the sanctions must be progressive, according to the number of offences committed (Lemennicier, 1992). Thus, public and sporting authorities could change the conditions for the sportsperson's rational choice by modifying the institutional environment that determines the parameters of the rational calculation (Kopp, 2006). The regulatory authority and the system for suppressing doping have to be a sufficient deterrent to discourage potential drug-takers. Therefore, two legal mechanisms could be effective in correcting doping, which is the main negative externality of the sporting spectacle: enacting an ex ante regulation (referring to an international quality standard, an ISO-type certification for athletes, and so on), bringing into play, ex post, the civil and criminal responsibility of the drugged sportsperson (compensation for damage caused by the drug-taker to ethics, and imprisonment, and so on).

Let us suppose that C.C.,[11] a cyclist with a rare talent as a climber and on the flat, is tempted to take a banned substance to improve his productivity and, therefore, his future income. To follow a programme of doping is expensive in terms of expenditure, risks of being caught and punished (in the short term) and health problems (in the medium to long term).

As far as investment in human capital is concerned (products and instructions for use, and so forth), three types of provision are put on the market: for €5000p.a., C.C. would receive a training scheme; for €45 000, he would enjoy a treatment adapted to his particular nature; in return for €100 000, he would find himself being given the most sophisticated hormones with the substances that mask their use and limit their side-effects, with personalized medical monitoring. Before deciding either to take drugs or to choose the programme, the cyclist C.C., as a rational individual, is going to compare the costs with current value of the extra income flow that the doping would give him. With the improvement of his ability, he would obtain better sporting results, which would be manifested in an increase in his salary. As it concerns a virtual sum of the earnings that C.C. would have received legally, it would be useful to determine the level at which he would abandon the idea of taking drugs. It goes without saying that the lower the initial income, the more the athlete will be encouraged to take drugs to increase it.

If the attitude of C.C. is neutral faced with the risk of being caught and punished, faced with possible future negative consequences for his health, and faced with feeling of cheating, C.C. would tend to give in to the temptation of drugging himself and express his preference for the present much more than the sportsperson who feels an aversion to these risks. A study carried out in 1997 by CBS, the television channel, amongst 198 top-level US athletes aged between 16 and 35, confirmed a preference for the present. The proposal was set out as follows: "We will supply you with a banned stimulant with two guarantees: you will not be caught and you will win all competitions in which you take part for the next five years. Then, you will die from the side-effects of the aforesaid substance. Do you accept?" More than half, 52 per cent, replied in the affirmative. Such neutral behaviour seemed to be the norm, and dating from a long time, among professional sportspeople.[12]

In such a set-up, C.C. the cyclist is going to benefit from significant net advantages: a gross annual income of €23m, an investment linked to the act of doping at €100 000, a value of abandoned legal income of €300 000, that is, the sum obtained in the same professional activity, but without resorting to illegal substances, and a "value" for the risk of being caught and punished close to zero. Moreover, if C.C. had not been a gifted rider, he would have had a more modest job in line with his meagre initial school training that would have brought him €15 000p.a. The difference between this real income and his sportsperson's income is a form of economic rent that C.C. profits from, because nature has made sure that riders of his class are very rare.

C.C.'s act of doping is, therefore, a consequence of his free choice and, especially within the framework of the inter-temporal choice, of his great preference for the present, linked to the special nature of his profession (short and hazardous careers). So, if C.C. is more efficient than others, and thus has a higher income, it is because he wanted it by "sacrificing" a part of his youth to a specific technical training course, excluding all others and low paid, and by forcing himself to apply an illegal medical assistance programme to his performance.

3   CRITIQUE OF THE PREMISE OF ECONOMIC RATIONALITY

We could wonder whether applying the principle of rationality,[13] with the premise of methodological individualism, and a cost/benefit analysis, are the appropriate means to understand the behaviour of the sportsperson who takes drugs and to define an "optimal" policy for controlling doping. Do we not need to go beyond the utilitarian framework conceived by Gary S. Becker, when he considered economics as the science of all human behaviour?[14] This opinion shows, in fact, the excessive and imperialist claim of a discipline that intends to reflect social relationships, as well as individual behaviour.

Admittedly, doping is an economic problem, but it is not just an economic problem. Are there not "higher values" to take into consideration – even if, for Pareto, "morality has got no place in economic reasoning? Not that it should be ignored, but that it is from another world" (Pareto, 1966, p. 16)? In other words, it seems to us questionable that the ultimate explanation of doping is to be found in the individual behaviour of sportspeople, in supposing that these are guided by the search for the maximum or minimum of an objective function (profit or cost), or even in their aggregation. This is for several reasons.

The microeconomic foundations are not developed enough and show omissions: a silence about the content of the objectives and values of the sportsperson, a simplification of reality through consistent hypotheses, the questionable premise of the overall consistency of behaviour, the lack of realism of the presupposition of the approach in terms of inter-temporal choice according to which the decision to dope is taken with a certain future, with properly expected future income, along with risks of sanction during the career and health problems throughout life.

In addition, the constituent ideology of this paradigm reduces the sportsperson to just the state of a calculating automaton and to a machine of productivist rationality to beat records, without any historical or moral dimension. Yet, the actions of sportspeople necessarily fit into a sporting structure, which must serve as the point of departure for an analysis, for the sporting movement (organization and very complex explicit and implicit contracts) predates athletes and conditions the choice of its members, whilst at the same time being shaped itself by these choices. This contradicts the premise of methodological individualism.

This double approach, theoretical and empirical, of the rational and maximizing behaviour of the sportsperson who takes drugs is also questionable and shows some shortcomings. Indeed, the paradigm likening the athlete to the *Homo oeconomicus* is based on several premises:

sportspeople do what they want and have the ability to compare the punishment incurred, balanced by the risk, with the satisfaction drawn from their act of doping (rationality). They are the best judges of their well-being; this consumer sovereignty supposes an ability to classify all possible combinations of drugs according to levels of satisfaction. Sportspeople are autonomous agents spurred by material and financial interests (individual and market choice), and those who take drugs have deviant behaviour with regard to ethics (the purity of sport).

All these hypotheses are incomplete, simplistic or erroneous. Contrary to what is said in utilitarian thinking, a sportsperson cannot be considered as a strict maximizer of personal interests, outside all social links and all institutional contexts (Sen, 1999). Forgetting the diversity and complexity of factors that determine behaviour, and in order to design universal laws, orthodox economics presupposes that anywhere and anytime the individual responds to the same model, that of *Homo oeconomicus*. However, human action has many dimensions and there is much rationality that does not limit it to that of a calculating automaton; humankind must be taken as an indivisible whole, not compartmentalized. Not everything leads from a calculation; beliefs, values and conventions influence choices and give them a meaning.

Similarly, only sportspeople capable of projecting themselves into the future could fear the risk of sanction. Taking their youth and immaturity into account, athletes are generally incapable of it, which makes them virtually impervious to modifications of the parameters relating to sanction. In addition, doping brings non-monetary gains (the pleasure of transgressing, fragmentation of the individual, body worship and so on), which considerably increase the net benefit of doping and we must not disregard them.

Consequently, the predictive capacity of the Beckerian approach to the sportspeople's reaction to the incentive system by costs is called into question by the very fact that the market alone cannot resolve all the faults of coordination of sportspeople's behaviour. A system of market regulation of doping (fines and suspension of activity, and so on) will not eradicate the cultural and sporting roots (the internal logic of performance), and will only stimulate resorting to undetectable products.

Let us take the example of two athletes, A and B. Either one could either take drugs or not. Three situations therefore arise. If neither of them takes drugs, a strictly sporting hierarchy appears. If one takes drugs, but not the other, the doping could be enough for the drug-taker to win. If both of them take drugs, and supposing that the effects of the substances consumed are identical, the sporting hierarchy is re-established (Ventelou, 2001).

What lessons can be drawn from these hypothetical cases? Everybody takes drugs, with everyone anticipating doping by others. In the end, the sports result is the same, but everyone has put their life in danger. It would be in the interest of every athlete to avoid illegal behaviour, but they adopt it despite everything to protect themselves from possible betrayal of the agreement.[15] We find ourselves in a situation comparable to that illustrated by the most famous dilemma of game theory, "the prisoner's dilemma" (Eber, 2006). In our example, the independent pursuit of personal interest by the two athletes means that both of them lose something: especially, in terms of health, life expectancy and ethics. The result is, in the meaning of Pareto, a suboptimum situation. Indeed, there are other situations where everyone could be better, if the behaviour were less "individualist". It is in the interest of everyone to develop in a climate of confidence, loyalty and cooperation. But economic agents prefer to work without coordination. The "prisoner's dilemma" calls into question the "theorem of the invisible hand", according to which, the search for personal profit is a good thing for the group, and therefore for its members (Guerrien, 2002).

In order to fight against the generalization of this opportunistic and cynical behaviour, the solution is "anti-economic" by nature since, in the same way that doping does not come down to just one economic cause, its suppression cannot come from the creation of a rights market to take drugs.[16]

The system of incentives by costs cannot properly influence sportspeople's behaviour, as the standard analysis does not take into account their strategic behaviour – particularly, their ability to organize themselves in order to continue doping with new products, since the old ones can be detected during tests. In this case, the utility of the drug-takers does not depend solely on their previously defined clear advantage, but on their ability to control the inherent risks of their profession that they intend to pursue by best managing this uncertainty. It is true that, temporarily, reorganizing their supply of new undetectable products will affect the opportunity costs that the sportspeople have to face. However, their decision to take drugs or not cannot be modified by variations in costs triggered by new scientific knowledge from the anti-doping regulatory authority (WADA).

4   AN ALTERNATIVE HYPOTHESIS: *HOMO SPORTIVUS*

The motives for doping cannot be reduced to a simple financial argument. Many other impulses are at work, such as the logic of training and performance, which explains the temptation to overdo it, or the pressure of the sporting background, which plays a structuring role in the psychological position of the athlete. This is why the hypothesis of *Homo sportivus* should be advanced, to whom "the model is more easily generalised than *homo oeconomicus*, because his motives greatly exceed the single interest" (Simonnot, 1988, p. 8). From this point of view, could it be said that the act of doping is attributable to the athlete's behaviour, or is it the consequence of a fixed and inevitable "risk" linked to the very nature of sporting competition? If not, and for example, how can the presence of 281 types of medicine be explained – 75 per cent of which should have been prescription-only – in the medicine cabinet of Juventus? This was a quantity that corresponded to that of a small hospital, according to an expert heard during the case of doping brought against the Italian football club in October 2002.[17]

The stakes are considerable since, using a neoclassical analysis, the drugged sportsperson is rational in his or her decision to break taboos or not. However, could the hypothesis not be put forward that doping could be considered as hyper-conformity to sporting values (Mignon, 2002)? Conversely, deviant and abnormal behaviour could be illustrated by the attitude of Christophe Basson in 1999, whose revelations about the practices of the pack excluded him from professional cycling: threats of reprisals by riders (especially, the future Tour winner, Lance Armstrong); indifference from his team mates in La Française des Jeux, the Société du Tour de France and the International Cycling Union to his lot; and non-selection for the lucrative rallies following the Tour, leading to his giving up his career.

The drug-taker does not, therefore, consider themselves as a deviant or cheat, but as an individual trying to do their work as an athlete as well as possible, to fully achieve their identity by looking to reach their best level so as to stay in the group.[18] As the sociologist Patrick Mignon (2002) has highlighted, the athlete makes the necessary sacrifices to be recognized, to overcome difficulties and to follow their dream.[19] They follow the Olympic motto, "Faster, Higher, Stronger" in their search for always more perfection. In the same way as training or improving techniques and equipment, doping maintains a legitimate relationship with performance. It is one means amongst others to play the game, respect the codes and uses of an environment whose culture is excellence and where self-achievement is strongly promoted.

These cognitive processes go beyond the power of tests and sanctions to dissuade and are much greater determining factors than the desire to earn money. If it were necessary to provide supplementary proof, it would be easy to find reasons to explain the products taken by amateurs. In this instance, they are linked to the very object of competitive sport. Thus, Georges Vigarello (2002) opportunely reminds us that the two cyclists sentenced in Arras on 7 November 1996 for "unauthorized acquisition of drugs" did not aim at being very famous and were not responsible to any sponsor, given their very modest national ranking (3326th and 8033rd respectively).

In an individualist society, everyone considers they have ownership of themselves, a legitimacy to move physical norms and to act on them.[20] The accounts of anonymous and regular doping, without any financial stake – especially those by body-builders, 75 per cent of whom take anabolic steroids – lend weight to this theory of "the symbolic issue of sport, of its aesthetic ethics (playing with death to surpass yourself)" as Claire Carrier (2002), the psychologist and psychoanalyst pointed out.

But the purpose of drugged behaviour in sport cannot always come down to looking for performance (Laure, 2004). It could be a means to prove that one possesses the necessary ability to join a group. The risky and dangerous game is helped by taking products that mark membership of the community. This process of initiation and integration is similar to that concerning other forms of consumption (alcohol, cannabis or cocaine, and so on).[21] This example shows very well the necessity of studying other determining factors for doping than those from an economic calculation.[22]

While standard theory postulates that individuals assess different alternatives in an absolute and objective way, would it not be better to admit that sportspeople assess situations in a relative way with regard to a reference point that could be subjective (Kahneman and Tversky, 2000; Eber and Willinger, 2006)? Taking decisions in an uncertain universe is not founded on abstract principles of calculation, but on the mental construction of his or her environment by the individual (a priori, emotions and intrinsic motives, and so on).

In its way, the hypothesis of *Homo sportivus,* whose method of reasoning and behaviour are not governed only by material incentives, could help to identify the multiplicity, complexity and intermingling of the causes of doping, which are of equal importance.

5 PERSPECTIVES

With the accumulation of proven facts about doping, which have been given wide media coverage for a dozen years at least, sport should have been profoundly suffering in its nature and morale. And yet, sport has not regressed; on the contrary, it has developed like never before.

Consequently, at the beginning of this century, has there not been a swing in how doping is perceived, the long-time shameful recourse to something proscribed implicitly becoming an accepted recourse, the long-time unpardonable misdemeanour being implicitly transformed into a permitted risk (Vigarello, 2002)?

The list of banned products has been drawn up by WADA and is based on three principles: the product has the potential to enhance performance, it represents a health risk and it is contrary to the ethics of sport. For a substance to be part of this list, it is enough for just two of the three criteria to be met. With the application of this definition to the list of French pharmaceutical specialities containing drug substances, 308 out of 950 specialities ceased to be proscribed in 2004, the date the World Anti-doping Code came into force (de Mondenard, 2004). This code also includes another standard of harmonization that suppresses, in certain cases, all proscribed substances: these licensed for therapeutic use.

Admittedly, the issuing of these licences is subject to an administrative and medical process in order to check the reality of the problems, but this recognition of doctors having the power to prescribe banned substances to sportspeople for therapeutic purposes illustrates one of the most spectacular forms of getting round proscribed substances. During the 2000-04 Tours de France, 210 out of 696 samples contained drugs and only four led to any sanction, insofar as all the others were covered by medical certificates (42 per cent of the 2004 pack benefited from a licence). For the Athens Olympics, 600 athletes had the opportunity of legally using drugs under the cover of treating themselves.[23]

After reducing the area of doping and licences, a third index authorizes the idea of a new permissiveness in the matter. The list of medicines having been the subject of a request for authorization from the French agency for health products sanitary safety (AFSSAPS) for importing into France by foreign cycling teams before taking part in the 2004 Tour de France, included several hundred different preparations, amongst which were medications whose use is often associated with taken drugged substances, or ones that have been changed from their therapeutic use (*Le Monde*, 27 July 2004).

In reality, most actors in the sporting spectacle industry lack credibility in their wish to eradicate doping. Sports institutions want to protect stars from suspension, to protect the commercial value of the competition. During the Sydney and Athens Olympics, nearly all the positive tests applied to second-rate athletes from Third World countries, who resorted to cheap products that were easy to detect. In addition, the creation, composition, working and direction of WADA depends, in the first place, on the IOC. Now, the economic success of the Olympic Games benefits the IOC, which holds the property rights of the Games. Moreover, the President of WADA was the President of the television rights and marketing commission of the IOC for many years that were marked by certain wheeling and dealing around the Olympic ideal. It would be necessary, conversely, for WADA to be really independent from the sporting movement, totally indifferent to the market value of sport and presided over by a personality showing a real aversion to doping and whose remuneration would be determined every year by the results of the fight against doping (Eber, 2002).

Another good example of conflict of interests could be illustrated with the Association of Tennis Professionals (ATP), which is, at the same time, a players' union, co-administrator of the international circuit and dope-tester. The ATP protects the anonymity of it drugged members, applies internal sanctions in an opaque way or clears them. Lastly, what are the ethics, the value of example and the legitimacy of television channel consultants broadcasting, for example, the Tour de France, whilst nearly all of them have been involved in the doping business? And what is the dissuasive effectiveness of immediate redundancy of a rider by a sponsor in the case of a positive test, insofar as the accused rider immediately finds a job in another team?

Therefore, the official culture of the sporting spectacle is changing imperceptibly. Doping appears as an accepted and irreversible fact for public opinion: 94 per cent of French people questioned by Sportlab in late 1999 thought that cycling was affected by doping (88 per cent for athletics). In the same survey, doping was considered to be an integral part of top-level sport: 85 per cent of those polled thought that wanting to suppress it was futile. Similarly, there was not, in their opinion, incompatibility between awareness of doping and the admitted interest for the given spectacle: 81 per cent found cycling pleasant to watch, and 95 per cent athletics. The dissociation between "values" in sport and the taste for spectacle was clear.

As Georges Vigarello (2002), has noted, the history of sport includes many examples when the denounced artifice at first was serenely accepted afterwards. Let us choose two of them from the fields of technology and finance. The derailleur, an instrument for changing gear, was banned until 1957, before becoming obviously established today, as it was seen as cheating and an unfair manoeuvre to save energy by adapting to the profile of the terrain. For a long time, professionalism seemed incompatible with sporting morality. Paying a professional was considered against the spirit of sport. Until the early 1980s, it was forbidden to pay an Olympic athlete for him or her to become efficient. So, and in the same way that it has accommodated the relationship between technical innovation and money, could not the morality of sport soon accommodate the relationship with doping?

Sport could thus shift its morality again by centring it on athletic perfection or the exceptional quality of the champion, whilst at the same time, drugged behaviour would be perfectly technically controlled, yet hidden.[24]

The generalization and trivialisation of doping mean that it could be considered as a by-product of the sports activity that accompanies it. Medically assisting performance and high-level sports practice work in such a way that it is impossible to have one without the other: the search for victory demands recourse to substances whose funding needs the organization of a network.[25] This is so true that many doctors are in favour of legalizing doping in order to obtain a biological readjustment of top-level athletes whose practice is not intended to improve, or even protect health. For the professional is an abnormal being, who is going to be intensely physically pushed to the limit in such a way as to reach a maximal efficiency from the human machine.

For these specialists, the real risks of top-level sport, well before doping, lie in this practice, which causes hormonal imbalances, saturates the organism with very toxic lactic acid and engenders poly-traumatologies that have to be compensated for (Yonnet, 1998). A second indication gives credit to the theory of by-products: the fight against doping through testing does not have the intention of eradicating this practice. Its intention is to give credit to the competition and, to do this, to watch over competitors in a strictly equal way, which guarantees the uncertainty of the spectacle, a condition for its media coverage and its commercialization. In other words, so that the spectacle continues to bring in money, the fight against doping must be permanent, but at the same time, doomed to failure, for it encourages resorting to undetectable products.

The sportspeople who takes drugs does not have the maximizing attitude of the *Homo oeconomicus* fiction, because its supposed rationality is affected by many constraints. Faced with a choice, the athlete could do, in certain cases, not what they would prefer, but what habit and the values that they have internalized dictate to them to do. The practice of doping in a sporting environment is a veritable initiation and integration rite, just like getting drunk in certain social groups.

Many sportspeople take drugs without behaving as maximizers and without necessarily being irrational. This paradox, which is similar to that identified by Maurice Allais in 1953, shows that individual rationality must not be reduced to just economic rationality, that is a maximizing behaviour under restraint. In this hypothesis, the attitude of athletes who select doped products, their doses and time of consumption can be interpreted

– according to a precautionary principle from a health point of view or with regard to risk aversion and their own conscience – as signs of great caution, the problem of being reasonable and respectful of sporting ethics, which are so many preoccupations that are not in the least irrational. The too narrow idea of rationality defined according to utilitarian presuppositions is confirmed by observing widespread drug practices in disciplines where material or symbolic earnings to be maximized are low (bodybuilding, fencing, rowing, canoeing and kayaking, shooting, and so on) or non-existent (most "amateur" competitions). The athlete who takes drugs does not always do so with the aim of making the best choice, as their choice could entail risks and lead to possible regrets. Their preferences depend partly on their environment and the history of their past actions. The moral climate that prevails in sport can affect the athlete's propensity to take drugs and, by interacting with their opponents, they are forced to play a role while, at the same time, keeping room for manoeuvre.

To conclude, the economic analysis of doping must be widened. Indeed, one should assess the social cost of it and define an optimal policy towards it. For every act of doping must be seen as an abuse of confidence by those who commit it against society. It distorts results by changing the criterion of measuring one against another, which is an unfair way of resolving a supposedly honest competitive relation. In addition, the fight against doping mobilizes major credits, mainly of public origin (funding tests and laboratories, information and prevention campaigns, medical monitoring of athletes and organizing suppression). Private expenditure, that is, that met by drug-takers, or public, that imposed on society, which are necessary for doping and its suppression, have a crowding-out effect on spending that could be devoted to the development of sport. This "function of social loss",[26] justified by damage caused by acts of doping to society as a whole, would also deserve to be studied.

Doping is not neutral concerning the value system. Drug-takers compete with non-drug-takers; drug-takers do not have uniform preparation and, with equal doping, the performance is profoundly different depending on the athlete. Doping obstructs the action of sporting and public authorities, the utility and legitimacy of which it lessens insofar as they appear ineffective in fighting this cheating. While destroying the ethical foundations of sport (rules, confidence, solidarity and the like), recognized doping has also a negative impact on the climate of investment in professional sport by reducing public, media and sponsor interest. A double consequence follows: investment diverted towards other activities that make a better association of images possible, and pressure to hide the extent of doping and reduce it to just some isolated acts. Lastly, doping affects sportspeople's health in the short, medium and long term:

injuries, infirmity, cardiovascular illnesses and cancers, etc., and reduces life expectancy.

Such an understanding is essential if mistakes are to be avoided as far as the fight against doping is concerned, and the health and social cost of the main negative externality of the contemporary sporting spectacle is to be limited. High-level sport is thus structured according to the idea of progress defined on strictly economic criteria of competitiveness and on a belief in the infinite surpassing of individual ability. But does not Utopia lie in maintaining the Olympic motto, "Faster, Higher, Stronger", as the ultimate goal of the sports community? For, unlike war, sport teaches people to measure themselves against each other without destroying each other and according to certain rules that tend to promote the uncertainty of results and fair confrontation, which exclude the freedom of the sportspeople to invent the conditions for their victory.

NOTES

1. For a presentation of this booming research method, see Eber and Willinger (2006).
2. The awarding of the 2002 Nobel Prize for Economics to a psychologist (Daniel Kahneman) and to an economist (Vernon Smith) consecrated the convergence and complementarity of these two social sciences.
3. See Laure (1995, 2000, 2004). According to Dr Patrick Laure, "drug-taking behaviour is a set of observable acts (the process of resorting to the product) by which, in a context of uncertainty, a person tries to adapt to the representation that he has from a given situation, with a view to performance" (Laure, 2000, p. 28).
4. There were 200 000 of them, worldwide, in 2006.
5. See Caballero and Bisiou (2000), Vigarello (2002) for an illustration of the various ways of getting round forbidden substances. For example, the Buffet law of 23 March 1999, replaced by Book V of the third part of the new health code enacted by the ruling of 15 June 2000, recognized doctors as having the power to prescribe banned substances to a sportsperson for therapeutic purposes.
6. That is why one of WADA's objectives is to "create uncertainty among cheats. They must not know whether we have a test or not for such and such a substance. If we do not have it, we will keep the samples to test them later", declared Richard Pound, its President (*Le Monde*, 13 August 2004).
7. Game theory in incomplete information makes it possible to take this type of situation into account and study the impact of asymmetric information on individual behaviour, as well as their effects on the resulting collective results of this behaviour. See Cavagnac (2006).
8. For a presentation of the supply, the demand and drug prices, and a market that has much in common with that of doping, see Kopp (2006).
9. See Becker (1964, p. 392), for whom "human capital analysis starts with the assumption that individuals decide on their education, training medical care, and other additions to knowledge and health by weighing the benefits and costs".
10. To illustrate the behaviour of a sportsperson who takes drugs, it would be desirable to be able to quantify every relevant element in calculating the opportunity cost of doping. Two levels of difficulty arise: on the one hand, one finds again that regarding doping all the traditional obstacles encountered when it is a question of evaluating an illegal

activity; on the other, at least two variants that are likely to sway the decision to take drugs (the values attributed to long-term health and to the infringements of sporting morality) escape any market calculation.

11.   This example is inspired by the case of a former champion, whose totally new perform-ances during the Tour de France appeared impossible to explain "naturally". However, and despite certain suspicion, this rider was never punished during his career.

12.   Thus, Jacques Anquetil declared in 1965: "Yes, I take drugs. . . So what? You must be an imbecile or incredibly hypocritical to imagine that a professional cyclist, who rides 235 days a year in all temperatures and in all conditions, can keep going without stimu-lants" (Yonnet, 1998, pp. 159–60). Mark McGwire, a star of Major League Baseball, commented on his publicity campaign on US television for an anabolic steroid that he took regularly: "I still believe that this is not bad at all. If you are an adult, then you must choose your destiny" (see *L'Equipe*, 9 September 1999).

13.   On the rationality of individual choices, in certainty or in a risky or uncertain environ-ment, see Eber and Willinger (2006), pp. 28–51.

14.   See Becker (1993), pp. 385–409.

15.   Admittedly, the hypotheses of this game are simplistic, but they convey very well the nega-tive consequences of a failure of cooperation between the sportspeople who take drugs.

16.   According to libertarians, for every problem of coordination, and therefore for every market failure, there would be a potential market likely to solve it. For example, the action of a polluter would be corrected by compensation to the polluted. This exten-sion, without limit, of the market does not solve any fundamental problem, since the market does not work autonomously, without regulation or morality. See Sen (1999).

17.   See *Libération*, 27 October 2002.

18.   "It was only to meet the demands of my job as a professional rider", explained Erwann Menthéour during the trial on the business of doping in the 1998 Tour de France, before the Tribunal de Grande Instance in Lille in November 2000.

19.   "The Tour is my reason for living . . . to be adored is an immense pleasure", said Richard Virenque (see *Le Monde*, 13 May 1999).

20.   "Doping is the man in the street, ready to go into consuming energy or drugged prod-ucts because we are in a society where the body has become a fundamental element of constructing the identity", analysed Jean Bilard, founder and president of Ecoute Dopage, for whom, and for example, "bodybuilding represents male aesthetic surgery" (*Libération*, 27 October 2002).

21.   The account of the trainer of the junior cyclist in Pôle France is eloquent: "He who didn't take drugs was considered naive and was marginalised. He had to hide himself so as not to take drugs" (*Le Monde*, 15 July 1999).

22.   The analysis by the psychiatrist, François Poyet, of the nature of professional cyclists' behaviour, of their recurrent views and their way of "doing the job" highlights the excessive pretensions of neoclassical microeconomics: "This growing psychosis is con-veyed by a non-perception of the simple realities of social life, a ritualisation of behav-iour, the development of a paralanguage, finding refuge in irrational beliefs, an insane egocentricity, a paranoia faced with real questions, a major inability to project into the future, an abolition of moral barriers, an addictive craving and unthinking suicidal behaviour, the suppression of natural feelings linked to effort and the depersonalisation induced by corporal modifications due to doping" (*Libération*, 11 July 1999).

23.   According to Marc Samson, President du Conseil de Prévention et de Lutte contre le Dopage (CPLD), "If one is ill, one rests, takes medicine and takes up the competition again a little later. . . With this system, one makes the use of banned substances com-monplace" (*Le Monde*, 16 October 2004).

24.   Ibid.

25.   The reasoning of Rudi Altig, world champion of road cycling in 1962, confirmed this idea: "We are professionals, we are not sportsmen", he explained, claiming the freedom to take drugs.

26.   See Becker (1968), pp. 169–217.

Conclusion

The organization of professional sport certainly comes at a turning point in its history. We have indeed shown that an ethical approach may put the observer ill at ease, when faced with the development of sport and its many unfortunate consequences (doping, corruption, peddling influence, distorting sporting rules, wasting public money, dualism of the athletes' conditions of employment, and so on). There have, admittedly, never been so many financial and logistic resources in sport as in the past decades. However, instead of being used to strengthen sport in society, these resources have become the ultimate objective. What is more, the fact that the effectiveness of sport as a business coexists with its social costs (doping, corruption and inequality, and so forth) is not just chance. On the contrary, it reveals a logical relationship, albeit a complex one, between the ever-increasing development of the "marketization" of professional sport with the increase in sporting abuses. The result of this is a natural propensity for this capitalist market economy to lead the sporting society towards an ethical dead end.

Such a conclusion can be considered as banal: sport is produced by a productivist system and possesses all of its features. We can therefore conclude that it is impossible to reform the model of sports organization from within, if we do not alter the overall system that produces it. As a matter of fact, we are dealing more with a crisis of capitalism than with a crisis of the sporting movement. However, it is therefore truly hypocritical or naive to think that we are going to make such reforms and thus fight more efficiently against all the abuses that affect professional sport, while at the same time remaining in an economic model that is dominated by the systematic search for profit at all costs.

Money can pervert sport in two ways: by altering the fairness of competitions and by affecting athletes' equality of opportunity. If sport is beholden to money and not the opposite, then it will be subjected to financial speculation. Thus, maximizing financial gains takes precedence over maximizing sporting gains. This has been the case for professional clubs in the North American Major Leagues for the past 40 years as well as for the major European clubs since the mid-1990s. Winning on the field is just one means among others to achieve the economic objectives that are considered the priority by shareholders.

Major economic interests coming into sport entail other risks and create new constraints: financial and organizational takeovers by broadcasters, sponsors and investors in professional sport, the unity of the pyramid of sport breaking down, the loss of legitimacy and power of sporting institutions (the IOC and federations), the fact that sporting results are increasingly determined by the size of the sums of money involved (in Formula 1 and sailing, as well as in team sports such as football), the individualization of disciplines that are essentially team sports because of the overexposure of their star players in the media (strikers claiming ownership rights when their feats are broadcast), and the abuses changing the authenticity of competitions and performances (scheduling according to commercial requirements, cheating, corruption and doping, and so on).

Although the issue of doping is not exclusive to sport, even though athletes are the main figureheads, doping has only a legal meaning and is criminalized only in sport. It is true that sport has been built around several myths (purity of effort, equality of opportunity, uncertainty of results and a natural and healthy activity, and so on) that explain its specificity, which itself is based on distinctive ethics. That is why it is necessary to keep these ethics, at least on the surface, to preserve the "meaning" of sport, as well as its symbolic and market value. Otherwise, sport would become an economic sector like any other and athletes would be reduced to the status of record-beating machines.

This is why it is imperative to determine the threshold over which surpassing oneself becomes the very denial of sporting ethics and public health. But if, in the twenty-first century, the "sporting ideal" must be something other than a business, that is, respect of the human being as opposed to the cult of the performance at all costs, and sport for sport's sake confronting a mercantilist system, then realism must not be sacrificed to the Promethean myth.

In the end, it seems that more socioeconomic work needs to be done to think out the future of the sporting phenomenon. In one respect, progress needs to be made to know better the abuses affecting professional sport and threatening its very existence. In another, a clarification of the word sport is a prerequisite in defining the conditions that must be met so that sport can become a global public good. These two problems logically imply a reflection on what is at stake in a new global governance of sport. From an internal point of view, not much can be expected from the effectiveness of the reforms of sporting institutions. From an overall point of view, global developments could very well toll the bell of international sporting spectacles as we know them today and could be the cause of the development of new eco-compatible sporting activities.

References

Adda J. (2006), *La Mondialisation de l'économie. Genèse et problèmes*, Paris, La Découverte.

Aglietta M. (1976), *Régulation et crises du capitalisme*, Paris, Calmann-Lévy.

Allais M. (1953), "Le comportement de l'homme rationnel devant le risque. Critique des postulats de l'Ecole américaine", *Econometrica*, **21**(4), 503–46.

Andreff W. (1988), "Les multinationales et le sport dans les pays en développement: ou comment faire courir le Tiers-monde après les capitaux", *Revue Tiers-monde*, **39**(113), January–March, 73–100.

Andreff W. (1989), "L'internationalisation économique du sport", in Wladimir Andreff (ed.), *Economie politique du sport*, Paris, Dalloz, pp. 203–36.

Andreff W. (1999), "Les finances du sport et l'éthique sportive", *Revue d'économie financière*, No. 55.

Andreff W. (2000), "L'évolution du modèle européen de financement du sport professionnel", in J.-J. Gouguet and D. Primault (eds), *Sport et mondialisation: quel enjeu pour le XXIᵉ siècle, Reflets et perspectives de la vie économique*, **49**(2–3).

Andreff W. (2001a), "A économie sous-développée, sport sous-développé", *Revue juridique et économique du sport*, Paris, Dalloz, June, No. 59, 7–42.

Andreff W. (2001b), "The correlation between economic underdevelopment and sport", *European Sport Management Quarterly*, **1**(4), December, 251–79.

Andreff W. (2002), "FIFA regulation of international transfers and the Coubertobin tax: enforcement, scopes and return. A rejoinder to B. Gerrard", *European Sport Management Quarterly*, **2**(1), 57–63.

Andreff W. (2003), *Les Multinationales globales*, Paris, La Découverte.

Andreff W. (2004a), "La taxe Coubertobin. Ou comment réguler les transferts des très jeunes athlètes en provenance du Tiers-monde", in *Apprendre à douter, questions de droit, questions sur le droit. Etudes offertes à Claude Lombois*, Limoges, Pulim, pp. 797–817.

Andreff W. (2004b), "The taxation of players' moves from developing countries", in R. Fort and J. Fizel (eds), *International Sports Economics Comparisons*, Westport, Praeger, pp. 87–103.

Andreff W. (2004c), "The taxation of players' moves from developing countries", in Jean-Jacques Gouguet (ed.), *Le sport professionnel après l'arrêt Bosman*, Limoges, Pulim.

Andreff W. (2006), "Sport in developing countries", in Wladimir Andreff and Stefan Szymanski (eds), *The Handbook of Economics of Sports*, Cheltenham, UK and Nothampton, MA, USA: Edward Elgar.

Andreff W. and Bourg J.-F. (2006), "Broadcasting rights and competition in European Football", in Claude Jeanrenaud and Stefan Késenne (eds), *The Economics of Sport and the Media*, Cheltenham, UK and Northampton, MA, USA, Edward Elgar.

Andreff W., Nys J.-F. and Bourg J.-F. (1987), *Le sport et la télévision: relations économiques*, Paris, Dalloz.

Arnaud P. (1997), *Les Athlètes de la République. Gymnastique, sport et idéologie républicaine 1870–1914*, Paris, L'Harmattan.

Arnaud P., Riordan J. (eds) (1993), *Sport et relations internationales pendant l'Entre-deux-guerres*, PPSH, Rapport final, Lyon, CRIS.

Arnaud P., Riordan J. (eds) (1998), *Sport et relations internationales (1900–1941)*, Paris, L'Harmattan.

Arnaut J.-L. (2006), *Independent European Sport Review*, report, www.independentfootballreview.com/doc/43619.pdf (accessed 8 July 2009).

Assidon E. (2004), *Les Théories économiques du développement*, 4th edition, Paris, La Découverte.

Augustin J.-P. (1995), *Sport, géographie et aménagement*, Paris, Nathan Université.

Augustin J.-P., Gillon P. (2004), *L'Olympisme – Bilan et enjeux géopolitiques*, Paris, Armand Colin.

Baade R. (1996), "Professional sports as catalysts for economic development", *Journal of Urban Affairs*, **18**(1).

Baade R. (2005a), "Be careful what you wish for: a cautionary note for city suitors for the 2012 Summer Olympic Games", working paper, unpublished.

Baade R. (2005b), "Evaluating subsidies to professional sports in the USA and Europe: a guide for the public sector", *Revue juridique et économique du sport*, No. 74, March.

Baade R., Matheson V. (2000), "An assessment of the economic impact of the American Championship, the Super Bowl, on host communities", in *Reflets et perspectives de la vie économique*, **39**(2–3).

Barde J.-P. (1992), *Economie et politique de l'environnement*, Paris, 2nd edition, PUF.

Barget E. (2001), "Le Spectacle sportif ponctuel: essai d'évaluation", economics thesis, University of Limoges.

Barget E., Gouguet J.-J. (2000), "L'impact économique des spectacles sportifs: analyse critique de la littérature", *Sport et mondialisation : quel enjeu pour le XXIᵉ siècle. Reflets et perspectives de la vie économique*, **39**(2–3).

Barget E., Gouguet J.-J. (2007), "Total economic value of sporting spectacle: theory and practice", *Journal of Sports Economics*, **8**(2), April, 165–82.

Barget E., Rouger A. (2000), "De l'utilité de la mesure de l'équilibre competitive", in J.-J. Gouguet and D. Primault (eds), *Sport et mondialisation: quel enjeu pour le XXXI'eme siècle? Reflets et Perspectives de la Vie Economique*, Brussels, De Boeck, 2–3, XXXIX.

Baumol W., Bowen W.G. (1966), *Performing Arts, The Economic Dilemma*, Cambridge, MA, Twentieth Century Fund.

Becker G. (1964), *Human Capital*, New York, NBER.

Becker G. (1968), "Crime and punishment: an economic approach", *Journal of Political Economy*, **78**, 169–217.

Becker G. (1993), "Nobel Lecture: the economic way of looking at behavior", *Journal of Political Economy*, **101**(3), 385–409.

Bennahmias J.-L. (2002), "Sport de haut niveau et argent", Paris, Rapport au Conseil Economique et Social.

Bernard A. and Busse M. (2003), "Who wins the Olympic Games. Economic resources and medal totals", *Review of Economics and Statistics*, **86**(1), 413–17.

Berry R., Gould W., Staudohar P. (1986), *Labour Relations in Professional Sports*, Dover, MA, Auburn House.

Bhagwati J. (1983),"The economic analysis of international migration", in R.C. Feenstra (ed.), *International Factor Mobility. Essays in Economic Theory*, vol. 2, Cambridge, MA and London, MIT Press.

Bolotny F. (2005), "La nouvelle télédépendance du football français", *Revue juridique et économique du sport*, Dalloz, No. 75, June.

Bolotny F., Bourg J.-F. (2006), "Demand for media coverage", in W. Andreff and S. Szymanski (eds), *The Handbook of the Economics of Sports*, Cheltenham, UK and Northampton, MA, USA, Edward Elgar.

Bonnieux F., Desaigues B. (1998), *Economie et politiques de l'environnement*, Paris, Dalloz.

Bourdeau P., Rotillon G. (1999), "L'impact de l'escalade dans le développement touristique du Briançonnais: une analyse coûts–bénéfice", *Revue juridique et économique du sport*, No. 51, Limoges.

Bourg J.-F. (1983), *Salaire, travail et emploi dans le football professionnel français*, Limoges, CDES, Dalloz.

Bourg J.-F. (1993), "Le sport dans le Tiers-monde: caractéristiques, obstacles, enjeux", *Revue juridique et économique du sport*, No. 27, 3–30.

Bourg J.-F. (1996), *Le Gouvernement du sport mondial*, Paris, Encyclopaedia Universalis.

Bourg J.-F. (2000), "Contribution à une analyse économique du dopage", *Reflets et perspectives de la vie économique*, **29**(2–3), Brussels, Editions De Boeck Université, 2000, reworked in: *Problèmes économiques*, 8 November, Paris, La Documentation française.

Bourg J.-F. (2003a), "Professional team sports in Europe: which economic model?", in Rodney Fort and John Fizel (eds), *International Sports Economics Comparisons*, New York, Praeger.

Bourg J.-F. (2003b), "Le sportif et le marché: le cas du dopage", *Revue internationale de psychosociologie*, Paris, **9**(20).

Bourg J.-F. (2004a), "Le dopage sportif", in G. Vigarello (2004) (ed.), *L'Esprit sportif aujourd'hui. Des valeurs en conflit*, Paris, Encyclopaedia Universalis.

Bourg J.-F. (2004b), "Le sport professionnel américain", in Georges Vigarello (ed.), *L'Esprit sportif aujourd'hui. Des valeurs en conflit*, Paris, Universalis.

Bourg J.-F. (2004c), "Les sports collectifs en Europe: quel modèle économique?", in J.-J. Gouguet (ed.), *Le Sport professionnel après l'arrêt Bosman*, Limoges, Pulim.

Bourg J.-F. (2004d), "L'économie du sport", in *Les Cahiers français*, Paris, La Documentation française.

Bourg J.-F. (2005), "Le champion et le marché: l'avenir du dopage", in Franck Nicolleau (ed.), *Où va le sportif d'élite? Les risques du star system*, Paris, Dalloz.

Bourg J.-F., Gouguet J.-J. (1998), *Analyse économique du sport*, Paris, PUF.

Bourg J.-F., Gouguet J.-J. (2004), "The economics of the Olympic Games", *Revue juridique et économique du sport*, Dalloz, September, pp. 107–26, reproduced in *Problèmes économiques*, Paris, La Documentation française, 8 December, pp. 37–45.

Bourg J.-F., Gouguet J.-J. (2005), *Economie du sport*, 2nd edition, Paris, La Découverte.

Bourg J.-F., Gouguet J.-J. (2006), "Sport and globalisation", in Wladimir Andreff and Stefan Szymanski (eds), *The Handbook of the Economics of Sports*, Cheltenham, UK and Northampton, MA, USA: Edward Elgar.

Bourguinat H. (1998), *L'Economie morale, le marché contre les acquis*, Paris, Arléa.

Boyer R. (1986), *La Théorie de la régulation. Une analyse critique,* Paris, La Découverte.

Boyer R., Saillard Y. (eds) (2002), *Théorie de la régulation. L'état des savoirs*, Paris, La Découverte.

Braudel F. (1967–79), *Civilisation matérielle, économie et capitalisme: XV-XVIIIᵉ siècle*, Book 1: *Les Structures du quotidien*, Book 2: *Les Jeux de l'échange*, Book 3: *Le Temps du monde*, Paris, Armand Colin.

Breillat J.-C., Dudognon C., Karaquillo J.-P., Lagarde F. (2004), *Code du sport*, 3rd edition, Paris, Dalloz.

Brohm J.-M. (1976), *Critiques du sport*, Paris, Christian Bourgois.

Brohm J.-M. (1983), *1936. Jeux olympiques à Berlin*, Brussels, Ed. Complexe.

Bullion M. (2002), "Les politiques d'investissement et de financement des clubs de football professionnel en Europe", HEC, Club de finance internationale, *Les Etudes du club*, No. 51, September.

Caballero F., Bisiou Y. (2000), *Droit de la drogue*, 2nd edition, Paris, Dalloz.

Cahuc P., Zylberberg A. (2003), *Microéconomie du marché du travail*, Paris, La Découverte.

Caillois R. (1967a) (ed.), *Jeux et sports*, Paris, Gallimard.

Caillois R. (1967b), *Les Jeux et les Hommes*, Paris, Gallimard.

Callède J.-P. (2000), *Les Politiques sportives en France. Eléments de sociologie historique*, Paris, Economica.

Callède J.-P. (2007), "Maires et ministres entreprenants: l'invention d'une politique publique des sports", in Tétart Ph., *Histoire du sport en France*, Paris, Vuibert.

Carrier C. (2002), *Le Champion, sa vie, sa mort. Psychanalyse de l'exploit*, Paris, Bayard.

Cavagnac M. (2006), *Théorie des jeux*, Paris, Gualino editeur.

Cavagnac M., Gouguet J.-J. (2006), "Talent sportif et équilibre compétitif. Une approche par la théorie des jeux", *Revue juridique et économique du sport*, No. 79.

Chamerois N. (2002), "La Mondialisation des Jeux Olympiques Séoul (1988) à la Sydney (2000)", doctoral thesis from University of Franche-Comté.

Chappelet J.-L. (2005), "Promouvoir le développement économique par le sport", 2nd Magglingen Conference Sport and Development, 4–6 December, Input Paper.

Charpiot R. (2004), "Les XIᵉ Jeux Olympiques et le Troisième Reich. Un mariage politiquement incorrect", in Milza et al. (2004), *Le Pouvoir des anneaux*, Paris, Vuibert.

Chavagneux C. (2004), *Économie politique internationale*, Paris, La Découverte.

Chovaux O. (2006), "Identité et représentation du football nordiste au premier XXᵉ siècle", in Yvan Gastaut, Stéphane Mourlane, *Le Football dans nos sociétés. Une culture populaire, 1914–1998*, Paris, Ed. Autrement.

Clastres P. (2007), "Le sport français au défi de l'Olympisme, 1892–1936", in P. Tétart (2007), *Histoire du sport en France*, Paris, Vuibert.

Clastres P., Dietschy P. (2006), *Sport, société et culture en France, XIXᵉ–XXᵉ siècles*, Paris, Hachette.

Coates D., Humphreys B. (1999), "The growth of sports franchises, stadiums and arenas", *Journal of Policy Analysis*, **18**(4).

Collin Y. (2004), "Quels arbitrages pour le football professionnel?", *Les rapports du Sénat*, No. 336.

Conseil d'analyse économique (2002), *Gouvernance mondiale. Rapport de synthèse*, Paris, La Documentation française.

de Coubertin. P. [1920] (1967), "La victoire de l'Olympisme", in *L'Idée Olympique*, Carl Diem Institut, Stuttgart, Karl Hoffmann Verlag.

Defrance J. (1995), *Sociologie du sport*, Paris, La Découverte.

Defrance J. (2000), *Sociologie du sport*, Paris, La Découverte.

Dejonghe T. (2004), "Restructuring the Belgian professional football league: a location – allocation solution", *Journal of Economic and Social Geography*, **95**(1).

de La Porte X. (2006), *La controverse pied/main. Hypothèses sur l'histoire du football*, Maisons-Alfort, Ere.

Deloitte (2000), *Annual Review of Football Finance*, Manchester, Sports Business Group at Deloitte.

de Mondenard J.-P. (1987), *Drogues et dopage*, Paris, Chiron.

de Mondenard J.-P. (2000), *Dopage, l'imposture des performances*, Paris, Chiron.

de Mondenard J.-P. (2004), *Dictionnaire du dopage. Substances, procédés, conduites, dangers*, Paris, Masson.

Denis J.-P. (2003), "Rapport à M. Jean-François Lamour, Minister for Sport, sur certains aspects du sport professionnel en France", http://lesrapports.ladocumentationfrancaise.Fr/BRP/034000712/0000.pdf (accessed 17 July 2009).

Dietschy P., Gastaut Y., Mourlane S. (2006), *Histoire politique des coupes du monde de football*, Paris, Vuibert.

Dion Y. (1987), "Le multiplicateur régional appliqué à un espace économique de petite dimension", thesis in economics, University of Bordeaux I.

Drevon A. (2000), *Les Jeux Olympiques oubliés. Paris 1900*, Ed. du CNRS.

Eber N. (2002), "Credibility and independence of the World Anti-doping

Agency, a Barro-Gordon-type approach to anti-doping policy", *Journal of Sports Economics*, **3**(1) February, 90–96.

Eber N. (2006), *Le Dilemme du prisonnier*, Paris, La Découverte.

Eber N., Willinger M. (2006), *L'Economie expérimentale*, Paris, La Découverte.

Ehrenberg A. (1991), *Le Culte de la performance*, Paris, Calmann-Lévy.

Elias N., Dunning E. (1994), *Sport et civilisation. La violence maîtrisée*, Paris, Fayard.

Fates Y. (1994), *Sport et Tiers-monde*, Paris, PUF.

Faure J.-M., Suaud C. (1999), *Le Football professionnel à la française*, Paris, PUF.

Filloux L. (2005), *L'Equilibre compétitif dans le football européen*, Rapport de stage Cdes Master1 AES, University of Limoges.

Fort R. (2003a), *Sports Economics*, Upper Saddle River, New Jersey, Prentice Hall.

Fort R. (2003b), "Thinking (some more) about competitive balance", *Journal of Sports Economics*, **4**(4), November.

Fort R. (2006), *Sports Economics*, 2nd edition, Upper Saddle River, New Jersey, Pearson Prentice Hall.

Fort R., Maxcy J. (2003), "Comment: competitive balance in sports leagues. An introduction", *Journal of Sports Economics*, **4**(2), May.

Foucard H., Torrenti J.-M. (1991), *Impact socio-économique de la Coupe du Monde de Football 1998. Approche méthodologique,* Paris, Ecole nationale des ponts et chaussées, unpublished.

Gabszewicz J. (2003), *La concurrence imparfaite*, Paris, La Découverte.

Gabszewicz J., Sonnac N. (2006), *L'Industrie des médias*, Paris, La Découverte.

Généreux J. (2001), "De la science économique à l'économie humaine", *L'Economie politique*, No. 9, 2001/1.

Gilliard H. (2001), "*Gestion de la qualité des hydrosystèmes: la concertation décentralisée*", economics thesis, University of Limoges, December.

Girard B. (2003), *Une histoire des théories du management en France de 1800 à 1940*, available at http://www.bernardgirard.com/management. pdf (accessed December 2009).

Gouguet J.-J. (1979), "Reconsidération de la théorie de la base", thèse complémentaire, University of Bordeaux I.

Gouguet J.-J. (1981), "Pour une réhabilitation de la théorie de la base", *Revue d'économie régionale et urbaine,* No. 1.

Gouguet J.-J., Nys J.-F. (1993), *Sport et développement économique régional*, Paris, Dalloz.

Gouguet J.-J. and Primault D. (2002), "Economic analysis of the functioning of the transfer market in professional football", *Revue des affaires européennes*, No. 2–3, March.

Gouguet J.-J., Primault D. (2003), "Formation des joueurs profession-nels et équilibre compétitif: l'exemple du football", *Revue juridique et économique du sport*, No. 68, September.

Gouguet J.-J., Primault D. (2004), "Economic analysis of transfer system", in Rodney Fort and John Fizel (eds), *International Sports Economics Comparisons*, Westport, CT, Praeger.

Gouguet J.-J., Primault D. (2005), "Agents in professional sport: an analy-sis of their role on competitive balance", 7th Annual Conference of the International Association of Sports Economists, Ottawa, 18–19th June.

Gouguet J.-J., Primault D. (2006), "The financial crisis in football in Europe: the French exception", *Journal of Sports Economics*, **7**(1), February.

Gratton C. and Solberg H.A. (2004), "Sports and broadcasting: compari-sons between the United States and Europe", in Rodney D. Fort and John Fizel (eds), *International Sports Economics Comparison*, Westport, CT, Praeger, pp. 175–87.

Grimes A.R., Kelly W.J., Rubin P.H. (1974), "A socioeconomic model of national Olympic performance", *Social Science Quarterly*, **55**(3), 777–82.

Guerrien B. (2002), *Dictionnaire d'analyse économique*, Paris, La Découverte.

Gygax J. (2004a), "Entre enjeux internationaux et nationaux. Le boycott américain des Jeux de Moscou (1980)", in Milza et al., *Les pouvoirs des anneaux*, Paris, Vuibert.

Gygax J. (2004b), "Le retrait soviétique des Jeux de Los Angeles. Enjeux idéologiques et diplomatie publique américaine 1983–1984", in Milza et al., *Les pouvoirs des anneaux*, Paris, Vuibert.

Harvey J., Saint-Germain M. (1995), "L'industrie et la politique cana-diennes du sport en contexte de mondialisation", *Sociologie et sociétés*, **27**(1), 33–52.

Hoehn T., Lancefield D. (2003), "Broadcasting and sport", *Oxford Review of Economic Policy*, **19**(4), 552–68.

Hoehn T., Szymanski S. (1999), "European Football – the Structure of Leagues and Revenue Sharing" , *Economic Policy*, **28**, April.

Horowitz I. (1974), "Sports broadcasting", in Roger G. Noll (ed.), *Government and the Sport Business*, Washington DC, The Brooking Institution.

Houlihan B. (2003a), "Doping and sport, more problems than solutions?", in Barrie Houlihan (ed.), *Sport & Society, A Student Introduction*, London, Sage Publications, pp. 218–34.

Houlihan B. (2003b), "Sport and globalisation", in Barrie Houlihan (ed.), *Sport & Society, A Student Introduction*, London, Sage Publications, pp. 345–63.

Ineum Consulting (2004), "Football professionnel, finances et perspectives", press release November.

Jennings A. (2000), *The Great Olympic Swindle*, Simon & Schuster UK Ltd, translated and published in French: *La Face cachée des Jeux Olympiques* (2002), Paris, L'Archipel.

Jennings A. (2006), *Carton rouge! Les dessous troublants de la FIFA*, Paris, Presses de la Cité.

Johnson D. and Ali A. (2000), "Coming to play or coming to win: participation and success at the Olympic Games", Working Paper, Wellesley College, 10 September.

Kahane L. (2003), "Comments on 'Thinking About Competitive Balance'", *Journal of Sports Economics*, **4**(4), November.

Kahneman D., Tversky, A. (eds) (2000), *Choices, Values and Frames*, Cambridge, Cambridge University Press.

Karaquillo J.-P. (2000), *Sport et droit*, Paris, Dalloz.

Kaul I., Grunberg I., Stern M.A. (eds) (2003), *Les Biens publics mondiaux. La coopération internationale au XXIᵉ siècle*, Paris, Economica.

Kenno Keimbou D.C. (2000), "L'Etat, le politique et le sport au Cameroun: le paradoxe d'une institutionnalisation (1949–1996)", *Regards sociologiques*, No. 20, 27–37.

Késenne S (1997), "L'affaire Bosman et l'économie du sport professionnel", *Revue du marché unique européen*, No. 1, 1996 (reproduced in *Problèmes économiques*, No. 2503, La Documentation française, Paris).

Késenne S. (2001), "Improving the competitive balance and the salary distribution in professional team sports", in M. Ibrahimo, Z. Mendes and F. Tenreiro (eds), *Economica do Desporto, Actas de la Conferência Internacional*, Lisbon, Cisep.

Kopp P. (2006), *Économie de la drogue*, Paris, La Découverte, 2006.

Lagadec P. (ed.) (2000), *Ruptures créatrices*, Paris, Editions d'Organisation.

Latouche S. (2001), *La Déraison de la raison économique. Du délire d'efficacité au principe de précaution*, Paris, Albin Michel.

Latouche S. (2003), *Justice sans limites. Le défi de l'éthique dans une économie mondialisée*, Paris, Fayard.

Latouche S. (2004), Survivre au développement, Paris, Mille et une Nuits.

Laure P. (1995), *Le Dopage*, Paris, PUF.

Laure P. (2000), *Dopage et société*, Paris, Ellipses.

Laure P. (2004), *Histoire du dopage et des conduites dopantes: les alchimistes de la performance*, Paris, Vuibert.

Lavoie M. (1997), *Avantage numérique. L'argent et la Ligue nationale de hockey*, Hull, Quebec, Editions Vents d'ouest.

Lavoie M. (2000), "La proposition d'invariance dans un monde où les équipes maximisent la performance sportive", in J.-J. Gouguet and D. Primault (eds), S*port et mondialisation: quel enjeu pour le XXIe siècle?, Reflets et perspectives de la vie économique*, Brussels, De Boeck.

Lavoie M. (2004), "Faut-il transposer à l'Europe les instruments de régulation du sport professionnel nord-américain?", in J.-J. Gouguet (ed.), *Le Sport professionnel après l'arrêt Bosman*, Limoges, Pulim.

Lemennicier B. (1992), *Economie du droit*, Paris, Cujas.

Lepetit C. (2005), *Potentiel économique local et performance sportive. L'exemple des championnats européens de football*, Mémoire master 1 Économie et finance, University of Limoges.

Lille F., Verschave F.-X. (2002), *On peut changer le monde. A la recherche des biens publics mondiaux*, Paris, La Découverte.

Loret A. (1995), *Génération Glisse*, Paris, Editions Autrement.

Maennig W. (2002), "On the economics of doping and corruption in international sports", *Journal of Sports Economics*, **3**(1), February, 61–89.

Maguire J. (2004), "Jeux olympiques l'envers de la médaille", *Alternatives Internationales*, July–August.

Michalet C.-A. (2003), "Les biens publics mondiaux", in Le Cercle des économistes (ed.), *L'Europe et la gouvernance mondiale*, Paris, Descartes et Cie.

Mignon P. (2002), "Le Dopage: état des lieux sociologiques", Documents du CESAMES, Université René-Descartes Paris V, No. 10.

Milza P. (2004), "Un siècle de Jeux Olympiques", in Milza P., Jequier F., Tétart P. (2004), *Les pouvoir des anneaux*, Paris, Vuibert.

Milza P., Jequier F., Tétart P. (eds) (2004), *Le pouvoir des anneaux. Les Jeux Olympiques à la lumière de la politique (1896–2004)*, Paris, Vuibert.

Moonjoong T. (2004), "The Color of Medals. An economic analysis of the Eastern and Western blocs' performance in the Olympics", *Journal of Sports Economics*, **5**(4), 311–28.

Moorhouse H. (1999), "The History, Functioning and Consequences of Mechanisms to Redistribute Income Between Clubs in English Professional Football", paper for the International Conference of Sports Economists, University of Limoges, July.

Motorsport Industry Association (MIA) (2003), *The Economic Impact of* the 2002 FIA Foster's British Grand Prix, Stoneleigh Park, http://www.ghkint.com/products/downloads/Publications/EIA_2002_British_GP.pdf (accessed 10 July 2009).

Neale W. (1964), "The peculiar economics of professional sports", *Quarterly Journal of Economics*, **78**(1).

Niggli N. (2004), "Helsinki 1952: Les Jeux Olympiques de la guerre?", in Milza et al., *Les pouvoirs des anneaux*, Paris, Vuibert.

Noll R., Zimbalist A. (eds) (1997), *Sports, Jobs & Taxes,* Washington DC, The Brookings Institution.

Ozden, C., Schiff M. (2006), *International Migration, Remittances and the Brain Drain*, New York, Palgrave.

Pareto V.F. (1966), *Manuel d'Economie Politique*, Geneva, Droz.

Passet R. (1975), *L'Economique et le vivant,* Paris, Payot.

Perroux F. (1970), "Les conceptualisations implicitement normatives et les limites de la modélisation en économie", *Economie et Société*, December.

Petrella R. (2004), *Désir d'humanité. Le droit de rêver*, Brussels, Labor.

Phelps E. (1990), *Economie politique*, Paris, Fayard.

PNUD [UNDP] (2005), *Rapport mondial sur le développement humain* [Human Development Report], Paris, Economica.

Pommerehne W., Frey B. (1993), *La Culture a-t-elle un prix?*, Paris, Plon.

Preuss H. (2000), *Economics of the Olympic Games. Hosting the Games 1972–2000*, University of New South Wales, Walla Walla Press.

Preuss H. (2003), "The economics of the Olympic Games: winners and losers", in Barrie Houlihan (ed.), *Sport & Society, A Student Introduction*, London, Sage Publications, pp. 252–71.

Primault D., Rouger A. (1999), "Concurrence sportive et concurrence économique sont elles compatibles?", *Les Ateliers de la concurrence*, DGCCRF, June.

Proceedings of CDES-CRIDEAU symposium (2000), *Outdoor Sports and Environmental Protection*, Limoges, PULIM.

Queval I. (2004), *S'accomplir ou se dépasser. Essai sur le sport contemporain*, Paris, Gallimard.

Redeker R. (2002), *Le Sport contre les peuples*, Paris, Berg International.

Regional Economic Sports Observatory (1998), "Sport and the Environment", CDES, Limoges, June.

Robert D. (2006), *Le Milieu du terrain*, Paris, Les Arènes.

Rosier B., Dockes P. (1983), *Rythmes économiques. Crises et changement social. Une perspective historique*, Paris, La Découverte.

Rottenberg S. (1956), "The baseball players' labor market", *Journal of Political Economy*, **64**(3).

Rozenblat C., Cicille P. (2003), *Les Villes européennes. Analyse comparative*, Paris, Datar.

Rütter H. et al. (2004), *Economic Impact of the UEFA EURO 2008 in Switzerland*, Lucerne.

Sacquet A.-M. (2002), *Atlas mondial du développement durable*, Paris, Ed. Autrement.

Saint-Martin J. (2007), "Sport, nationalisme et propagande, 1918–1939", in P. Tétart (2007), *Histoire du sport en France*, Paris, Vuibert.

Samuelson P. (1964), "Public goods and subscription TV: correction of the record', *Journal of Law and Economics*, **7**, October.

Sanderson A., Siegfried J. (2003), "Thinking about competitive balance", *Journal of Sports Economics*, **4**(4), November.

Sandy R., Sloane P., Rosentraub M. (2004), *The Economics of Sport, An International Perspective*, New York, Palgrave, Macmillan.

Sapir J. (2006), *La Fin de l'eurolibéralisme*, Paris, Seuil.

Scully G. (1995), *The Market Structure of Sports*, Chicago, The University of Chicago Press.

Sen A. (1999), *L'Economie est une science morale*, Paris, La Découverte.

Sen A. (2000), *Un nouveau modèle économique. Développement, justice, liberté*, Paris, Odile Jacob.

Sen A. (2003), *Un nouveau modèle économique. Développement, justice, liberté*, Paris, Odile Jacob.

Simonnot P. (1988), *Homo sportivus*, Paris, Gallimard.

Siri F. (2000) (ed.), *La Fièvre du dopage*, Paris, Editions Autrement.

Siri F. (2002), *Dopés: victimes ou coupables?*, Paris, Editions Le Pommier.

Sloane P. (1976), "Restrictions of competition in professional team sports", *Bulletin of Economic Research*, **28**(1), May.

Souchaud Y. (1995), *Situation sportive dans les pays les moins avancés d'Afrique: bilan*, Division de la jeunesse et des activités sportives, Paris, UNESCO.

Staudohar P. (1996), *Playing For Dollars*, New York, Cornell University Press.

Stringer Y. (1980), "Le faux miracle des retombées économiques", *La Presse*, 18 December, Montreal.

Szymanski S., Kuipers T. (1999), *Winners and Losers, the Business Strategy of Football*, London, Penguin Group.

Tétart P. (ed.) (2007), *Histoire du sport en France. Le temps de la conquête*, Paris, Vuibert.

The Boston Consulting Group (2004), "Evaluation des impacts économiques des JO à Paris. Principaux éléments d'analyse", 17 June, unpublished.

Thomas R. (1997), *Histoire du sport*, 2nd edition, Paris, PUF.

Tobin J. (1978), "A proposal for international monetary reform", *Eastern Economic Journal*, **4**(3–4), 153–9.

Traité établissant une Constitution pour l'Europe (2005), Paris, Ministry of the Interior, March.

Treillet S. (2005), *L'Economie du développement*, 2nd edition, Paris, Armand Colin.

UNDP (2005), *World Report on Human Development 2005*, Paris, Economica.

Van den Hove S. (2000), *Approches participatives pour la gouvernance en matière de développement durable*, University of Saint-Quentin, Cahiers du C3ED.

Vaury O. (2003), "Ces cerveaux qui peuvent rapporter gros", *Alternatives internationales*, No. 7, March–April.

Ventelou B. (2001), *Au-delà de la rareté*, Paris, Albin Michel.

Veyne P. (1976), *Le Pain et le Cirque. Sociologie historique d'un pluralisme politique*, Paris, Seuil.

Vigarello G. (1990), "Les premières Coupes du monde, ou l'installation du sport moderne", *Vingtième siècle. Revue d'Histoire,* No. 26, April–June 1990, pp. 5–10.

Vigarello G. (2002), *Du jeu ancien au show sportif. Naissance d'un mythe*, Paris, Le Seuil.

Waddington I. (2000), *Sport, Health and Drugs: A Critical Sociological Perspective*, London, E. & F.N. Spon.

Wahl A. (1989), *Les Archives du football. Sport et société en France (1880–1890)*, Paris, Julliard-Gallimard.

Wahl A. (1991), *La Balle au pied. Histoire du football*, Paris, Gallimard.

Wahl A., Lanfranchi P. (1995), *Les Footballeurs français des années trente à nos jours*, Paris, Hachette.

World Bank (2006), World Development Report 2005, Washington, DC, The World Bank.

Yonnet P. (1998), *Systèmes des sports*, Paris, Gallimard.

Yonnet P. (2004), *Huit leçons sur le sport*, Paris, Gallimard.

Zimbalist A. (2002a), "Reply. Competitive balance conundrums. Response to Fort and Maxcy's comment", *Journal of Sports Economics*, **4**(2), May.

Zimbalist A. (2002b), "Competitive balance in sports leagues. An introduction", *Journal of Sports Economics*, **3**(2), May.

Index